Ulster and North America

Ulster and North America

Transatlantic Perspectives on the Scotch-Irish

edited by

H. Tyler Blethen

and

Curtis W. Wood, Jr.

With a foreword by

T. G. Fraser

THE UNIVERSITY OF ALABAMA PRESS

Tuscaloosa and London

First paperbound printing 2001.

9 8 7 6 5 4 3 2 1
10 09 08 07 06 05 04 03 02 01

∞

The paper on which this book is printed meets the minimum requirements of
American National Standard for Information Science-Permanence of Paper for Printed
Library Materials, ANSI Z39.48-1984.

The essay by Warren R. Hofstra, "Land , Ethnicity, and Community at the Opequon
Settlement, Virginia, 1730–1800," originally appeared in the Virginia Magazine of
History and Biography, vol. 98, no. 3 (July 1990): 423–48.

Library of Congress Cataloging-in-Publication Data

Ulster and North America : transatlantic perspectives on the Scotch-
  Irish / edited by H. Tyler Blethen and Curtis W. Wood, Jr. : with a
  foreword by T. G. Fraser
      p. cm.
    Includes bibliographical references and index.
    ISBN 0-8173-1135-1 (pbk. : alk. paper)
    1. Scots-Irish—North America—History. 2. Ulster (Northern
Ireland and Ireland)—Civilization. 3. Ulster (Northern Ireland and
Ireland)—Emigration and immigration—History. I. Blethen, Tyler.
II. Wood, Curtis.
E49.2.S4U47 1997
970.004'9163—dc20   96-25002

British Library Cataloguing-in-Publication Data available

Contents

Foreword
The Ulster–American Heritage Symposium: A Retrospect

T. G. Fraser

The first Ulster–American Heritage Symposium was held at the New University of Ulster in the bicentennial year of 1976. Sessions at the University of North Carolina at Asheville followed two years later, setting a pattern—still flourishing after nearly two decades—of biennial alternate sessions in Northern Ireland and Appalachia. From the start, the purpose of the symposium was to explore the many facets of Ulster migration to North America, particularly southern Appalachia. As with many academic enterprises, its origins combined a perceived academic need sustained by the drive and commitment of particular individuals who, in this case, are separated by the Atlantic.

The academic need was clear enough. In 1963, Nathan Glazer and Daniel Patrick Moynihan published their seminal "beginning book," *Beyond the Melting Pot,* in which they pointed to the need for a deeper understanding of the role of ethnicity in American life. "We had hoped," they explained in the introduction to the 1970 edition, "that some higher level of intellectual effort and scholarly attention might be paid to the persistence of ethnic ties in American society, a phenomenon that had not been forecast and had to be explained."[1] Superficially it might seem that the substantial eighteenth-century migration from Ulster was an unlikely candidate for such attention, for the predominantly Presbyterian migrants had long since been seen as absorbed into the mainstream of American life, an essential element in the making of "old-stock" America. But that had not always been the assumption, for in the 1890s the Scotch-Irish had flaunted their distinctive place in the making of the republic. At the first convention of the Scotch-Irish Congress, held at Columbia, Tennessee, in May 1889 "to preserve the history and perpetuate the achievements of the Scotch-Irish race in America," delegates had warmed to the message of how they helped forge contemporary America. Not only did they hear a litany of illustrious men of Scotch-Irish blood—Patrick Henry, Thomas Jefferson, John Paul Jones, Andrew Jackson, James Buchanan, Abraham Lincoln, and Ulysses S. Grant—but they were reminded that the "Scotch-Irish people have been second to none in their influence upon modern civilization."[2] What prompted such hyperbole is clear enough: those descendants of the Ulster immigrants wished to mark a clear division between themselves and more recent immigrant groups, not least the Catholic Irish who had come in large numbers in the wake of the Famine. Established German Jews held similar attitudes at that time toward the poorer Ashkenazim flooding in to escape persecution in the czarist empire. The proceedings of the Scotch-Irish Congresses are an invaluable source from which to gauge the attitudes—and prejudices—of the time.

Echoing Glazer and Moynihan, the 1960s saw a modest, and more scholarly, revival of interest in the history of the Scotch-Irish as an ethnic group with the publication in the United States of James G. Leyburn's *The Scotch-Irish: A Social History* (1962) and of two Ulster-based studies: R. J. Dickson's *Ulster Emigration to Colonial America, 1718–1775* (1966); and E. R. R. Green's collection of *Essays in Scotch-Irish History* (1969). It was a time when higher education in Northern Ireland was opening up with the establishment of the New University of Ulster, which combined a new campus at Coleraine with the nineteenth-century Magee University College in Londonderry. It was a creation not without controversy, for many believed that Derry, Northern Ireland's second city, should have been awarded a full-fledged university. Part of the origin of the symposium lay in an attempt to float an Institute of Ulster–North American Studies at Magee College, focusing on Derry's historic role as an emigration port and its more recent links with the United States Navy in the Second World War. Although this failed to materialize, it set the scene for the discussions that gave rise to the symposium in 1976.

Northern Ireland must have seemed an unlikely port of call for Americans in the early 1970s, for it had become a byword for violence and civil unrest. In 1975, however, the New University of Ulster was visited by Dr. James Stewart, former head of the Philosophy Department of the University of North Carolina at Asheville, then active in the Overseas Programs of the University of North Carolina. As the result of his discussions with Professor Frank Lelievre of Magee College and W. T. Ewing, registrar of the New University, the first symposium convened the following year. Dr. Stewart's interest was not fortuitous. Born in Moneymore, County Londonderry, and educated in Belfast, he had never lost his Ulster links throughout his distinguished career in American education. The southern Appalachian region in which he worked had been the classic area of Scotch-Irish settlement in the eighteenth century, defining the region's culture and development. In that part of the southern interior the Scotch-Irish had been the predominant ethnic element among the white population for much of the eighteenth and nineteenth centuries.[3] As such, they had been well to the fore in all of America's wars, as the names Andrew Jackson, Davy Crockett, Stonewall Jackson, and George S. Patton, among countless others, amply testify. But the Civil War, Reconstruction, and the problems of declining industry and small farms had all left their mark on southern Appalachia, a region characterized by East Tennessee State University's Richard Blaustein as "overwhelmed by despair and exploitation."[4] By the 1960s, Appalachians were ready to fight back, to understand and assert the merits of their distinctive culture, and in this they were led by dedicated scholars in their universities.

From the start, then, the Ulster–American Heritage Symposium filled a need in both societies. Its premise was that the Scotch-Irish brought the culture of Scotland and Ulster to this distinctive region of North America, leaving an indelible stamp on its development and way of life. An essential principle of the symposium has been that culture is broadly defined to embrace history, language, folk life, music, and technology. Studies have reached out to include the Scottish background of the Ulster migrants and to examine other areas of Scotch-Irish settlement in Canada, Pennsylvania, and the Ozarks. The primary focus has been on Ulster Presbyterian migration, but this emphasis has not been interpreted in any sectarian sense. Indeed, the Scotch-Irish congresses of the 1890s were keen to avoid accusations of religious exclusion, their constitution explicitly stating that "no man" would be "excluded from this association, whether he be Catholic, or Presbyterian, or of any other denomination."[5] There is a growing awareness of the Catholic influence embedded in the Ulster migration of the eighteenth and early nineteenth centuries, evidenced not least in the career of Archbishop John Hughes of New York, who emigrated from County Tyrone.

The symposium's work has been underpinned by key institutions and individuals. In 1984 the New University of Ulster and the Ulster Polytechnic merged to form the University of Ulster, now one of the largest universities in Britain or Ireland. Peter Roebuck and Steve Ickringill of the university's history department sustained the symposium on their side of the Atlantic, their task immeasurably eased by the generosity of the trustees of the Garfield Weston Trust, who have backed the project financially from its earliest days. The "Ulster end" of the symposium has increasingly, and appropriately, become a partnership between the university and the Ulster-American Folk Park near Omagh. Inspired by Eric Montgomery, this was constructed adjacent to the boyhood home of Judge Thomas Mellon at Camphill as a working museum of Ulster-American migration. Under its two directors, Dr. Denis MacNeice and John Gilmour, it has become an essential pillar of the symposium's work, as has its American counterpart, the Museum of American Frontier Culture. American support has been directed through a group of Appalachian universities, the University of North Carolina at Asheville, Appalachian State University, East Tennessee State University, and Western Carolina University. While many scholars in these universities have been closely involved with the symposium, they would be first to acknowledge the guiding hands of Western Carolina's Tyler Blethen and Curtis Wood, without whose interest and commitment over many years this volume could never have appeared.

University of Ulster

Preface

This project had its origins in the early stages of the Ulster–American Heritage Symposium, when it became clear that the research presented there would prove valuable should it achieve an afterlife. That aspiration, though quick to germinate, has proved slow to bear fruit, only in part because it was an international collaborative project. One of the great virtues of an ongoing symposium is that it creates a community of individuals who, sharing the same interests, offer a continuing dialogue that identifies and clarifies important issues and that challenges, stimulates, and supports new and better scholarship. We have reaped the benefits of just this kind of community and express our heartfelt gratitude to those scholars who have contributed to this book through their commitment to the symposium over the years. Some of these scholars are in print here. Many are not, yet their research, their questions, and their support have been integral to the symposium and have helped to shape the work found here.

Many people have assisted and supported us throughout the years that the preparation of this book has taken. Pride of place goes to three persons—Mr. William Ewing, Dr. Frank Lelievre, and Dr. James Stewart—whose original fervent belief in the notion of a transatlantic collaboration created the symposium from whose proceedings the following selections are taken. This volume would not exist without their dedication and hard work in establishing a symposium that has recently celebrated its twentieth year.

Others who have sustained the biennial meetings and given us encouragement include Tom Fraser, Steve Ickringill, Eric Montgomery, Peter Roebuck, and Brian Trainor. Our colleagues in the Department of History at Western Carolina University have been the source of valuable suggestions and advice. Mark Huddle in particular helped us with our research and with our organization. The staff of Western Carolina University's Mountain Heritage Center, past and present, have shared our interest in the Scotch-Irish influence on the historical development of mountain society. June Shuler efficiently typed much of the manuscript when the scanner refused to deliver the level of efficiency that its adherents promised. We are also grateful for the support of Western Carolina University's Hunter Library faculty and staff, particularly the bibliographic research of Carole Wood.

We appreciate the commitment of Malcolm MacDonald of The University of Alabama Press to the project. His early confidence in it, his courteous prompting, and his long-suffering patience ensured that we would somehow eventually shepherd it through our myriad academic responsibilities to completion.

A special thanks to our wives, Deborah Blethen and Carole Wood, for their unfailing support, encouragement, and understanding.

Curtis W. Wood, Jr.
H. Tyler Blethen

1 Introduction

H. Tyler Blethen
Curtis W. Wood, Jr.

The Scotch-Irish are one of many ethnic groups that the people of North America have studied in order to understand their own origins in terms of family, community, and nation. A century ago the contribution the Scotch-Irish made to the New World seemed clear and straightforward: they settled the frontiers, founded countless families, and gave Canada and the United States many of their leaders. When we both first came to live in western North Carolina over two decades ago, we soon learned that the families who have lived here for generations cherish a strong memory of their Scotch-Irish origins. Beyond that general ethnic awareness, however, they retain little knowledge of who in fact those forebears were and to what their legacy amounted. The Scotch-Irish have throughout their history been a difficult group to identify and define. Even their name is misleading, for most of them were not what the hyphen implies: they were not the offspring of a biological union of Scottish and Irish people. Rather they emerged from the process of cultural fusion that so often occurs in migration history. Their origins go back to the late Middle Ages, when Scots from the Western Islands settled in Counties Antrim and Down in the eastern part of Ulster, the northernmost province of Ireland. In the seventeenth century many more Scots emigrated from the western Lowlands, and they were joined by sizable numbers of English from the borderlands of northwestern England. Most of this wave were Presbyterians and English speakers. Over time they have collectively come to be known in Ulster as "Ulster Scots."

The term "Scotch-Irish" is an American usage. It was seldom used in the eighteenth century, when "Irish" was far more common. After the massive migration to America driven by the Irish Potato Famine of the 1840s, many Americans of Protestant Irish ancestry seized on the name to distinguish themselves from the culturally different Catholic Irish immigrants, whom the Scotch-Irish perceived as inferior.[1] Recently the term "Scots-Irish" has appeared, but "Scotch-Irish" continues to be more widely used and recognized in America. Although in this collection we have used "Scotch-Irish," the terms should be considered synonymous.

In addition to their diverse origins, other reasons why the Scotch-Irish are so hard to define include their language, their mobility, and their adaptability. As English speakers, they were largely indistinguishable from the majority of other white Americans in the eighteenth and early nineteenth centuries. Not segregated by language, they blended easily into the mainstream. Their high mobility placed them in close contact with people from other ethnic groups, and they proved extremely adaptable, readily borrowing cultural elements they found useful. One of the difficulties of studying their history in North America is the problem of identifying ethnic boundaries, of deciding just what was uniquely Scotch-Irish. Most scholars agree that in terms of material culture, it is much more difficult to isolate a Scotch-Irish style than a German or English style, whether in the arts or crafts, dress, or architecture. The essence of Scotch-Irish style was simplicity and practicality. The settlers from Ulster were a people whose life was made simple by poverty, a people practiced in abandoning their past. Twice in living memory they had moved; and less recently they had rejected a religion rich in style and tradition for an austere Calvinism that scorned outward appearance and stressed the private and individual. The consequence was a minimal style and an extraordinary willingness to learn from and adopt the ways of others at the expense of their own culture and tradition. It should come as no surprise that they made few significant efforts, until the heavy migration spurred by the Potato Famine, to articulate a distinct ethnic identity.

Like all Americans, the historical origins of the Scotch-Irish are found elsewhere. Europe in the seventeenth and eighteenth centuries experienced many population shifts caused by war, religious violence, and nascent colonization. In the British Isles and Ireland this potent mixture combined to create a migration of Protestant English-speakers from the border regions between England and Scotland to Ulster. Their desire to escape poverty coincided with the official policy of James Stuart, king of England and Scotland from 1603 to 1625, to pacify his rebellious Irish subjects by planting loyal Protestants among them. These immigrants created an agricultural society of landlords and tenants who, facing conflict with the native Irish and the continuing influx of significant numbers of Scottish settlers, retained many characteristics of a frontier for much of the seventeenth century.[2] By the mid-eighteenth century, however, the transformation of Ulster was quite dramatic, for agricultural improvement and the rise of the linen industry had made the province the most prosperous in Ireland.

Despite economic improvement, Ulster Scots experienced a number of problems that made their lives difficult. As Presbyterians in an Anglican state, most of them faced religious hostility from their own government. They were subject to penal laws barring them from higher education and the professions and forcing them to pay tithes to the Church of Ireland, although by the 1720s these laws were only loosely enforced. In the eighteenth century they suffered from cycles of short-term economic depression, as a series of poor harvests and a rapidly rising population intensified competition for land and drove rents mercilessly upward. Even the linen industry, which offered supplementary income to farmers as well as alternative employment, suffered from sporadic but serious downturns.[3]

Throughout the eighteenth century large numbers of Ulster Scots migrated once again, this time across the Atlantic to the British colonies in North America. From the 1680s until the American Revolution temporarily cut off shipping, at least 250,000 sailed to North America. After the Revolution an even larger wave crossed, perhaps 500,000 more, peaking in the period between the Napoleonic Wars and the Potato Famine. These pre-Famine Irish migrants were predominantly Presbyterians from Ulster. Philadelphia was their preeminent port of entry, but they settled all along the Eastern seaboard, from Nova Scotia to Georgia. The migration was not a consistent flow. Surging and ebbing in response to changing conditions in Ireland and North America, at different times it called forth immigrants of varying occupations and status. Those who were artisans typically preferred cities and towns, while those who were farmers, along with most latecomers, were drawn inland. Although Scotch-Irish migrants settled a great swath of the backcountry all along the Appalachian chain, most settled the southern frontier. Amid echoes of their Ulster past, they lived in a frontier environment, often facing natives angered by the forcible expropriation of their land. It was on these many frontiers, from Ulster to the American South, that the creativity and complexity of the Scotch-Irish that now challenge those who would understand them was expressed.

The essays that follow represent the best scholarship from the eighteen-year history of the Ulster–American Heritage Symposium. These years have witnessed a resurgence of interest in Scotch-Irish migration, and the symposium is an important expression of that interest. This collection reflects the nature of contemporary Scotch-Irish studies, in particular the issues, approaches, and methodologies that engage scholars. In the context of recently published research, this collection has several unique qualities. First, it is interdisciplinary, bringing together the work of the historian, archivist, geographer, linguist, historical demographer, and Scottish-studies specialist. One of the enduring challenges of writing about the Scotch-Irish is an elusiveness that comes from their capacity for change, their ability to assimilate, and, in North America, to take on the colors of a new environment and create a variety of new cultural forms. Years ago E. Estyn Evans, commenting on this phenomenon, observed that a successful history of the Scotch-Irish would require the cooperation of many scholarly disciplines.[4] This collection does not offer a comprehensive history—there are important issues not addressed—but these essays do demonstrate the value of a multidisciplinary approach.

Second, the essays are in every sense transatlantic. The community of scholars who appear here are Scottish, Irish, American, and Canadian, and the perspective they collectively offer bridges the ocean dividing them. Those who would study the Scotch-Irish must possess a thorough and sophisticated understanding of Scottish, Irish, and American history. Few American historians studying the Scotch-Irish have mastered the source materials and scholarship available on both sides of the Atlantic. This criticism is frequently expressed about the work of James Leyburn, David Hackett Fischer, Rodger Cunningham, and Forrest McDonald and Grady McWhiney.[5] At the same time, British and Irish scholars of their own national histories seldom pursue their countrymen to America with the same confidence they exhibit when discussing their own societies. The authors in this collection speak from well-grounded knowledge of their subjects, and several offer good examples of a scholarly synthesis of sources from both sides of the Atlantic. One of the important points this volume puts forward is that the Scotch-Irish were, in this age of migration, not irrevocably leaving home but were in fact participants in the creation of a transatlantic community, with its own traditions of goings and returnings. Finally, this collection is the product of an extended dialogue among the symposium's participants, many of whom have been coming together to share and refine ideas and viewpoints for nearly two decades.

The eleven essays that follow address many important topics and issues concerning Scotch-Irish history—from the seventeenth through the early nineteenth centuries—emphasizing social and economic history. The essays by Cowan, Connolly, Macafee, and Pollock focus on the dynamic nature of Ulster society in the seventeenth and eighteenth centuries and the evolving cultural, religious, economic, and social conditions shaping those Scotch-Irish who chose to emigrate. Edward J. Cowan directs our attention to the neglect of Scottish history and culture in this story of the Scotch-Irish. He focuses on the role of the prophetic mentality in Scottish history, suggesting that this mentality was a significant element of the Scotch-Irish legacy, particularly its legends of religious persecution. Critiquing James Leyburn's depiction of the Scottish Reformation as liberating and enlightened, Cowan instead links it to the prophetic tradition, stressing its irrational, reactionary, and superstitious nature. He questions the role of the prophetic mentality as either a catalyst for migration or a barrier to action and reexamines its contribution to the Scotch-Irish search for identity in the nineteenth century.

Most scholars agree that the most persistent and visible aspect of the Scotch-Irish culture as they dispersed and adapted across many frontiers was their Presbyterian faith. Presbyterianism was a strong bond between the Ulster settlers and Scotland, but the Ulster experience brought about significant change. A new Presbyterianism, which scholars are still defining and evaluating, had begun to emerge by the late seventeenth century. S. J. Connolly examines the development of Ulster Presbyterianism from the seventeenth through the nineteenth centuries. His analysis stresses the uniqueness of Ulster Presbyterianism and its success in maintaining a well-defined separate identity within Ulster society. He identifies the main components of the Presbyterian community during the period of emigration: a comprehensive system of religious and moral discipline that produced a high degree of community cohesion, and the economic independence that helps to explain the community's ability to reject the Anglican church of the landlord class. This cohesiveness and independence, Connolly argues, also helps account for the survival of cultural traits from Lowland Scotland—traits such as a fierce spirit of independence and the "dour incivility" that accompanied it, religious revivalism and superstitious beliefs, and a tradition of political radicalism. It is generally agreed among contemporary scholars that religious grievances were not a primary cause of Ulster migration, but Connolly makes clear that the disabilities these Protestants experienced in Ulster were quite real. Over the course of the eighteenth and nineteenth centuries, Ulster Presbyterianism evolved away from its primary focus on community to one in which individual salvation and the personal experience of conversion were paramount. This process was accompanied by economic and demographic change, the homogenization of accent and customs, and the rise of a pan-Protestant Unionism. All this is further evidence of a society in the midst of rapid and important change.

William Macafee's essay extends his important, previously published work into the nineteenth century and places Ulster's demographic history in the context of earlier research on Ireland as a whole. Macafee argues for a new chronology for population growth based on evidence of unprecedented annual growth rates after 1750 (1.3–1.9 percent per annum for 1753–91 and 1.3–1.4 percent for 1791–1821), even as Ulster lost population to North America. This new interpretation is inspired in part by a revision of Irish economic history that posits significant growth in the Irish economy beginning in the 1730s rather than the 1780s and by a growing appreciation of significant regional variations within the island. Macafee observes that, though the age at marriage of Ulster women was younger than elsewhere and though Ulster had long experienced higher fertility rates than most of Western Europe, marriage ages and fertility levels showed little change over the period studied. Instead, the driving force in population growth must have been the significant decline in child mortality rates that allowed more children to survive to become parents twenty years later. Specific reasons for this decline are not fully understood, but Macafee links them to general economic betterment—in particular the growth of the linen industry—and to accompanying improvements in diet, transportation, and disease prevention. Macafee's findings underline the dynamic qualities of Ulster society in the age of emigration, particularly its modernizing tendencies.

Recent approaches to the research and interpretation of preindustrial America, referred to as the "new rural history," have examined economic strategies at the household level in order to evaluate community and individual values and behaviors. Proponents have debated the role of market forces versus self-sufficiency in the development of settlement patterns, the evolution of community, and the creation of a rural *mentalité.*[6] Vivienne Pollock adapts the perspective of the "new rural history" to examine seventeenth- and eighteenth-century Ulster economy and society. She describes seventeenth-century Ulster as "an early modern enterprise zone," increasingly commercialized and dramatically stimulated by large agricultural profits and, at the end of the century, by a new wave of Scottish immigrants. Ulster's economic environment stimulated a high degree of agricultural diversification and the development of the rural linen industry by the early eighteenth century. This emerging economy was characterized by rising land rents, dependency on textile production to pay rents and to buy food, and marked regional variations and specializations within the province. Pollock examines farm accounts of the Orrs of County Down and the Holmeses of southern County Tyrone to elucidate "the extent to which the domestic needs of 'ordinary' Ulster people were met by a commercially based strategy." Pollock shows that neither the Orrs nor the Holmeses attempted to reach independence of the market and attain self-sufficiency. Their actions suggest that neither family regarded their farming activities as sufficient to meet the everyday needs of their households. The author draws on the research of J. B. Pruitt and Mick Reed to present Ulster households as thoroughly integrated into a market economy, but with the impact of centralizing market forces mediated by significant local networks of exchange of goods and labor. Pollock concludes that a detailed study of economic behavior can enrich our understanding of the effects of emigration on the development of social and economic structures in Ulster and North America. Her essay also reminds us that emigrants from Ulster, who were coming from a dynamic society in flux, were subject to changing values and attitudes over the span of the four or more generations in which migration took place.

Essays by Kirkham and Parkhill address the process and experience of migration from Ulster. Graeme Kirkham's essay provides a valuable revision of the seminal work of R. J. Dickson, who suggested that only a small number of Ulster emigrants came to America before 1717. Kirkham presents new evidence for significant emigration in the years 1680–1717 and argues that movement from Ulster to North America was well established by 1700. While contemporary accounts emphasized political and religious grievances as causes of the earliest migration, Kirkham stresses the importance of economic and social disturbances at the end of the seventeenth century, the opening of trade between Ireland and North America in 1680, and conflict between Dissenters and the

Anglican elite that was primarily social and economic in nature rather than religious. Even in this early period, promotional efforts by Quaker leaders in Pennsylvania and New Jersey and the colonial government of South Carolina spread awareness in Ulster that America was a good place to settle.

Dickson and Kirkham agree that the first large-scale emigration occurred in the period 1717–19. On the basis of new information, however, Kirkham suggests that as many as 7,000, nearly twice Dickson's estimate, sailed to America during those years. This surge of emigration was caused in part by economic distress, in particular by rising rents; but, as Kirkham points out, this period also saw the emergence of emigration as a commercial enterprise. The availability of information about America and the opportunities presented by affordable passage aboard merchant vessels provided significant incentives. Kirkham's essay also suggests the possibility of significant Catholic migration to America in this early period.

Trevor Parkhill utilizes emigrant letters found in the Public Record Office of Northern Ireland—both public letters printed in Ulster newspapers as advertisements for shipowners and private letters—as a source for the period 1750–1875. He vividly demonstrates their value by studying the motives for emigration, the expectations and experiences of Ulster settlers in America, and the differences between Ulster and America. Letters home were essential stimuli to migration, providing encouragement and support. They also illustrate the movement of migrants back and forth, for the decision to come to America in the eighteenth and early nineteenth centuries was not an irreversible one. Returning emigrants formed yet another link connecting the communities and cultures of Ulster and North America and provide intriguing evidence of strong, continuing ties. Parkhill also examines evidence of the skills emigrants brought. Ulster settlers mainly sought land to farm, but they demonstrated a growing adaptability and mobility. In contrast to Catharine Anne Wilson's migrants, the subject of chapter 8, Parkhill's evidence suggests that pre-Famine migration was dominated by single young people rather than families. Here, letters home often took a crucial part in a process of extended migration, through which the new immigrant encouraged family members left behind to follow.

The remaining essays, which deal with Scotch-Irish settlement in North America, contribute to the growing literature on ethnicity and cultural diffusion, suggesting both confirmation of and correction to the important work of Fischer, McDonald, and McWhiney. In particular they illustrate the debate between cultural diffusionists, who stress the importance of the immigrants' cultural heritage, and proponents of the developmental and materialist viewpoint found in literature on the "new rural history."

Catharine Anne Wilson applies the methodology of a genealogical group study to a small and identifiable migration to Canada: 105 families from the United Parish of St. Andrews on Ireland's Ards Peninsula to Amherst Island, near Kingston, Ontario, from 1820 to 1860. Using land records to construct genealogical profiles and trace individuals over time, she challenges the traditional stereotype of Scotch-Irish materialistic individualism, arguing that these people did not migrate entirely for individual gain. Instead, like Warren Hofstra's Opequon settlers of chapter 10, they were cautious, familial, and communal. While individual gain was clearly a motive for emigration, so too were advancement of family and the maintenance of community ties. Where Parkhill's eighteenth-century emigrants to Pennsylvania were overwhelmingly single people, about 95 percent of Wilson's group migrated as families. In addition, most lived within five miles of each other at St. Andrews, and at Amherst Island they settled together. They went to great lengths to replicate their Old World society, even choosing to rent land from an Irish landlord in a continuation of their traditional landlord-tenant social system, which she argues illustrates their desire to place security before riches. Like Parkhill's migrants, hers also traveled back and forth to Ireland to maintain family ties. Wilson suggests that the behavior and values exhibited at Amherst Island are more typical of actual Scotch-Irish emigrants than is the traditional stereotype of grasping individualistic frontier folk. She calls for more studies using family reconstruction and individual-level tracing informed by a greater sensitivity to the more mundane and less heroic aspects of migration and settlement. Certainly more work needs to be done to discover the extent to which the Scotch-Irish migration experience of Canada differs from that of the United States.

Russel L. Gerlach, arguing that the Scotch-Irish experience west of Appalachia has been neglected, pursues their settlement into the Missouri Ozarks. Applying the techniques of cultural geography to compare these Scotch-Irish to Germans also in Missouri, he finds inferential but substantial evidence of a large Scotch-Irish population possessing an identifiable "critical mass" of historical cultural traits that distinguish them from other groups. Using high-culture/low-culture categories of analysis, he argues that riverine and other productive low-elevation lands of northern Missouri were settled by migrants of English stock from Virginia and Kentucky and by a "relatively cultivated class" of clan-related, high-culture Scotch-Irish from the westernmost Carolina Piedmont, the Valley of Virginia, and East Tennessee. These "yeoman-cum-bourgeois" possessed an "almost ethnic self-consciousness." The rougher landscape of the Ozarks, on the other hand, was settled by *low-culture* Scotch-Irish, described by Gerlach as "restless frontier type[s]" who hunted, farmed, and displayed high mobility. Questioning whether this Scotch-Irish element in the Ozarks possessed identifiable elements of an ethnic culture, Gerlach argues that their ethnic traits, while largely invisible, were deeply embedded, making them, rather than an ethnic group, carriers of an ethnic culture, a distinction he clarifies by contrasting them with the Germans. Drawing on E. Estyn Evans's ideas about cultural preadaptation, he argues that their origins in Ulster preadapted them in a variety of ways with a capacity for change and an ability to endure in a landscape that no one else wanted.

Warren R. Hofstra's study of Opequon, a rural community in the Lower Shenandoah Valley, like Catharine Anne Wilson's essay on Amherst Island, challenges conventional images of the Scotch-Irish as restless backwoods strivers after individual freedom and material self-betterment at the expense of stable and supportive communities. He concludes instead that, at least in the beginning, they were primarily concerned with preserving the cohesiveness of their community. Unlike Gerlach's "preadapted" Scotch-Irish, who willingly settled rough mountain lands, Hofstra's families chose the best land available, based on its commercial potential. The Scotch-Irish of Opequon were strongly ethnocentric, preferring to marry, convey land, and worship within their own community. Only in their trade and financial dealings did they enter into relationships with the German, English, and Virginia-born settlers of Opequon. Family, kin, ethnicity, land, and congregation provided the cohesion that sustained this eighteenth-century frontier community for two generations, but these elements proved unable to retain their hold on the third generation, seduced by unprecedented opportunities to obtain western lands following the American Revolution. Hofstra's more mobile and materialistically individualistic third generation, which compares in interesting ways with the antebellum western North Carolina frontier society Blethen and Wood describe in chapter 12, raises another set of questions about the ongoing adaptability of the Scotch-Irish to new conditions.

Michael B. Montgomery has undertaken to redress the relative absence of substantive research on the linguistic heritage of Appalachia. As the promising but unfinished work of the Linguistic Atlas of the United States and Canada Project illustrates, many difficulties stand in the way of tracing that heritage—including problems of methodology; the sparseness of the early documentary record; the constant changeability of language; and the need to be as knowledgeable about the history, sources, and construction of language in Britain and Ireland as in Appalachia. Drawing on his extensive research on both sides of the Atlantic to identify grammatical features—which are more resistant to change than vocabulary or pronunciation—Montgomery traces forty characteristic Appalachian grammatical features to their Scotch-Irish, Southern British, or General British source and then outlines the linguistic processes that account for their preservation in mountain speech. In finding that seventeen (43 percent) of the grammatical features are of Scotch-Irish origin, he makes a strong case for Ulster's contribution to Appalachian speech. Using linguistic theory to distinguish among three types of processes characterizing transatlantic linguistic connections—straight retentions, disguised retentions, and reinterpretations—he shows how and why Old World patterns have been preserved in New World English down to the present day and helps explain why the Scotch-Irish impact on Appalachian English has been underestimated in the past.

Like Catharine Anne Wilson and Warren R. Hofstra, H. Tyler Blethen and Curtis W. Wood, Jr., examine the transmission of culture in the process of migration, although on a larger scale, that of the mountainous region of antebellum western North Carolina. As do Wilson and Gerlach, Blethen and Wood argue that migrants brought their cultural baggage with them, hoping to replicate life in the homeland, but they had mixed success. The authors also discuss Gerlach's notion of cultural preadaptation. As in Hofstra's Opequon, they find that Scotch-Irish influence in western North Carolina weakened over time. Using a wide variety of sources and techniques, including surname analysis, census records, family histories, and land records, they conclude that the Scotch-Irish arrived in numbers large enough, and assumed social and economic roles powerful enough, to shape significantly the region's development. Although their early numbers were large, perhaps 40 percent of all settlers, their proportion declined to about 20 percent of the population by the Civil War. Religion was another area in which Scotch-Irish influence diminished. The original Presbyterianism of the majority of the settlers was not sustained, for mountain communities found it hard to attract seminary-educated pastors. Eventually the Baptist faith, with its openness to ministerial calling regardless of the level of formal education, displaced Presbyterianism as the dominant church in the region.

Land-use and settlement patterns tell a different story about the extent of Scotch-Irish influence. Their Irish heritage of "mixed" farming, based on both grain and livestock, and of the "infield-outfield" system survived to shape the new environment they found in the mountains. Adaptation occurred as they replaced wheat, rye, and oats with Indian corn and sheep with hogs. But they preserved their basic agricultural and stock-raising techniques, such as infield-outfield farming and free-range grazing. They also preserved their settlement patterns, carving out dispersed farms instead of nucleated farm villages in their new land. Admitting that the Scotch-Irish are not easy to separate from the mainstream in terms of their ethnic identity, Blethen and Wood nevertheless conclude that, in some ways, primarily their land-use and settlement patterns, they left their ethnic mark on the landscape of western North Carolina.

Although this volume represents some of the latest research in Scotch-Irish studies, much remains to be done. Despite decades of intense popular and scholarly scrutiny, the whole question of ethnicity remains very much unresolved. It is still not clear exactly what being Scotch-Irish constitutes. Scholars have not progressed much past the United States Census Bureau's current practice of asking each individual to declare his or her own sense of ethnic identity. How far can ethnicity be refined beyond individual perceptions of identity? Progress in identifying broad cultural markers has come slowly. This is particularly true in understanding the Scottish element of the Scotch-Irish. Most research so far has begun with the plantation of Ulster. A great deal more needs to be done in identifying the Scottish dimension of Scotch-Irish culture and history.

Recent developments in cultural history have had a profound impact on our understanding of the past, and their application to the Scotch-

Irish is promising. Some cultural markers have been investigated, but with varying results. A good start has already been made in the field of language, where Karl Nicholas and Hal Farwell have built on Michael Montgomery's work investigating the transmission of language across the Atlantic.[7]

Along the same lines is the provocative transatlantic study of folkways recently published by David Hackett Fischer in *Albion's Seed: Four British Folkways in America*. Though many of his conclusions have been challenged,[8] his interpretations have stimulated new thinking about our cultural definitions of ethnicity. A closer examination of folkways—family, gender, material culture, food, work, leisure, and worship—from a transatlantic perspective, would add much to our understanding.

Some questions about the eighteenth-century Irish migration process have barely been asked. For instance, what role did Irish Catholics play in this overwhelmingly Protestant migration? David Doyle has done some preliminary investigation,[9] but many questions remain unanswered: How many Catholics migrated? Where in Ireland did they come from? And where in North America did they go? How did they assimilate into an overwhelmingly English-speaking, Protestant, British colonial society? We also know little about reverse migration. Some emigrants always return home. How many of this migration group did so? Why? And what influence did they have on the continuing migration and on the homeland to which they returned?

It would also be valuable to have a better understanding of the revival and reconstruction of Scotch-Irish ethnic identity in the late nineteenth and early twentieth centuries, evidenced by the rise of Presbyterian and Scotch-Irish societies and the efforts of various Scotch-Irish congresses. What were the causes and consequences of this strong movement to define ethnic identity? And what was its impact on those regions, such as Appalachia and the South, which had a significant Scotch-Irish heritage?

Finally, the recognition that this migration was a *North American* phenomenon, not confined to just the South or even the United States, has come only slowly. The Scotch-Irish settled all across British America, including New England and Canada.

The rewards of comparative studies are apparent in this volume, and future study will undoubtedly bring even more. If this volume suggests one thing above all else, it is the value of regional and local studies in providing a basis for comparisons that will produce a fuller and richer picture of the Scotch-Irish experience. Readers are directed to the notes for each chapter and to the select bibliography at the end of this volume for information about primary and secondary sources for the study of the Scotch-Irish in Ulster and North America.

2 Prophecy and Prophylaxis: A Paradigm for the Scotch-Irish?

Edward J. Cowan

I have seen a dreary dream
Beyond the Isle o Skye;
I saw a dead man win the fight,
And I think that man was I.
—F. J. Child, *English and Scottish Popular Ballads*

This well-known stanza from the ballad "The Battle of Otterburn" is not only prophetic but also, perhaps, appropriate to an essay whose author may be destroyed or demolished by the conclusion, leaving the fight unwon, the audience (or readership) totally unconvinced. This discussion will focus on the aboriginal component of the Scotch-Irish, namely the Scots who have hitherto been either totally ignored by commentators or violently wrested out of context, their role subjected to incredible distortion. What Americans have written about the Scottish part of the Scotch-Irish—for example, James G. Leyburn,[1] or more recently, David Hackett Fischer[2]—is frequently hilarious, a haphazard hodgepodge of miscellaneous misinformation drawn from all over Scotland, irrespective of temporal or cultural considerations, and designed to reflect the characteristics of a section of the population who are themselves, in the best American tradition, a myth.

Myth, however, is not to be despised by historians. On the contrary, they should strive to understand and analyze the phenomenon as a codification of historical truth.[3] This statement is made in a spirit of admiration, for Americans may be one of the few peoples in the world with a greater capacity for self-mythologization than the Scots. What follows is a brief discussion of one of the most potent forces in Scottish history, one almost totally ignored thus far in recent Scottish historiography: the role of prophecy. Though it must be left to American scholars better able to judge than the present author, this chapter suggests that the prophetic mentality was part of the cultural baggage imported into eighteenth-century America by the people we call the Scotch-Irish.

Throughout history people have believed that the future was as knowable as the past. In prediction, learned or popular, about the Second Coming of Jesus Christ, as well as in vaticinatory statements promising the dawn of a golden age, prophecy and myth coalesced. Popular culture observed and preserved dates in the calendar that were deemed particularly propitious for obtaining knowledge of the future, and countless portents and signs were interpreted for information about all aspects of everyday life, from birth, marriage, and death to the weather and crop yields.

Existing at the dawn of documented human activity, prophecy was the triplet sibling of poetry and history. Not only does the oldest extant Scottish poem, *The Gododdin*,[4] deal with prophetic themes, but the prophecies attributed to Merlin, King Arthur's great sage and sidekick, were already known in Scotland by the tenth century. These prophecies would be further reinforced and popularized by Geoffrey of Monmouth in the twelfth century in vaticinatory language as infuriatingly dense and obscure as that of the Book of Revelation. Geoffrey's prophecies held out the glorious promise that the Celtic peoples of Scotland, Ireland, Wales, Cornwall, and Brittany would reunite under an Arthur redivivus who would rule the whole of Britain and drive the accursed Anglo-Saxons back into the North Sea from whence they came.[5] This idea of a reborn King Arthur grew into one of the most potent prophetic myths in British history, for, through time, it was believed that Arthur would take the form of a real historical personage who would be the first to unite the four kingdoms of the British Isles under his rule. Bad King John had his nephew Arthur, Count of Brittany, a potential focus for opposition to the monarch, killed because of his name. In 1307, during the Scottish Wars of Independence, the English authorities had two friars executed for asserting that Robert Bruce, king of Scots, was the subject of the prophecies of Merlin. After his great victory over the English at Bannockburn in 1314, Robert sent his brother Edward to Ireland to stress the common origins of the Scots and the Irish; later, Edward Bruce marked the prophetic heritage by attempting to stimulate the Welsh into rebellion against the English.[6] The Scots, therefore, attempted to exploit the prophecies concerning Arthur to their own political advantage, and English propagandists became equally insistent that if a second Arthur did appear, he would undoubtedly be an Englishman.

The early sixteenth century saw the rise of skeptical voices like that of the philosopher and historian John Mair, who attempted to discredit prophets because he was profoundly disturbed by the growing popularity of political prophecy. By now the Arthurian myth had been anglicized, and distinctly imperialistic emphases had been added. Henry Tudor invoked the prophecies of Merlin to justify his overthrow of Richard III, and Henry named his eldest son Arthur in order to speed the fulfillment of the prophecy. Arthur was the prince who should and would have been king had he not died and been succeeded by his younger brother, Henry VIII. Not to be outdone, both James IV and James V of Scotland called their sons Arthur. The anonymous author of the *Complaynt of Scotland*, alarmed that the Scots were on the receiving end of Arthurian prophecy, warned his countrymen against "diverse prophane prophecies of merlyne and other ald corruptit vaticinaris, the quhilkes hes affermit in rusty ryme, that scotland and ingland sal be under ane prince to which the inglismen gifis ferme credit."[7]

The Reformation should have sounded the death knell of Scottish prophecy, for the Protestants were inclined to consign it to the garbage bin of history, along with other alleged medieval or Romish superstition. That they did not is attributable to the penchant of the Reformers, John Knox among them, for prophecy on the biblical model. Ironically, the religious elite thus sustained prophetic belief while trying to suppress folk seers and popular predictions, which they considered to be subversive and potentially destructive to the status quo.

One of the best-known prophets of medieval Britain was born in southern Scotland and lived during the thirteenth century. Curiously, but appropriately, he occurs in something of an Arthurian context. Thomas the Rhymer, also known as True Thomas, or Thomas of Erceldoune (Earlston), is the subject of the famous ballad in which he is seduced by the Queen of Fairyland—King Arthur's last resting place, also named Applelad or Avalon—during a seven-year stint in her kingdom.[8] Thomas would become the most famous of all Scottish seers, and he is still quoted to this day. In 1773 Sir David Dalrymple, Lord Hailes, the historian and annalist who energetically attempted to purge Scottish historiography of embarrassing myth and legend, could lament that the Rhymer's name "is not forgotten in Scotland nor his authority slighted even at this day." His prophecies had not only been reprinted "but have been consulted with a weak, if not criminal curiosity." As it happened, Thomas's reputation had recently had a close squeak. His famous prophecy about the Haig family—"Betide, betide, whate'er betide /

Haig shall be Haig of Bemerside"—appeared to be doomed when Zerubabel Haig, seventeenth baron of Bemerside, who died in 1753, had twelve daughters before he fathered a son, an ancestor of Field Marshall Earl Haig of First World War notoriety.[9]

True Thomas was to be invoked once more at one of the most profound historical moments in Scottish, or for that matter, British vaticination, namely the Union of the Crowns in 1603 when James VI of Scotland succeeded Elizabeth I of England. For complex reasons put forward elsewhere,[10] James not only convinced himself that he was indeed the Arthur of the prophecies but also, for good measure, the second Constantine, the last emperor who would reign in the Last Days.

As part of the propaganda effort to bolster the legitimacy—or the inevitability—of James's position, the royal publisher in Edinburgh, Robert Waldegrave, printed in 1603 a collection known as the *Whole Prophecies of Scotland*. The volume is a ragbag of bits and pieces, most totally obscure in meaning and drawn from Merlin; the Venerable Bede; Waldhave, abbot of Melrose; and others; but primarily citing Thomas the Rhymer. Even the most skeptical of commentators was deeply impressed that Thomas in the thirteenth century had allegedly prophesied:

> From the North to the South Sey
> A French wife shall beare the son
> Shall rule all Bretane to the sey
> that of the Bruce's blood shall come
> As neere as the ninth degree.[11]

The French wife was none other than Mary, Queen of Scots, who could indeed be counted as descended in the ninth generation from Robert Bruce. The significance of Waldegrave's *Whole Prophecies* is twofold; first, crucially, it spliced together religious and profane prophecy; second, it greatly fostered and reinforced popular vaticination during the following two hundred years and beyond.

Waldegrave was reprinted in 1615 and 1625; at least twelve editions appeared between 1680 and 1746.[12] More editions are turning up all the time, and the volume survived in the chapbook literature right through the nineteenth century, an era that was to be fascinated, as many people still are, by the prophecies of one of the great Gaelic seers, the Brahan Seer—also known as Coinneach Odhar, or Kenneth Mackenzie—whose prophecies, the subject of a volume by Alexander Mackenzie first printed in 1899, are still being reprinted.[13] The Seer is credited in some quarters with predicting television, North Sea oil, and acid rain. John MacInnes of the School of Scottish Studies at the University of Edinburgh was recently assured that Coinneach Odhar had predicted that when two women ruled Britain, the kingdom would be coming to an end.[14] At the time of writing, Margaret Thatcher has been deposed, and Queen Elizabeth and the United Kingdom cling to survival.

MacInnes cautions against seeing such predictions as genuine precognition. They are, rather, "cultural items which have their place in the social construction of reality,"[15] a statement with which I must concur. However, there is some suggestion in the folk tradition that unusual events or experiences do dictate the assumption that a prophecy *must* exist. A study of nightmares and the Old Hag tradition provides a useful analogy. A dreamer assaulted by the Old Hag experiences terror, pressure on the chest, and suffocation, but these and other symptoms are real and experiential. The presence of the Old Hag simply offers an explanation. "It is not tradition"—and here we might substitute prophecy—"that pre-dates experience but experience that pre-dates tradition."[16] Prominent prophets such as Thomas the Rhymer or the Brahan Seer clearly, like epic heroes, attracted the utterances and deeds of lesser mortals through the passage of time or were attributed with predictions that they somehow *ought* to have made.

On the other hand, one example neatly illustrates the lengths to which people would go to prove not only the efficacy of prophecy but also the enhanced significance of the event allegedly predicted. A prediction about a battle at Gladmoor was originally composed (presumably retrospectively) with the battle of Barnet during the Wars of the Roses in mind. Through time, Gladmoor in England became associated with the village of Gladsmuir in East Lothian, Scotland, and the Gladmoor battle loomed so large in Scottish tradition as to be considered a veritable Armageddon. When Bonnie Prince Charlie defeated Johnny Cope at the battle of Prestonpans in 1745, the name and site of the battle were moved down the road six miles eastward to Gladsmuir:

> The battle of Gladsmoor, it was a noble stour
> And weel do we ken that oor young prince wan.
> The gallant Lowland lads, when they saw the tartan plaids
> Wheel round to the right and away they ran.[17]

The past predicts the future, and the present confirms the past.

What, then, is the significance of all of this for the Scotch-Irish?

Whether or not we approve of that label, there is no doubt that the overwhelming proportion of Ulster Scots who migrated to the New World in the eighteenth century shared one solid common heritage that was both religious and cultural—namely, Presbyterianism. It was radical Presbyterianism at that, the Presbyterianism of dissent and nonconformity, of the heady days of the National Covenant and the Solemn League, of opposition to Stewart despotism, of the Killing Times, of martyrdom and death at conventicles, of the Hillmen and the Suffering Bleeding Remnant—altogether a radical tradition that, if John Knox and others are to be believed, went all the way back to the Lollards of Kyle in the fifteenth century. Throughout the whole of the seventeenth century, covenanting preachers—men whose intellects were as acute as their outlooks were frighteningly blinkered—went back and forth across the Irish Sea to reinforce prejudice and political extremism. Particularly important to the Scotch-Irish heritage were legends of the persecution, torture, and execution suffered by Covenanters in the name of their faith, which culminated in the so-called Killing Times, 1684–88, when the brutalities inflicted by government dragoons undoubtedly intensified.[18] Persecution was particularly severe in the southwest of Scotland, which during this period resembled nothing so much as modern Ulster with its occupying forces. Most important of all, religious radicals—inspired by the stories of victims, who soon acquired the status of martyrs—generated their own folklore and tradition. Indeed, such traditions provided a true martyrology for the first time in the annals of Scottish Presbyterian history, and one that, despite the radicalism of the Covenanters, the Church of Scotland would eventually subsume as its own.[19]

These men and women of humble position who attempted to establish the republic of Jesus Christ on the mountains and moors of Galloway and Lanarkshire were truly heroic, brave, and steadfast beyond belief; but so richly layered was the legend they created that even today, historians[20] have, thus far, failed to penetrate the thick texture in order to recover their history. Especially significant for the theme of this chapter is the fact that virtually all of those who were executed uttered prophecies before their demise, and those who survived had no hesitation in committing these predictions to print. These prophecies, along with accounts of the sufferings, were printed and distributed in the thousands during the next three centuries. In political terms the heroes of the covenants were the original Whigs, a term of derision first applied to the

Covenanters in the mid-seventeenth century, but they were much purer and more severe than those who came to parliamentary prominence during the eighteenth and nineteenth centuries. The covenanting leadership—the prophets, if you will—not only harbored chiliastic or millenarian beliefs but assumed the mantle of folk seers. Fiercely convinced of their own righteousness and ultimate salvation, they were at best the elect, the chosen of the Lord, and at worst pathetic specimens of degenerate antinomianism.

James Leyburn's study of the Scotch-Irish paints a canvas of unrelieved gloom, misery, lawlessness, and barbarity in depicting the Scottish homeland of the Ulster Scots. From all of this the Reformation supposedly brought relief: "Protestantism was exciting news to the Scots. For the first time in their history the people had been given something to think about, seriously and deeply."[21] Whereas Leyburn clearly views this as the beginning of enlightenment and civilization, some of us might want to argue that there was another side to this story, that in 1560 the Scots (or some of them) stepped out of the gloom and into the *glaur* (mud). For well over a century the black hand of Calvinism was to seize the soul, if not necessarily the mind, of Lowland Scotland. But the men and women of southwest Scotland and of Ulster[22] were in the tightest grip of all, and they did not want to be released, because they perceived they were fighting a rearguard action against the forces of skepticism and atheism—a word they loved to use. They were, in short, confronting the first shock troops of what was to become the Scottish Enlightenment, and against those Satanic hordes they felt compelled to defend themselves. These forces of reaction armed themselves with the defensive shield of providentialism, stressing the God-dominated universe against innovation and enlightenment. In so doing, the later Covenanters developed ideas the very antithesis of Leyburn's argument.

Right at the end of the seventeenth century there appeared a rash of publications with such titles as *Satan's Invisible World*, *The Secret Commonwealth of Elves and Fairies*, and *Deuteroscopia Commonly Called the Second Sight*, largely written by worthy ministers who, to reinforce the providential, argued that witches, fairies, and other paranormal phenomena were created by God as part of his Divine Plan. The upshot was—and it was truly ironic given the views of the early Protestant Reformers—that by the late seventeenth and early eighteenth centuries, the most fanatically religious Presbyterians were also the most superstitious. Indeed, there is a case to be made that the Scottish Enlightenment was, at least initially, a reaction against superstition and folk belief and, as such, was fundamentally an elitist attack on Scottish popular culture.

It was this package of religion and folk belief—including sacred and profane prophecy—that the Scotch-Irish brought to the Americas as part of their cultural baggage. This tradition, as it gained strength, was even able to absorb elements of Celtic vaticination, presumably because ultimately all prophecy is equally efficacious, although to Lowland Presbyterians the beliefs of the Gaels were as alien as those of the native peoples of North America. The myth of the eternal return applied whether the warrior was King Arthur or Bonnie Prince Charlie; and Sir Walter Scott—even if he did not, as Mark Twain suggested, contribute to the outbreak of the Civil War—was to encourage a sentimental attachment to the last Jacobite Pretender among his considerable Scotch-Irish readership.[23]

This chapter has offered some suggestions about the Scotch-Irish by examining the role of the prophetic mentality, but prophecy can be perceived as a double-edged, or even a multi-edged, weapon. It can act as a spur to the elect, leading them to the apex of achievement or predestining them to prosperity. But prophecy may also have conditioned many to the very notion of emigration. All recorded prophecies—whether of Merlin, Thomas the Rhymer, or the Brahan Seer—are heavily preoccupied with the end of things, the demise and disappearance of prominent and not-so-prominent families, the decay of great buildings, birds nesting in the castle tower, vixens whelping in the fireplace of the great hall, the alien takeover of property, the blighting of the landscape, and "the sheep's jawbone on the land," a reference to the nineteenth-century process whereby people were cleared from the land to make way for sheep. All such existing prophecies could have served to reinforce both a fatalistic acceptance of departure and the inheritance of the earth by the meek and the mighty alike.

And finally we come to the prophylaxis of my title. The model here is drawn from Scottish evidence, and I leave it to others to judge its applicability to the Scotch-Irish. Prophecy acts as a preventive: for those who believe in it, all things will come to pass, if not now, then in the future. Viewed in this way, prophecy can become an excuse for passivity, for idleness, for inaction; or to put it another way, if the dead hero always returns, then no one is ever actually defeated. Is it possible that the

Scotch-Irish shared the Scottish characteristic described by Gregory Smith as a "strange union of opposites,"[24] the notion of "The Caledonian Antisyzygy," which so inspired Hugh MacDiarmid, Scotland's greatest twentieth-century poet?[25] The idea discussed by both Smith and MacDiarmid is that inherent contradictions exist within every individual as well as within societies, ethnicities, or nations. Modern Scots find their reason tempered by passion; they are hard-headed yet sentimental, friendly yet violent, enterprising yet cautious. It must be left to others better able to judge whether these and numerous other tensions were part of the Scottish legacy to the Scotch-Irish.

When the Scotch-Irish in the nineteenth-century United States created their own myth, they were ransacking the past to find prophetic corroboration for their own present. The label Scotch-Irish was intended to distinguish one part of the population from the Catholic, or "bog," Irish on both sides of the Atlantic. Thomas Dixon's repugnant novel *The Clansman* (1905) links the inspiration for the Ku Klux Klan to the values of the "suffering bleeding remnant" of the "Killing Times" in southwest Scotland. Thus, though we may at worst condemn and at best regret some of the values and attitudes of those Scotch-Irish, it would be difficult to deny an essential reality at the core of their findings. Their quest, after all, was part of the same engine that drives a greater amount of historical research than we are usually prepared to admit. If we cannot always let the dead man win the fight, we at least have an obligation to try to understand what the struggle was about.

3 Ulster Presbyterians: Religion, Culture, and Politics, 1660–1850

S. J. Connolly

The origins of Ulster Presbyterianism lie in the violence and uncertainty, both religious and political, of the 1640s and 1650s. For several decades Scots had been moving into Ulster—some as part of the formal plantation scheme initiated in 1609, others through spontaneous movement into a thinly populated area newly pacified and opened for settlement. By 1630 they made up perhaps 60 percent of a total settler population of around 40,000.[1] The Protestantism they brought with them already differed markedly from that of England and Ireland. The established Scottish church was still at this point episcopal, but presbyteries and synods, made up of parish ministers and lay elders, had won for themselves a role in the church's government. Popular religious traditions were also different, as was demonstrated in the spectacular surge of revivalist enthusiasm that commenced in the area around Sixmilewater River in County Antrim in 1625, spreading from there both to other parts of rural Ulster and to Lowland Scotland.

Initially, however, potential religious divisions were muffled, as all concerned concentrated on the immediate task of establishing a British and Protestant settlement in Ulster. The thoroughly Calvinist official theology of the Church of Ireland, well to the left of its English counterpart, made it easier for Scottish settlers to remain within the establishment, and its loose administrative structures permitted local accommodations between presbytery and episcopacy. Such accommodations were becoming more difficult by the late 1630s, as the Crown began to impose a tighter religious uniformity throughout its dominions. But open rejection of the episcopal church did not come until after these same religious policies had plunged all three kingdoms into civil war. The first Ulster presbytery, established at Carrickfergus in June 1642, was in fact set up by ministers and elders from four regiments of the Scottish army under Robert Monro that had arrived in Ulster two months before. Within a short time congregations were also set up in the surrounding countryside. Initially these were served by itinerant ministers sent on short tours of duty from Scotland. But by 1653 there were more than 20 resident ministers.[2]

This extension across areas of Scottish settlement by a network of Presbyterian congregations took place against a background of great political confusion. Monro's army had come to protect settlers in Ulster from the Catholics who had risen in arms in October 1641. Initially the Ulster Scots were allies of the English Parliament, opposed to both the Catholics and the Protestant supporters of Charles I. By 1648 the Scots, disillusioned with Parliament's religious and political aims, had turned back to the king. For a time their forces in Ireland cooperated with the Irish Royalists. But this alliance was progressively eroded by the growing association of the king's cause in Ireland with militant Catholicism.

The Cromwellian regime of the 1650s initially harassed the Presbyterians for their support of the exiled Charles II, but improved relations after 1655 permitted Presbyterians to consolidate and further extend their ecclesiastical organization. By the end of the decade the number of ministers had risen to at least seventy.[3] Their numerical strength and cohesion, at a time when the Anglican clergy had either conformed to the congregationalist structure established by the new government or retreated into quietism, made Presbyterians in fact the most considerable Protestant grouping. For a short time, in the hectic maneuverings that followed the death of Cromwell and the collapse of his regime, it seemed as if the return of monarchy might be combined with a restructuring of the state church along Presbyterian lines. But the episcopalian loyalties of the returning Royalists, and the retreat into conservatism of a landed class frightened by the anarchy they had glimpsed in 1659, ensured that the old Anglican regime was restored without modification.[4]

Official treatment of Presbyterians over the next twenty-five years was, like other aspects of the religious policies of Charles II, ambiguous and inconsistent. In the 1660s the restored bishops, backed by the civil authorities, sought to prevent Presbyterian assemblies and, in some cases, imprisoned or excommunicated the ministers involved. The Act of Uniformity, passed in 1666, made it illegal for anyone not episcopally ordained to administer communion and required that all schoolmasters be licensed by the Anglican bishop.[5] In 1672, during the king's brief experiment with religious toleration, Presbyterian ministers began receiving a payment, the *regium donum*, toward the cost of their maintenance. Yet the Dublin authorities continued to regard the Ulster Presbyterians as potentially disloyal. There was particular concern that they might unite with the Covenanters or other Scottish opponents of the Restoration settlement. Repeatedly during the 1670s the Dublin administration responded to word of disturbances in Scotland by drafting extra troops into Ulster. In 1683–84, following the supposed Whig conspiracy known as the Rye House plot, local authorities in Ulster closed down Presbyterian meeting houses and began levying fines on those who failed to attend Anglican worship.[6]

Presbyterian-Anglican hostilities were briefly suspended during 1685–91, as both parties united against the apparent plans of James II to turn Ireland into the main stronghold of his Catholic monarchy. But as soon as the war for Ireland had been won, the old tensions reappeared. Anglicans were now seriously alarmed by the Presbyterian presence in Ulster. Fresh immigration in the 1650s and 1660s had come from both England and Scotland, boosting Presbyterian numbers but not their share of the Protestant population: in the late 1660s Scots still made up around 60 percent of the British population, now increased to about 120,000. A last great flood of immigrants in the 1690s, by contrast, came entirely from Scotland. Although contemporary estimates of 50,000–80,000 new arrivals were too high, Presbyterians now comprised by far the largest Protestant group in Ulster, and they may have equaled or outnumbered Anglicans in the country as a whole.[7]

In 1691 Presbyterian ministers in Ulster set up an overall governing body, the General Synod. At a time when Presbyterianism had just displaced episcopacy as the established religion in Scotland, this growth in numbers and organizational strength was deeply alarming to Anglicans. Hostility intensified after the accession of Queen Anne in 1702, as the High Church movement, concerned to reassert the authority of the established church, gained ground among clergy and some laymen in both Britain and Ireland. Ecclesiastical and local authorities sought to block the establishment of new Presbyterian congregations, and church courts prosecuted the participants and officiating ministers at Presbyterian weddings. Meanwhile, a clause attached to the major anti-Catholic statute of 1704 introduced the Sacramental Test, in force in England since 1673. This act required all holders of offices of profit or trust under the Crown to obtain certificates that they were communicants in the

Church of Ireland. At the peak of the Anglican reaction, in the summer of 1714, the Dublin government suspended payment of the *regium donum*, High Church mobs in Ulster attacked Presbyterian meeting houses, and there was a rash of prosecutions under the Act of Uniformity.[8]

The accession of George I ended the immediate pressure on Ulster Presbyterians but did not bring any fundamental change in their status. The Whigs who now monopolized political power in Great Britain were explicitly committed to the principles of the Glorious Revolution and of Protestant unity against the threat of popery at home and abroad. The circumstances of the Irish Protestant gentry, confronted by Catholic and Presbyterian rivals, both of whom were numerically far more formidable than their English counterparts, meant that the great majority wholeheartedly supported the first part of this political stance but were less enthusiastic about the second. Thus, attempts by the London government to improve the legal position of Irish Presbyterians rapidly ran into difficulties. Although the new government acted to prevent further direct harassment of Presbyterian ministers and congregations, Anglican hardliners used the church courts, which were outside the immediate control of the executive, to fight a vigorous rearguard action lasting well into the 1720s. Meanwhile, governmental attempts to persuade the Irish Parliament to admit Dissenters to civil and military office were wholly unsuccessful. Parliament did pass a Toleration Act in 1719, but this act, conceding no more than the right of Protestant Dissenters to attend their own services without incurring legal penalties, was in fact a cleverly designed preemptive measure introduced by supporters of the established church as a means of blocking anything more substantial. A further attempt to remove the Sacramental Test in 1733 was abandoned in the face of overwhelming opposition.[9]

Throughout the eighteenth century, and for most of the nineteenth, Ulster Presbyterians thus remained on the middle rung of a tripartite hierarchy of status and privilege: Anglican, Presbyterian, and Catholic. Marriages of two Presbyterians by their own minister were legalized in 1737, but it was not until 1844 that the state clearly recognized the right of ministers to officiate where one of the parties was not a Presbyterian. Second, and far more burdensome, was the requirement that Presbyterians pay tithes to the Church of Ireland. This issue became less visible after 1838, when the tithe became a charge on landownership rather than occupancy, but the underlying grievance was not removed until the disestablishment of the Church of Ireland in 1870. The other major grievance, the Sacramental Test, remained in force up to 1780. It was undoubtedly of importance in excluding Presbyterians from municipal corporations at a time when their strong position in Ulster's commercial life would have ensured local political dominance in many places. But in other respects the effect of the test must be set in the context of a society dominated by networks of patronage extending downward from an overwhelmingly Anglican landed class. The absence of any great purge of office holders after the imposition of the Sacramental Test in 1704 makes clear that, even before the test, not many Presbyterians had managed to gain seats on the gravy train of Irish public employment. By the same token the absence of a significant landowning element continued long after 1780, preventing Presbyterians from joining the political establishment. It was not until 1857, for example, that a Presbyterian was returned for an Irish county seat. Even in the borough constituencies, where landlord influence was less important and commercial and manufacturing interests could generally expect to carry more weight, only four Presbyterian candidates had been returned in the period 1832–57.[10] Anglicans also continued to make up a wholly disproportionate number of judges, magistrates, and senior civil servants. As late as 1880 a Presbyterian journal could complain that "from the highest official to the lowest, there is a disposition to keep episcopacy in a position of ascendancy."[11]

The Presbyterians of Ulster remained throughout the eighteenth century and into the nineteenth a well-defined separate group within Irish society. Their distinctive identity had three main components: religious, economic, and cultural.

The religious system that Ulster Presbyterianism had developed in the fifty years after 1642 was highly organized and all-embracing. The affairs of each congregation were regulated by the kirk session, made up of the minister and lay elders. Wider issues were dealt with by the presbytery, representing a group of congregations, or, from 1691, by the General Synod—with each of these again made up of both ministers and elders. Much of the business of the kirk session was concerned with the scrutiny of members' moral conduct. It was a discipline hard to avoid. Elders were expected to inquire into the behavior of their neighbors and report transgressions to the session. There were also meetings at which each elder in turn left the room while his behavior was discussed by the rest. Those complained of were summoned for examination; if the offence was proved, they were made to perform public penance. New members were required to bring with them a certificate of good conduct from their former congregation.[12]

It was this comprehensive system of religious and moral discipline that, more than anything else, alarmed Anglican critics of Presbyterianism. William King, archbishop of Dublin, defended the Sacramental Test by arguing that Irish Dissenters were wholly different from their English counterparts: "they make laws for themselves and allow not that the civil magistrate has any right to control them, and will be just so far the king's subjects as their lay elders and presbyteries will allow them." Laymen, King alleged, were "under an absolute slavery" to their ministers and elders, obliged to buy and sell only with those whom church authorities approved.[13] What such comments overlooked was the relatively democratic nature of Presbyterian church government. Ministers—most of them the sons of farmers—were chosen by the congregations they were to serve, and laymen played a part in decision making at every level. The discipline of the local session, backed up by the threat of excommunication and ostracism, may have been burdensome to the individual, but it reflected the values and preferences of a whole community. Precisely for this reason, Presbyterian discipline extended well beyond strictly religious concerns. Eighteenth-century session books show members being disciplined for dishonesty in business dealings, for quarrelling with neighbors, even for seeking to outbid a fellow Presbyterian for land on which he was regarded as having first claim.

The high degree of cohesion maintained in the difficult years of the seventeenth century gave way during the calmer period after 1714 to an equally striking indulgence in internal controversy. In 1726 ministers unwilling to subscribe to the Westminster Confession of Faith broke away from the General Synod to form the separate Presbytery of Antrim. Shortly afterward theological conservatives who remained dissatisfied with the synod's commitment to orthodoxy withdrew to set up the Secession Church, which itself later split into rival burgher and antiburgher factions following a dispute that had arisen in the Scottish church on the issue of lay patronage. These fissures in the monolith of Ulster Dissent were reassuring to Anglican observers. Together with the beginning of large-scale Presbyterian emigration from around 1718, they help to account for a certain softening of denominational rivalries after the 1720s. From another point of view, however, such internal divisions fought out to the point of schism were a further demonstration of the fierce spirit of independence that was central to the growth and continuation of Ulster Presbyterianism in all its forms.

Establishment hostility toward Presbyterians was further reinforced by a second characteristic: their relative economic independence. English settlers in seventeenth-century Ulster had in many cases come as sponsored migrants, taking their positions as laborers, petty tradesmen, or small farmers within a passable replica of the hierarchical world of rural England. The Scots, by contrast, had more commonly arrived as independent migrants, untrammeled by bonds of clientage and with resources of their own. Before long they dominated not only the counties of Antrim and Down but also some of the most fertile parts of other Ulster counties, relegating not just Catholics but also Anglicans to more remote and unprofitable lands.[14]

Although at the highest level of all, that of the landowning class, Presbyterians remained very poorly represented—Presbyterian landed families, small in number, tended over time to drift to the established church—they remained the most privileged group within Ulster society. The eighteenth-century counties of Antrim, Londonderry, and Down, the chief strongholds of Presbyterianism, maintained a pattern of mixed farming on reasonably large holdings quite different from the fragmented and overburdened agriculture characteristic of most other regions. In addition, the linen weavers of these counties retained their status as independent craftsmen producing directly for the market—this at a time when weavers in south Ulster were being forced to work as wage laborers for piece rates on materials put out to them by middlemen. Census statistics from the nineteenth century confirm that Presbyterians continued to be significantly overrepresented among merchants, businessmen, white collar, and skilled workers and that even working-class Presbyterians were better housed and better educated than either their Catholic or Church of Ireland counterparts.[15]

It was these favorable circumstances that made it possible for the Ulster Scots to persist in their rejection of the church of the landlord class. (By contrast the nonconformist congregations that the Cromwellian army had left behind in the south, where economic underdevelopment strengthened the ties of vertical dependency, had by the early eighteenth century dwindled into relative insignificance.) In addition, and accounting for at least part of the hostility that Presbyterians awakened among the ruling elite, economic independence encouraged an aggressive rejection of that dependence which the age expected of social subordinates.

Thus the rector of Dungiven, County Derry, writing in 1814, contrasted the "natural politeness and urbanity" of the Catholic inhabitants with "the rough and ungracious salutation but too common among the descendants of the Scotch."[16] A report on the parish of Mallusk in County Antrim, twenty years later, noted that the predominantly Presbyterian inhabitants "are rather rough and blunt, though honest in their manners. A stranger would term them rude, but politeness they look on as servility." In Ballymartin, in the same county, "their manners, even when intending civility, are far from being courteous, but their ideas and principles are generally honest and manly. They are more than a little stubborn. . . . They may be led but they won't be driven."[17]

The dour incivility of the Presbyterians of the northeast can also be seen as part of their distinctive cultural inheritance, preserving in an Irish context the traditions of Lowland Scotland. In the early decades of settlement, Scots were still recognized by their dress. An anonymous memorandum circa 1660 recommended that they be required to wear hats rather than bonnets so that "it would not be so visible to themselves in a short time that they were so numerous, nor so great a discouragement to the English, who in all fairs and markets see a hundred bonnets worn for one hat."[18] One of the women accused of witchcraft in Island Magee in 1711 wore "a dirty biggy (which is the head clothes which the farmers' and tradesmens' wives in Scotland usually wear)."[19] By the later eighteenth century such differences appear to have disappeared. Distinctions in accent lasted longer. An account of the parish of Killead in southern County Antrim in 1838 noted that accents delineated "the purely Scottish districts immediately north of it, and those as purely English immediately south of it. In it, in proceeding southward, the traveller first notices the disappearance of the strong Scottish accent of the more northern parishes, and in it he first perceives in their orchards, gardens and taste for planting (particularly the elms in the hedgerows along the roadside) the characteristics of an English colony." Another, slightly earlier account, however, noted that the distinctive accent still retained by the descendants of Scottish settlers had also been acquired by "the English colonists . . . where the intercourse is frequent."[20] A national accent was becoming a regional one.

In other cases, too, interchange had blurred cultural boundaries. The Island Magee trials of 1711 grew out of a distinctively Scottish tradition. Formal witchcraft accusations of this kind had never been common elsewhere in Ireland and had been tacitly abandoned in England by the 1680s. In the early nineteenth century, Ulster Presbyterians continued to live as if in a universe of unseen forces that some could manipulate either for good or for evil. But references to their regard for fairy bushes and even holy wells make clear that the magical beliefs of Lowland Scotland had by now become inextricably intermingled with those of Catholic Ulster.[21] In the same way the game of shinty, originally a Scottish import, appears to have become largely indistinguishable from the similar game involving crooked sticks and a ball known throughout most of Ireland as "common" (*caman* in Irish).[22] Some cultural traditions, however, resisted assimilation. In the early nineteenth century, Presbyterians in Ulster—like Scots today—still paid less attention than others to the festival of Christmas.[23] Cultural ties with Scotland were also kept alive by the religious connection: prior to the establishment of the Belfast Academical Institution in 1815, Ulster ministers were trained at the University of Glasgow, and Scottish controversies like the burgher-antiburgher dispute of the 1740s quickly spilled over into Presbyterian Ulster.

National identity, of course, is as much a matter of self-definition as of ethnicity or even culture. Here the seventeenth and eighteenth centuries were for all sections of Irish society a time of uncertainty and readjustment. Up to the end of the seventeenth century, and for some time beyond, "Irish" and "English" usually meant "Catholic" and "Protestant." The Ulster Presbyterians, in such a scheme, were "Scots," and they continued to be regarded as such. Governments in the 1660s and 1670s had been alert to the risk that the Presbyterians of Ulster might join the Scottish Covenanters in rebellion. In the same way, Queen Anne's ministers, in the period of heightened Anglo-Scottish tension that preceded the union of 1707, saw the Ulster Presbyterians as a potentially dangerous fifth column in the event of war.[24] Indeed, at this stage the Presbyterians themselves thought in very similar terms. Ulster students registering at Glasgow University were entered on its rolls as "Scotus Hiberniae," and a judgment of the Lord Advocate in 1722 referring to them as "Irishmen" aroused great indignation. By the middle of the eighteenth century, however, Ulster Presbyterians, like other denominations of Irish Protestants, had begun to define themselves, though with some continuing inhibitions, as Irish.[25]

This change in self-definition prepared the way for a new stage in what was already a complex political history. In the middle decades of the seventeenth century, the Ulster Scots had acted a wholly separate role. They had at different times allied themselves with, and taken up arms against, each of the other major groups contending for power—the Royalists, the Parliamentarians, and the Irish Catholic Confederation. In the decades after 1660, by contrast, more settled conditions and firm control by the restored monarchy had sharply reduced the opportunities for independent political action. The Scottish Presbyterian population reemerged as an important force in the war of 1688–91, when they were in the forefront of resistance to James II and his Irish allies. Their stand was initially part of a general Irish Protestant movement for self-defense, at a point when the immediate threat of Catholic domination had pushed ethnic and denominational distinctions into the background. Once the conflict was over, however, rivalry between Anglicans and Presbyterians once again came into the open, in the form of bitter squabbles over the relative contribution of the two groups toward the defeat of the common enemy. The mutual hostility of the two main Protestant denominations was also central to the bitter party conflict that marked the reign of Queen Anne (1702–14), with Tories defending the privileges of the established church while Ulster Presbyterians acted as the main electoral power base of the Irish Whigs. As late as March 1718 a group went about the streets of Armagh City assaulting local Tories to cries of "scour the Tories and Papists, for they are much alike, and damn the Church of England people for the most of them are Jacobites."[26] Already by this time, however, the eclipse of the Tories at the national level was making such local partisanship redundant. Significantly, the leadership of the Whig party had passed, by the early 1730s, from the heirs of the Ulster magnate William Conolly to the faction led by Henry Boyle, a Munster-based politician to whom the problems of northern Dissenters were of no direct electoral concern. The political marginalization of the Ulster Presbyterians was forcefully demonstrated in the ignominious failure of attempts to repeal the Sacramental Test in 1733.

Political eclipse was never total. Throughout the early and middle decades of the eighteenth century, Presbyterian Ulster constituted one important base for the continued tradition of radical political thought that Caroline Robbins, in a classic study, has called the "Commonwealth" school. These "Commonwealthmen," heirs to the republican writers of the seventeenth century, defended the values of representative government, civil liberties, and active citizenship; some called themselves "real Whigs," implicitly rejecting the oligarchic Whiggism whose dominance in both Ireland and Great Britain had been confirmed by the Hanoverian succession. The most prominent Irish representative of this tradition was Francis Hutcheson, the son and grandson of Presbyterian ministers from County Down, who taught for ten years in Dublin before taking the chair of philosophy at the University of Glasgow in 1730. Hutcheson's defense of representative government and of the right of resistance to tyranny, carried to America by former students, was to be an important influence on the development of colonial radicalism. Other significant figures included James Arbuckle, editor of the *Dublin Weekly Journal;* the publisher William Bruce; and Thomas Drennan, who taught with Hutcheson in the Dublin Academy and whose son William was to be a founding member of the Society of United Irishmen. These men were linked, not only by their advanced political views and a common Ulster Presbyterian background, but also by close personal and family ties. For example, Hutcheson—who was a cousin of William Bruce, who published Hutcheson's early work—had been a pupil at the academy in Killyleagh, County Down, founded by Bruce's father. How far these sophisticated intellectuals, part of a closely knit network of friends and relatives, were representative of a wider body of opinion remains difficult to say. The most recent study, that by A. T. Q. Stewart, emphasizes their isolation from the mainstream of Ulster Presbyterianism.[27] But the radical tradition was strong enough for the lord lieutenant, the Duke of Bedford, to complain in 1759 of a faction of Presbyterians who were in his view "totally republican and averse to English government."[28]

Over the next four decades, what was in 1759 an alarmist response to purely theoretical writings evolved into something close to reality. In the 1770s Ulster Presbyterians were both sympathetic to the cause of the American revolutionaries and active in supporting local agitation for the removal of restrictions on Irish trade, for the independence of the Irish Parliament, and later for electoral reform. In 1776 the predominantly Presbyterian voters of County Antrim, in an unprecedented departure from the pattern of proprietorial control normal in county elections, returned James Willson, a reform candidate with no landed property.[29] Although the collapse of the parliamentary reform agitation of 1783–85 temporarily dampened radical spirit, events in France after 1789 brought a new wave of reforming enthusiasm. Thomas Paine's *Rights of Man* became, using Wolf Tone's famous phrase, the "Koran" of Belfast. The Society of United Irishmen, founded in October 1791, drew its initial membership almost entirely from the local Presbyterian commercial community of the same city. Later, as it expanded to include a popular following, it found its first and most receptive recruiting ground among the Presbyterian farmers and weavers of Counties Antrim, Down, and Londonderry.[30]

That the Presbyterians of Ulster should thus have provided the most active and committed supporters of the movement for political reform, and eventually of French-inspired revolutionary conspiracy, is in no way surprising. As religious dissenters in a state dominated by Anglican landowners they possessed both memories of past oppression and a continuing sense of grievance. Their members, as already noted, included a high proportion of independent small producers who, largely free of the bonds of clientage and dependency, were sufficiently confident of their own status to resent the manifold inequalities of a society based on hereditary privilege. Levels of literacy were also high, reflecting both the relative prosperity of the Presbyterian population and a religious tradition that emphasized individual bible reading. The 1780s and 1790s saw a proliferation of book clubs and reading societies among farmers and tradesmen in Antrim and Down. The United Irish leader Arthur O'Connor told Charles James Fox that Ulster had "perhaps the best educated peasantry in Europe."[31]

All this made Presbyterian Ulster a classic milieu for the development of late-eighteenth-century popular radicalism. At the same time it would be wrong to interpret its politics solely in terms of the Enlightenment virtues of literacy, rationality, and economic independence. Recent research has shown, for example, that support for the United Irish movement was not, as was long imagined, uniquely or even particularly associated with the theologically liberal "New Light" wing of Presbyterianism. Of those ministers actively involved in the movement whose theological views can be determined, about half were in fact "Old Light" supporters of doctrinal orthodoxy. Here it is important to remember that the cause for which the Scots of Ulster had fought in the mid-seventeenth century had not been the combination of rationalistic religion and classical republicanism seen among Dublin- and Belfast-based intellectuals like Arbuckle, Bruce, and Hutcheson. Rather, it had been the cause of Charles II, in his guise as the godly monarch, pledged by his adherence to the Solemn League and Covenant to uphold true religion throughout his realms.

In the 1790s, similarly, there seem to have been elements among both clergy and laity to whom events in France were notable less as the victory of political liberty than as the downfall of popish absolutism or, in millenarian terms, as the fall of the Antichrist. The printed propaganda of the United Irishmen included not just such classics of secular radicalism as Paine's *Rights of Man* but prophetic and other writings from the seventeenth-century covenanting tradition. In this as in other respects the revolutionary movement of the 1790s was a coalition of widely differing elements, briefly fused into one whole by the pressures of the immediate crisis.[32]

Not all Ulster Presbyterians, of course, were revolutionaries. The Synod of Ulster was from the start strongly hostile to French-inspired radicalism. Others who were initially drawn to the United Irish movement drifted away during the 1790s as the movement's politics became more extreme. Because the suggestion that Presbyterians should unite with Catholics to force radical political change was particularly problematic, the United Irish movement was never as successful among Presbyterians living in south and west Ulster, where Catholics were numerically strong, as it was in Antrim and parts of the surrounding counties, where Protestants made up two-thirds or more of the population. Within this northeast corner, however, the cause of revolution achieved a degree of popular support seen nowhere else in Ireland. When in December 1796 a French invasion fleet attempted a landing on the southwestern coast, the Irish government was enormously relieved that it had not appeared instead off County Antrim. When the authorities, soon after, moved against what was by that time a formidable revolutionary underground, it was in Ulster that they began their work. Despite the repression that followed, the United Irishmen of Antrim, Down, and Londonderry were able, in June 1798, to stage armed insurrections in support of an uprising in the south. Those involved included more than twenty Presbyterian ministers, four of whom were later executed.

The events of 1798 did not, as is sometimes imagined, bring about the instant collapse of Ulster Presbyterian disaffection. Once the immediate shock of the rebellion was over, there was in fact a revival, beginning around 1806, of radical political activity in Belfast. For another twenty years or so the city remained the center of a recognizable body of Protestant, overwhelmingly Presbyterian, radicalism, expressing itself over such issues of the day as the scandal, centered on the duke of York, over corruption in the army; the claims of George IV's estranged wife, Queen Caroline; and such longstanding causes as parliamentary reform and control of patronage. In 1816 the government was alarmed to learn of a dinner attended by teachers and governors of Belfast Academical Institution, the training college for Presbyterian ministers, at which toasts were drunk to the American and French revolutions.[33] Nor was the expression of such sentiments wholly confined to after-dinner conviviality. In 1806 it was reported that the clandestine Defender movement around Kells in County Antrim still contained "more dissenters . . . than Catholics." As late as 1814 there were accounts of "a few Protestant traitors, a remnant of the views and projects of 1798," active in Belfast and the surrounding countryside. Edward Wakefield, a reasonably liberal English commentator, argued in 1812 that the Presbyterians as a whole were "republicans in principle, in their hearts decided enemies to the established government," their apparent passivity "the quietness of expedience alone."[34]

Even so, it remains undeniably true that after 1798 the Presbyterians of east Ulster retreated from their role as the vanguard of Irish popular radicalism. Official concern over their possibly treasonable predilections appears to have died out by the start of the 1820s. By 1835 a visitor to the parish of Connor in County Antrim could note complacently that the inhabitants "were almost to a man engaged in the rebellion of 1798. . . . However since that time their politics have changed, and they now seem indifferent and careless on the subject."[35] Six years later Daniel O'Connell, leader of the movement for repeal of the Act of Union, wrote off the whole past and present political commitment of Ulster Presbyterianism in a contemptuous phrase: they had, he said, "fought badly at Ballynahinch . . . and as soon as the fellows were checked they became furious Orangemen and have continued so ever since."[36]

That the Presbyterians of east Ulster should have moved away from their earlier commitment to revolutionary politics is not in itself a matter for much comment. The events of the 1790s had after all been exceptional, part of an international crisis. After 1815 the vocabulary of politics was changing everywhere in the United Kingdom, among Irish Catholics and English working-class radicals as well as the Protestant, former United Irishmen. But there were also other changes, more closely reflecting the particular circumstances of Ulster Presbyterians. In the 1790s the radicals among them had accepted the idea that there should be a "brotherhood of affection" uniting Catholics and those Protestants not part of the political establishment. They had done so partly out of expediency, partly out of a belief that Irish Catholicism was becoming more moderate and less monolithic, and partly, as already mentioned, out of the confidence born of a strong local numerical superiority. Events in the south in the summer of 1798, when the ostensibly republican and democratic insurrection initiated by the United Irish leaders turned into a bloody religious civil war, brutally exposed the dangers of such a strategy. As early as June 3, 1798, an informant in Ulster reported "a great change in the sentiments of many of the Presbyterians, in consequence of the massacre of so many Protestants in the south." Five years later the judge who presided over a special commission in Ulster reported that, although the spirit of rebellion was now "completely down" among the Dissenters of the north, what kept them loyal was not a change in political principles but rather their conviction "that the country is in danger from the Catholics."[37]

That conviction was strengthened rather than weakened by the events of the next three or four decades. From the 1820s a new generation of Catholic political leaders, headed by Daniel O'Connell, set about organizing—in close alliance with the Catholic clergy—a new and formidable system of popular agitation. In 1813 the Synod of Ulster was still able to support the principle of Catholic emancipation, but by the mid-1820s there were indications that a growing majority of Presbyterians were now hostile to further concessions. The renewed necessity of seeing themselves as part of a threatened Protestant minority within Ireland as a whole also forced Ulster Presbyterians to look again at the idea of an Ireland independent of Great Britain. The disappearance of separatist sentiment after the 1790s can in part be attributed to the growing dependence of east Ulster, with its flourishing manufactures, on English markets and raw materials. But the main reason was the growing realization that only a close continuing connection with Great Britain could protect the Protestant minority from the tyranny of aggressive Catholicism.[38]

O'Connell's dismissive comments in 1841 are vivid testimony to the estrangement that had taken place by this time between the Presbyterians of the northeast and their former Catholic and nationalist allies. As a summary of Presbyterian political development since the 1790s, however, his words are less than satisfactory. It is true that Ulster Presbyterians had by this time abandoned even the diluted radicalism they had shown in the first decades after 1800. But they had not all become conservatives, much less "furious Orangemen." Some had indeed responded to the threat of Catholic domination by giving wholehearted support to the existing establishment. The notorious example is Henry Cooke, the most prominent minister of his generation, who in 1834 appeared at a rally organized by the leaders of Ulster Toryism in Hillsborough, County Down, to announce "the banns of marriage" between Presbyterianism and the established church, henceforth bound together in defense of the constitution. But Cooke's open identification with the Tory cause was in fact widely criticized by other leading Presbyterians, who preferred to give their support to Whigs or Liberals, as well as to agitators of agrarian issues: during the major campaign for tenant rights of the late 1840s and early 1850s Cooke complained of "perfect communist interpretations" put forward by some ministers.[39]

At the popular level antiestablishment politics were more fragmented. Poll book analysis suggests that Ulster Liberalism was, from at least the 1830s, dependent for electoral support on the alliance of an overwhelming majority of Catholic voters combined with a minority of mainly more affluent Presbyterians. Poorer Presbyterians were more likely to respond to the claims of Protestant unity and vote Conservative.[40] But this does not mean that they had lost the truculent independence, combined with dislike of an Anglican-dominated establishment, that had earlier made them such willing recruits to the radical cause. In Ballyrobert, County Antrim, for example, a "memoir" compiled in 1838 for the Ordnance Survey reported "a strong prejudice" against both Anglicanism and Catholicism, "which creeds they look on as being closely allied," adding that "all classes have absurd notions as to independence in religious and secular matters." An account of Doagh similarly attributed the "cold, stiff and disagreeable" manners of the inhabitants to "a notion that they have no superiors, and that courtesy is but another name for servility. This last notion is chiefly to be attributed to their independent circumstances, holding leases in perpetuity at trifling rents, and to the information they have attained by reading without its being matured by intercourse with the world."[41] Sentiments like these could still, in the right circumstances, be mobilized in the service of antiestablishment politics, as they were in the tenant right campaign of the immediate post-Famine years. Where electoral politics are concerned, the heyday of Ulster Liberalism in fact came relatively late, in the period following the Reform Act of 1867 and the unsatisfactory Land Act of 1870. In the general election of 1880, against a background of agricultural depression and bitter conflict between landlord and tenant, Liberal candidates are estimated to have taken up to half the Presbyterian vote in the Ulster counties. It was only over the next few years, as the prospect of Home Rule imposed by a Liberal government became impossible to ignore, that Ulster Presbyterian Liberalism was finally eliminated as a significant electoral force.[42]

At the same time that the political outlook of Ulster Presbyterians was being gradually reshaped, major changes were also taking place in religious attitudes. By the 1820s an evangelical party, committed to the centrality of the individual's personal conviction of salvation through God's grace, was rapidly gaining ground among both clergy and laity. In 1829 a group unwilling to accept evangelical demands for a strict definition of belief in the divinity of Christ and for the scrutiny of the personal religious experiences of future ministers was forced to secede from the Synod of Ulster. These religious differences in some cases overlapped with political divisions. The chief spokesman for the evangelicals was Henry Cooke, whereas the leader of the seceding Remonstrants, Henry Montgomery, was a prominent supporter of Ulster Liberalism. In other cases, however, there was no direct correlation between religious and political views.[43]

Yet the triumph of evangelicalism did have a wider significance. The emphasis of Ulster Presbyterianism in the eighteenth century had been on community. What was important was membership in the kirk session and submission to its discipline. The conversionist evangelicalism of the nineteenth century, however, brought a crucial change of emphasis. In place of the goal of a self-contained society regulated according to a distinctive set of religious, moral, and even political principles, Presbyterians now became preoccupied with the salvation of the individual, achieved through and manifested in the intensely personal experience of conversion.[44] This shift in focus came at a time when the tight communal discipline of the eighteenth century was beginning to break down, as population grew and rapid economic change disrupted settled communities.[45] It was also a time when the peculiarities of accent, custom, and behavior that had continued to mark out the descendants of Scottish settlers as a separate cultural group had begun to erode. All three developments are clearly related. Taken together with gradual political absorption into a pan-Protestant Unionism, they reflect the extent of the transformation that was taking place. Ulster Presbyterians, for the better part of two centuries a separate people, were becoming instead a religious denomination.

4 The Demographic History of Ulster, 1750–1841

William Macafee

At the beginning of the eighteenth century the population of Ulster was probably just in excess of half a million people. By the middle of the century little change had taken place, but by 1841 its population had risen to some 2.4 million. The first serious explanation of this dramatic rise in population was advanced by K. H. Connell in 1950.[1] Connell's work related to Ireland as a whole, but his general explanation applies to Ulster. He argued that population in Ireland began to grow rapidly from the 1780s and that the major cause of that growth was an increase in fertility resulting from a fall in age at first marriage. Since Connell's seminal study, work on sources such as parish registers and Hearth Returns coupled with a reinterpretation of Irish economic history has called into question both his chronology of growth and his explanation of that growth.[2] At the same time a convincing alternative explanation to the one proposed by Connell has not been forthcoming. Indeed, one of the reasons for such a state of affairs is the growing appreciation of the regional contrasts within the island as a whole. Before the complete demographic history of Ireland can be written, it may be necessary to have a fuller understanding of regional variations. This chapter explores, in the light of recent research, the demographic history of Ulster during the period 1750–1841.

Clearly any study of population growth requires reasonably accurate counts of the population for as many years as possible throughout a period. Such a statement is self-evident to present-day demographers, who have census figures usually on a decennial basis. However, for the decades before 1850, census figures for Ulster are only available for the years 1821, 1831, and 1841. Any counts for the eighteenth century have to be estimated from Hearth Tax Returns. This involves adjusting the raw figures to allow for exemption and evasion and, because they refer to households, multiplying them by an appropriate household size. The figures, therefore, that appear in Table 4.1 reflect adjustments used by different scholars.

The first set of estimates in Table 4.1 are based on the work of Connell. Working back from the 1821 census, Connell suggested a correction factor of 20 percent for the 1791 Hearth Returns.[3] He then assumed that the further back into the eighteenth century one went, the more inefficient the collection of the hearth tax became. This prompted him to increase the raw figures for the first half of the eighteenth century by 50 percent for Ireland as a whole. On the question of household size, Connell postulated multipliers in excess of five for the eighteenth century: 5.25 for 1725, 5.38 for 1753, and 5.65 for 1791.[4]

When Connell applied these adjustments and multipliers to the tax returns for Ireland as a whole, he found little growth in the population until the second half of the eighteenth century. His adjustments suggested an annual growth rate of 1.05 percent for the period 1753–91 and a rate of 1.2 percent for the period 1791–1821.[5] Connell never made any separate calculations for Ulster, regarding the statistics as too inadequate and too insecure to point with any certainty to regional trends in population growth. However, recent research by Dickson et al. has questioned Connell's reservations about the inadequacy of the regional statistics.[6] Table 4.1 shows population estimates and annual growth rates for Ulster based on the work of Connell, Clarkson, Dickson et al., and Macafee. In all instances the pattern for Ulster shows population growing rapidly between 1753 and 1791, with a falling off in growth after 1791. This is in contrast to Connell's national picture of slightly slower growth from 1753 to 1791, with continued increase between 1791 and 1821.

The chronology of growth postulated by Connell for Ireland as a whole was consistent with G. A. T. O'Brien's interpretation of Irish economic development.[7] This view contrasted the long-term depression of the earlier part of the century under repressive English mercantilist policy with the growth and prosperity experienced under the legislative encouragement of Grattan's Parliament. Thus Connell's contention was that population began to expand rapidly from the 1780s because of the encouragement given to grain under the Corn Laws passed by the Irish Parliament in 1784. This swing from pasture to arable land made it possible, he argued, for the Irish to realize their long-felt desire to marry early. The inevitable increase in fertility that resulted from these earlier

Table 4.1 Estimates of Ulster Population, 1712–1841
(in millions)

	Connell (1950)	Clarkson (1981)	Dickson et al. (1982)	Macafee (1987)
1712	0.82		0.54–0.63	
1725	0.84	0.61	0.56–0.65	
1744	0.83		0.55–0.64	
1753	0.93	0.66	0.62–0.72	0.63–0.77
1791	1.50	1.40–1.50	1.43	1.28–1.33
1821	1.99			
1831	2.30			
1841	2.40			

Annual Growth Rates for Ulster Population, 1712–1841 (in percentages)

	Connell (1950)	Clarkson (1981)	Dickson et al. (1982)	Macafee (1987)
1712–1753	0.3		0.3	
1753–1791	1.3	1.9–2.1	1.7–2.2	1.3–1.9
1791–1821	1.0	1.0–1.2	1.1	1.3–1.4
1753–1841	1.1	1.5	1.3–1.5	1.3–1.5

SOURCES: K. H. Connell, *The Populations of Ireland, 1750–1845* (Oxford: Oxford University Press, 1950), 25; D. Dickson, C. O'Grada, and S. Daultrey, "Hearth Tax, Household Size and Irish Population Change, 1672–1821," *Proceedings of The Royal Irish Academy* 82 (1982), 125–81; L. Clarkson, "Irish Population Revisited, 1687–1821," in *Irish Population, Economy and Society: Essays in Honour of the late K. H. Connell,* ed. G. M. Goldstrom and L. Clarkson (Oxford: Clarendon Press, 1981), 26; W. Macafee, "The Population of Ulster, 1630–1841: Evidence from Mid-Ulster" (unpublished D.Phil. thesis, University of Ulster, Coleraine, 1987), 352, 362; Parliamentary Papers 22 (1824), 39 (1833), 24 (1843).[a] The 1712–1791 population estimates are based on Hearth Tax Returns. The 1821–1841 figures are taken from official census returns.
[a]These are normally referred to as British Parliamentary Papers; conventionally they are taken to be publications of the British House of Commons. Anyone wishing to consult these papers needs to know the volume number and the year of publication. Most of the Irish Census Papers, to which these three refer, were published originally by Alexander Thom, 87 Abbey Street, Dublin for H.M.S.O. These three volumes have been reprinted by Irish Microforms, Dublin, 1978.

marriages was, in his view, the key factor explaining the post-1780 population explosion.

The reinterpretation of Irish economic development advanced by L. M. Cullen, however, suggests a different explanation of demographic development than that postulated by Connell. Central to Cullen's thesis is the view that Irish society changed rapidly from an essentially medieval one in the early seventeenth century to one which, by the eighteenth century, was beginning to take on the trappings of a modern society.[8] Cullen regarded the growth of foreign trade and the mechanisms of trade—markets, fairs, and towns—as the motor forces in this transition.[9]

His early work, published during the 1960s, questioned the traditional view that Ireland's external trade, agriculture, and industry had been seriously hampered during the first eighty years of the eighteenth century by repressive English policy, resulting in long-term economic depression until the legislative encouragement of Grattan's Parliament after 1782.[10] This view, he argued, was based on the uncritical use of the polemic writings of contemporary pamphleteers.[11] Instead, Cullen pointed to the fact that, despite these restrictions, Ireland's external trade had begun to expand from the 1730s. Within Ulster, for example, exports of linen to England had increased fivefold by the 1770s. As W. H. Crawford has shown, this expansion in the linen trade stimulated a demand not only for yarn but also for agricultural foodstuffs to feed weavers. The effects of this even spilled over into the provinces of Connaught and Leinster.[12]

Cullen saw this trade and the internal economic development accruing from it as laying the foundations for the greater prosperity of the 1780s, which earlier historians had attributed to the legislative encouragement of Grattan's Parliament. Any further development during the period of Grattan's Parliament was, he argued, the result of industrialization in Britain and the resultant widening of demand.[13] Such a view of Irish economic development during the eighteenth century calls into question Connell's chronology of pre-Famine population growth, which suggested little growth before 1780.

More recent work by L. A. Clarkson and by Dickson et al. has suggested a different chronology, more consistent with the model of economic development postulated by Cullen. As Table 4.1 shows, they propose a scenario that, like Connell, suggests little growth before 1753. However, for the years 1753–91 both suggest exceptionally high growth rates for Ulster, ranging 1.7–2.2 percent. Once again it has to be stressed that, like Connell, Clarkson did not calculate rates for Ulster. His suggested national adjustments to the Hearth Returns and his household multipliers have simply been applied to Ulster. On the other hand, Dickson et al.'s work was regionally based. Both would agree that the growth during the period 1753–91 would have started much earlier than 1780. Perhaps the most interesting point to emerge from both studies is the dramatic fall in growth rates for Ulster during the periods after 1791, and more will be said about that later.

These drastic revisions result from a reassessment of both the adjustments that need to be made for exemption and evasion and the level of the household multiplier used. Working independently, both Clarkson and Dickson et al. presented evidence to suggest that, at least during the period 1712–53, the collection of the tax was probably more efficient than later in the century. Clarkson[14] has suggested, for Ireland as a whole, an adjustment as low as 15 percent, and Dickson et al.[15] have suggested a lower-bound adjustment of 14 percent and an upper-bound of 34 percent.

In addition to producing estimates for the national level, the Dickson et al. study produced estimates for the four provinces of Ireland. Although not specifically stated in their paper, it is possible to calculate the lower- and upper-bound adjustments for each province. They appear to suggest for Ulster a lower-bound adjustment of 12 percent and an upper-bound of 30 percent. These adjustments are very similar to that proposed for Leinster and Munster but much lower than the 23 percent and 54 percent suggested for Connaught. Clarkson[16] used the same adjustment as Connell for the 1791 returns (20 percent), but Dickson et al.[17] suggested a much lower adjustment of 8 percent. With regard to household multipliers Clarkson argued for an average household size of 5.0 throughout the eighteenth century for the whole of Ireland, but evidence from many parts of Ireland suggests that regional rather than national multipliers ought to be established.[18] Dickson et al. have suggested a household multiplier for Ulster of 4.8 for 1753 and 5.9 for 1791.[19]

Clearly, as shown in Table 4.1, these revisions suggest exceptionally high growth rates for Ulster. Those calculated from the Clarkson revisions might be deemed invalid on the grounds that national parameters have been applied to regional figures. However, the Dickson et al. growth rates are based on regional adjustments. Work by the author of this chapter supports the view of Dickson et al. that growth rates were high throughout Ulster during the period 1753–91 and that there was probably a slowing down of growth during the early part of the nineteenth century. However, it questions the level of growth during 1753–91 and the extent to which growth was inhibited in the later period.[20] Certainly a case could be made for a growth rate in Ulster of around 1.3–1.9 percent during the period 1753–91 and of 1.3–1.4 percent for the period 1791–1821. As will be shown, such a scenario of growth for Ulster is more consistent with the evidence from parish registers.

When viewed within the wider context of Western Europe, these proposed annual growth rates appear remarkable. Even within Ireland, Ulster's rate of population growth stands out, and certainly by 1841, with 406 persons per square mile of arable land, it was the most densely populated province. Connaught came next with 386, Munster with 332, and Leinster with 247.[21] Within Ulster, densities were highest in the linen areas of north Armagh and east Tyrone. When annual growth rates are compared with other countries in Europe, once again Ulster stands out. During the period 1753–1841, when annual growth rates for Ulster were probably 1.3–1.5 percent, comparable figures for England, Scotland, Sweden, and France were 1.0, 0.8, 0.7, and 0.4 percent, respectively.[22]

Why then did such unprecedented growth occur in Ulster during the second half of the eighteenth century, and were the factors causing the growth any different from those operating in the rest of Ireland? In searching for causes, immigration can be dismissed as a factor; indeed until the 1770s, Ulster was losing migrants to America. We need, therefore, to look to a fall in the death rate, a rise in fertility, or some combination of both as the direct cause of growth. At the same time these direct causes need to be considered within the wider economic and social context of which they were a part.

Let us turn first to possible changes in the death rate. Connell did not see a falling death rate as being of much importance in accelerating population growth in eighteenth-century Ireland. He believed that the death rate remained high throughout the eighteenth century, but population was able to grow in the latter part of the century because of an increase in fertility arising from a fall in the age at marriage sufficiently steep to offset the mounting losses from death.

M. Drake, critiquing Connell's work, argued for a fall in the general levels of mortality as the potato became more dominant in the diet of Irish men and women.[23] This reopening of the fertility versus mortality argument led to some studies, particularly by V. Morgan, into levels of mortality in the Ulster parishes of Blaris and Magherafelt. Despite suggested unrepresentativeness and other inadequacies that will be discussed later, such studies revealed high levels of mortality during the seventeenth and early eighteenth centuries, particularly among children.[24] I have used and extended these studies to build a picture of changing mortality during the seventeenth and eighteenth centuries, particularly with regard to the changing pattern of child deaths. Figure 4.1 gives details of child burials as a percentage of total burials in each year during the period 1650–1785.

The data relating to the parish of Templemore (which includes the city of Derry) for the years 1653–1703 indicate that on average 60 percent of the burials each year were of children. The percentage rarely fell below 50; in fact in only eight of the fifty years was it less than 50 percent. Furthermore, it could reach as high as 82 percent as it did in 1668. A similar pattern occurred in the parish of Blaris (Lisburn) where, during the years 1662–1700, 56 percent of those buried were children. Indeed, if the years 1689 and 1690 were removed from the calculation on the grounds that burials for those years were swollen by soldiers from outside the area, then once again we have a figure of 60 percent. Likewise in only six of the years during the period (and two of these were 1689 and 1690) did the percentage fall below 50, and it reached as high as 80 percent in 1666.[25]

The first half of the eighteenth century saw little change in this pattern. In Blaris during the period 1701–40 the figure fell slightly to 57 percent. In ten of these years it fell below 50 percent, and it reached its high of 73 percent in 1713. In the parish of Loughgall (not shown in Figure 4.1) in County Armagh the figure was 54 percent for the years 1701–15, and in the parish of Magherafelt in County Londonderry it reached a staggering average of 75 percent for the years 1717–36. This latter figure was caused, to some extent, by the fact that the number of deaths recorded each year was relatively small.[26]

Even by the 1750s the average could still be high; in the parish of Armagh, for example, it was 57 percent for the years 1750–57, and in Shankill parish (which includes the town of Lurgan) it was 58 percent for the period 1751–56. Of course, time spans as short as these can artificially increase or decrease the percentage. At the same time there is evidence that after the 1750s the periods of time when child burials were greater than 50 percent were both shorter and less frequent. Cer-

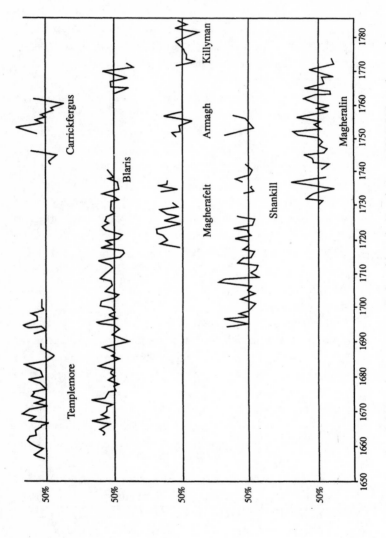

Figure 4.1 Child burials as a percentage of total burials in each year, 1650–1785, in the parishes of Armagh, Blaris, Carrickfergus, Killyman, Magheralin, Magherafelt, Shankill, and Templemore.

tainly by the latter part of the eighteenth century, as the following figures suggest, there was a considerable decrease in the percentage of child burials: Blaris 1763–71, 44 percent; Armagh 1771–74, 43 percent; Killyman 1776–87, 44 percent.[27]

Although limited and to some extent inadequate, this evidence certainly lends support to the view that mortality levels, particularly those of children, were falling throughout the eighteenth century in Ulster. Such a view would be consistent with the Cullen model of economic development, which argues for a commercialization of the Irish economy from the 1730s. Such a process not only led to earnings being monetized but also to their being increased.[28] Within Ulster, particularly in the linen areas, even the poor became involved in the process: the better-off small holders engaged in weaving, the poorer families in spinning.[29] This extra money, Cullen argued, could in better times allow the more substantial tenants to buy luxuries, but more important, it allowed the poorer sections of the community to buy food when times were bad. This injection of cash into the poorer sections of the community meant that they could now enter the market as buyers of grain from the spring onward until the next year's potato crop ripened.[30]

Improvements in transport, such as the opening of the Newry Canal by the 1740s, meant that grain and other foodstuffs could be moved around many parts of the country more easily. Such developments coupled with the spread of the potato may have prolonged life in general and, in particular, provided young children with nutritious food. Certainly the suspension of severe famines after the 1740s probably made an important contribution to the increase in population during the second half of the eighteenth century. In addition, disease, primarily smallpox, had been responsible for many child deaths, and, despite Connell's skepticism, some historians believe that the adoption of inoculation, particularly after 1760, may have saved young lives.[31] At the same time the relationship between disease and famine is far from clear. Indeed, as J. Walter and R. Schofield suggest, one of the consequences of the more effective distribution of food was the concomitant spread of diseases like smallpox and measles.[32] Clearly, the unraveling of the causal chain between disease, famine, and general economic conditions will require more research before firm conclusions can be reached on the exact timing and causes of falling mortality.

If, as in the rest of Western Europe, a falling death rate was making a substantial contribution to the growth of population in Ulster from the middle of the eighteenth century, was it sufficient to have caused the level of annual growth rates suggested in Table 4.1? Such a question seems appropriate given E. A. Wrigley and R. S. Schofield's findings with regard to the dynamics of English population growth in the eighteenth century.[33] They found that whereas a fall in the death rate had made some contribution to the rise of English population in the late eighteenth century, the main cause of growth was a rise in fertility following a lowering in the age at first marriage and a decline in celibacy. This, they argued, explains why England at that time had higher growth rates than any other country in Western Europe, with the possible exception of Ireland. If the Wrigley-Schofield thesis is correct in circumstances where growth rates only reached 1.0 percent, then might it not also apply to Ulster where, as was argued earlier, growth rates were certainly in excess of 1 percent? Indeed the Wrigley-Schofield findings could be seen as lending support to Connell's original explanation of Irish population growth.

Connell believed that the prime cause of the acceleration of population growth in Ireland during the late eighteenth century had been an increase in fertility resulting from the earlier marriage of both men and women. This earlier marriage, he contended, became possible because of the greater ease, by the 1780s, of acquiring a holding. This situation resulted from a number of interrelated factors: a swing from arable land to pasture, the increasing subdivision of estates, and the spread of the potato.

For his evidence on age at marriage Connell placed considerable reliance on the Reports of the Poor Law Commissioners, in which many of those interviewed gave details of exceptionally young marriages. Examples were given of women marrying at the ages of 15 to 20; indeed, in some areas 14 and even 13 were regarded as common ages for the marriage of girls.[34] However, this essentially oral evidence does not appear to stand up when compared with the census figures. J. Mokyr and C. O'Grada, using the 1841 census, calculated the median age at marriage for Ireland as a whole, on the eve of the Famine, at 24–25 for women and 27–29 for men. They also pointed out that of the 375,975 women aged 14–16, only 487 (1.3 percent) were married. Moreover, of the 756,726 women aged 17–25, only 146,257 (19.3 percent) were married.[35]

Work by Morgan and Macafee, based on Enumerators' Returns for a number of parishes in County Antrim, produced an average age at first marriage of approximately 26 for men and 24 for women.[36] This research also confirmed that there was some variation between social groups; certainly substantial farmers were more inclined to marry in their late twenties and early thirties. At the same time, among small farmers, weavers, and laborers there was no evidence of the widespread early marriage of the kind suggested by Connell or by contemporary observers. O'Neill, in a study of marriage ages in County Cavan during the early nineteenth century, found a difference of up to two years between the ages at which farmers and laborers married. But, once again, the average age at which laborers married, 24.5 years, was not particularly low.[37]

Though evidence from parish registers on age at marriage is scant, some analyses have been done. In particular Morgan's work on the register of baptisms, burials, and marriages for the Church of Ireland parish of Coleraine pointed to an increase in the age at marriage from an average age of 21.7 for men and 21.0 for women in the decade 1820–30, to 24–26 for men and 22–25 for women during the 1830s and 1840s.[38] Unfortunately, the inadequacy of the register in the latter years of the eighteenth and the first few decades of the nineteenth centuries makes it impossible to calculate age at marriage for this crucial earlier period.

Another problem was the fact that the sample referred, in the main, to an urban population that, it could be argued, might have a different socioeconomic structure and therefore a different pattern of marriage from the rest of rural Ireland. Preliminary work on the Blaris (Lisburn) register for the late seventeenth and early eighteenth centuries suggests a relatively early age at marriage: late teens and early twenties.[39] This could, of course, have resulted from the fact that, at that time, many of the residents of the parish would have been recently arrived immigrants. However, there is also evidence from Cromwellian Transplantation Certificates of the seventeenth century that indicate an average age at marriage of 22 for a sample of women in the counties of Dublin and Waterford.[40] D. E. C. Eversley's work on Quaker records has shown that the average age at marriage for Irish Quaker women was 23–25 throughout the period 1650–1849, and there is no evidence of a substantial fall in age at marriage in the late eighteenth century.[41] Once again the age at marriage for women is not excessively low, but it is noticeable that Irish Quaker women married, on average, at an age four years younger than their counterparts in England, a fact reflected in the higher fertility rates in Ireland.

Thus, apart from Eversley's work, there is no hard evidence on age at marriage for the latter half of the eighteenth century, which is the crucial period when population was growing rapidly. Recent work[42] on parish registers in the mid-Ulster area has produced interesting evidence on age at marriage during the period 1770–1845. The most productive of these registers was that for Killyman, where, apart from a short period of incomplete registration from 1770–75, the register had been well kept, particularly with regard to baptisms, from 1745 through to the Famine, which began in 1845.[43] The parish of Killyman is southeast of the town of Dungannon in County Tyrone and extends across the county boundary into Armagh. It lies within the area of Ulster that during the eighteenth and early nineteenth centuries was dominated by the linen industry. Because of this the region was characterized by very small farms and by cottier and weaver houses, creating high densities of population; by 1841 there were 582 persons per square mile in the parish. The register gives the occupations of the fathers of children baptized from 1837 onward, and of 317 families identified, 147 of the heads of households were weavers, 132 were farmers, 31 were in various trades, 15 were laborers, 5 were listed as professional, 1 was a servant, and 1 was a beggar. It is very probable that many of those listed as farmers were also engaged in the linen trade.

There are some 1,000 marriage entries in the Killyman register, and it was possible to trace both marriage and baptismal dates for 291 females and 200 males. In the case of males, two sets of figures were used in order to boost the size of the sample: 105 men whose actual date of marriage was known from the register, and a further 95 whose date of marriage was estimated as one year before the birth of their first child.[44]

Table 4.2 shows clearly that there was no significant change in the male age at marriage from decade to decade; the mean and indeed the median stayed around 25–26 years. Furthermore, throughout the entire period 1771–1845, only 18 percent of men marrying were aged 22 years or younger; indeed only 6 percent were 20 years or below. The stability of the male age at marriage during the period 1771–1845 was one of the most significant points to emerge from this research.

Of course fertility is not controlled by the age at which men marry; it is far more dependent on the age at which women marry. As Table 4.3 indicates, the mean age at marriage for women in Killyman during the period 1811–45 was 23.6 years, a figure very close to the findings, already mentioned, of Mokyr and O'Grada and of Morgan and Macafee. This contrasts, however, with the earlier period 1771–1810, when the

Table 4.2   Parish of Killyman: Male Age at First Marriage

	Sample Size	Mean	Standard Deviation	Median	Mode
1771–1810	92	25.7	3.3	26	27
1771–1780	17	25.4	2.3	27	27
1781–1790	25	26.4	3.6	26	30
1791–1800	12	25.2	2.7	25	24
1801–1810	38	25.4	3.6	27	27
1811–1845	108	26.1	4.1	26	23
1811–1820	30	26.1	2.8	26	25–26
1821–1830	30	26.7	4.9	26	27
1831–1840	35	25.4	4.5	24	24
1841–1845	13	26.0	3.8	26	22

SOURCE: PRONI, T.679/383, 384, 386, 387, 393.

Table 4.3   Parish of Killyman: Female Age at First Marriage

	Sample Size	Mean	Standard Deviation	Median	Mode
1771–1810	121	21.8	3.7	21	18/20
1771–1780	13	22.6	2.9	21	21
1781–1790	28	22.4	4.4	21	19
1791–1800	26	21.3	4.7	20	22
1801–1810	54	21.5	2.7	20	20
1811–1845	170	23.6	4.3	22	21/22
1811–1820	26	24.0	4.8	22	21
1821–1830	44	23.0	3.8	22	22
1831–1840	66	23.4	4.0	23	20/22/26
1841–1845	34	24.4	4.9	23	19

SOURCE: PRONI T.679/383, 384, 386, 387, 393.

Table 4.4 Parish of Killyman: Female Age at First Marriage (as share of total marriages)

	Total Marriages	Percent Aged 19 and below	Percent Aged 20 and below	Percent Aged 23 and below	Percent Aged 26 and up
1771–1810	121	31	45	73	16
1811–1845	170	15	24	58	31

SOURCE: PRONI, T.679/383, 384, 386, 387, 393.

mean age at marriage for women in Killyman was 21.8, a difference of almost two years.

Essentially the difference in age at marriage between the two periods can be explained by the percentage of those women 20 years old and younger who were marrying in each period. Table 4.4 shows clearly a high percentage of those aged 20 or below marrying in the decades between 1771 and 1810. During this period they formed close to 50 percent of the total, whereas in the period after 1811 the figure was nearer to 25 percent. Conversely the percentage aged 26 years or above was as low as 16 for the period 1771–1810, a figure that nearly doubled in the later period. The evidence, therefore, points to a perceptible shift toward slightly later marriages for females after 1811. This evidence lends support to the proposition by Mokyr and O'Grada that, in all likelihood, the age at marriage for Irish women turned upward from 20–22 to 24–25 during 1800–45.[45]

Another interesting point to emerge from the study of marriage ages in Killyman was not only the fact that women married at a relatively early age but that, in many cases, males marrying in their late twenties chose brides much younger than themselves. The reasons for this practice are not altogether clear. The decision when to marry was not entirely the result of economic motives; social custom and practice also played a part. Unfortunately, evidence on such matters is scarce. There is no hard evidence to suggest why men chose relatively young partners. There is, however, evidence to suggest that a man was unlikely to marry until he was in a position to acquire a holding. This would explain the average age at marriage for males of around 25–26 years. Also, certainly until at least the 1750s, levels of mortality were extremely high and life expectancy was low. In such circumstances a husband and wife were likely to lose up to half of the children born to them, and it was also very possible that a wife would die giving birth to children.

In a community where the labor of children was valued (and there is evidence to suggest that it was, particularly in the linen areas of Ulster), the decision to take a wife aged 20–22 years may have been based on the experience that there was a better chance of her giving birth to a larger number of children than a woman of 25–27. To some extent the upward shift in female age at marriage during the early nineteenth century, although partly resulting from land shortage, the restriction of subdivision, and the contraction of the linen industry, may also have been related to the fact that child mortality, although high by modern standards, had fallen substantially and that life expectancy had risen. The problem with this theory is that it suggests a change in the way people thought about marriage; because such thoughts were rarely written down, it is difficult to substantiate.

Thus, though there is no evidence of the extremely early marriages suggested by Connell, the Killyman marriage ages for women, when viewed in a European context, are early. During the period 1780–1820 the mean age at marriage for women in Killyman was 22.1 years, a figure two years younger than women during the same period in England and as much as five and almost eight years younger than their counterparts in Germany and Scandinavia.[46]

If relatively early marriage had always been the case in Killyman before the 1770s and 1780s and fertility levels consequently high, then the key factor triggering the takeoff into sustained population growth in the parish during the second half of the eighteenth century must have been a fall in mortality. If, as Clarkson has suggested, the saving of lives was principally among children, then the effects would become cumulative as increasing proportions of children survived to become parents themselves.[47] Cullen has argued that if the reduction of the death rate was concentrated on the young (0–5 years), then a sharp rise in the number of marriages would follow some twenty years later.[48]

Table 4.5 (column a) shows the number of marriages recorded in the Killyman register during each decade from the 1750s into the 1840s. Comparison of the baptismal entries with the marriage entries for the parish suggests an underregistration of marriages. Given the relative absence of a floating population (names that only appear once or twice)

Table 4.5 Parish of Killyman: Number of Marriages per Decade, 1751–1845

	(a) Recorded in Register	(b) Estimate
1751–1760	38	83
1761–1770	17	108
1771–1780	44	163
1781–1790	86	186
1791–1800	105	178
1801–1810	137	233
1811–1820	106	204
1821–1830	165	290
1831–1840	228	415
1841–1845	93	161
Total	1,019	2,021

SOURCE: PRONI, T.679/383, 384, 386, 387, 393.

in the register, it was possible to produce estimates, accurate enough to be assigned to a particular decade, of the probable dates of marriage for many families. The results of this exercise are shown in column b.[49]

Table 4.5 shows an increase of some 45 percent (relative to previous decades) in the number of marriages contracted during the 1770s and 1780s. The bulge of children produced by the marriages of the 1770s and the 1780s, shown in Figure 4.2, was reflected, as Cullen suggested, some twenty to twenty-five years later when the number of marriages rose sharply. These marriages in turn produced their bulge of children around the 1820s. By the late 1840s, emigration and the devastating effects of the Famine had removed the next potential bulge. However, the pattern of periodic "boom" shown in Figure 4.2 was modified by the effects of economic depression. For example, there was a decline of 4 percent in the number of marriages contracted during the decade 1791–1800. This decline probably reflected deteriorating conditions within the linen industry. Likewise, during the decade 1811–1820 there was also a 12 percent decrease in marriages contracted. Part of this decrease could probably be attributed to the postwar depression, but a close inspection of the figures reveals that depression in the linen industry, at its worst in the year 1811, was probably also responsible.[50] Clearly, then, the evidence from the Killyman register (Figure 4.2) lends support to both Clarkson's and Cullen's hypotheses regarding the cumulative effects of a fall in child mortality.

However, the question still remains as to the representativeness of the Killyman register. It is difficult to answer this question because of the lack of good data from other parish registers, even within those areas in Ulster where Church of Ireland records are still extant. Analysis of the nearby Donaghmore register[51] for the period 1800–50 suggests a mean age at marriage for males of 26.9 years, a median of 26 years, and a mode of 25–26 years. Only 13 percent of men married at age 22 or younger, and there was only one instance in the sample of marriage at age 20 and one at 19. However, these figures were calculated from a sample of only thirty-one marriages.

With regard to female age at marriage for the same period, a sample of forty-four cases produced a mean of 22.3 years, a median of 22 years, and modes of 22 and 23 years; 73 percent of these marriages were at age 23 and younger, but only 16 percent were age 19 and younger. The indifferent quality of the Donaghmore register during the second half of the eighteenth century, coupled with the fact that the parish was divided in 1775 in order to create the new parish of Pomeroy, made it almost impossible to trace many marriages in the 1780s and 1790s. Data from the parish register for Magheralin[52] during the period 1750–70 suggest a mean age at marriage for males of 25.4 years. However, this figure was calculated from only eight cases. In the case of women the mean age at marriage for the same period was 22.5 years, a figure calculated on the basis of thirteen cases.

Although these data lend some weight to the picture emerging from the Killyman data, because the vast majority of these registers refer exclusively to the Church of Ireland population, some doubt has been raised as to their representativeness. It was precisely for this reason that Connell did not consider them a useful demographic source, believing that members of the Church of Ireland "differed from the remainder in occupation, custom and wealth."[53] More recently Mokyr and O'Grada have reemphasized this point, suggesting that studies using primarily Church of Ireland records "may not reflect the demographic characteristics of the Catholic majority."[54] Certainly the socioeconomic data derived from the Killyman register would challenge the contention that

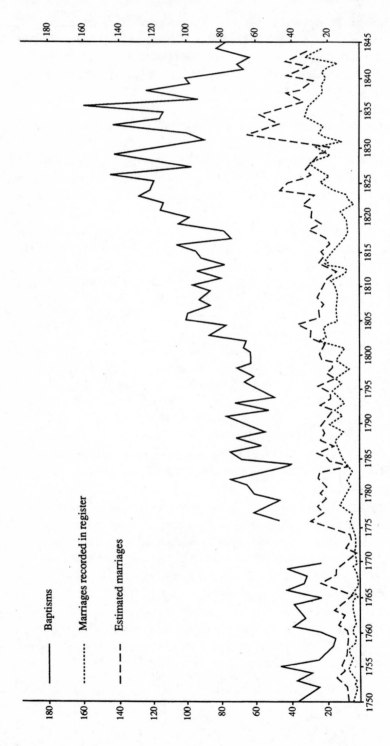

Figure 4.2 Baptisms and marriages in the parish of Killyman, 1750–1845.

the Church of Ireland population differed from the rest of the community in occupation and wealth. Furthermore, because they formed 46 percent of the total population in the parish, it can hardly be said that they were an insignificant part of the area.

It must also be recognized that throughout many of the parishes in north Armagh and south Antrim, the Church of Ireland population formed well over 50 percent of the total population.[55] Given that these same parishes lay within the linen triangle of Ulster, there is no reason to suppose that their socioeconomic structure was radically different from that of Killyman. Thus the demographic behavior of the Church of Ireland population in the rural linen parishes of north Armagh, although perhaps not representative of Ireland as a whole, cannot simply be dismissed, particularly when one considers that these same areas experienced densities of population as high as any other parts of Ireland. The obvious implication for the rest of Ireland of the marriage ages found in parishes such as Killyman is that it clearly would not require women in other parts of Ireland to marry exceptionally young in order to produce the levels of fertility necessary for the annual growth rates postulated by Dickson et al. for Connaught, Munster, and Leinster.[56]

Clearly, then, Ulster's population grew rapidly during the second half of the eighteenth century. But there does appear to have been a slowing down of that growth during the nineteenth century. Although rates of growth were probably not quite as high as those proposed by Clarkson and by Dickson et al., they could have been as high as 1.5 percent during the period 1753–91, a figure well in excess of the average for many parts of Western Europe. The evidence of recent research suggests falling mortality as the prime proximate cause. Down to the mid-eighteenth century, in common with that of all early modern societies, Ulster's population suffered from high levels of mortality, particularly among children.

The analysis of parish registers provides clear evidence of frequent and severe mortality crises, when child burials constituted up to 80 percent of all burials recorded in a particular year or years. Sometime around the middle of the century there appears to have been a fall in the general level of mortality, but even more important there was a significant drop in the number of child deaths. As yet the exact causes of the fall in mortality levels are not fully understood, but it is probable that it is linked to the general economic improvements that Cullen and others have suggested were evident from the 1730s. Certainly, within Ulster the growth and geographic spread of the linen industry from the beginning of the eighteenth century would have made a major contribution to this process.

Such a scenario places Ulster within the general Western European experience of an acceleration in population growth, beginning around the middle of the eighteenth century and caused initially by a general fall in the levels of mortality.[57] However, what appears to have made the Ulster experience different from many other parts of Western Europe was the probability that Ulster already had higher levels of fertility. This high fertility, which produced short periods of rapid growth during the seventeenth and eighteenth centuries, had been persistently thwarted by high levels of mortality. The easing, around 1750, of this preventive check allowed the demographic system to move forward into a much longer period of sustained growth.

The basic cause of this high fertility was, as Connell thought, early marriage. However, care needs to be taken to define what is meant by the term. Certainly there is no evidence in the parish registers of the very early marriages postulated by Connell. This essay suggests that Ulster women, on average, married earlier than their counterparts in western Europe: at around 22 years as opposed to age 25 or older. In the case of males the average age was 26, as opposed to age 28–30.

Thus, no substantial fall in age at marriage occurred, particularly around the 1780s, that might have initiated the original takeoff in population growth. The evidence on male age at marriage shows clearly that this did not take place. Nor was it the case during the eighteenth century for women. Any changes that did take place in marriage ages seem to have been upward: during the early nineteenth century, the average age at which women married appears to have risen by as much as two years. This change in marriage behavior, coupled with growing numbers emigrating to Britain and America, was probably responsible for the slowing down of growth during the decades immediately prior to the Famine. This emigration was to increase more dramatically during and after the Great Famine, and would, when combined with a further rise in age at marriage and increased celibacy, lead to a very different demographic regime in the post-Famine period.

5 The Household Economy in Early Rural America and Ulster: The Question of Self-Sufficiency

Vivienne Pollock

Strong notions of self-sufficiency color perceptions of the rural past on both sides of the Atlantic. Time and again we are asked by various agencies to accept a historical reality in which money and markets played a minimal role in securing, for country dwellers at least, the essentials of human existence. The power of this evocation is undeniable. In an increasingly complex, industrialized, and impersonal world, household self-sufficiency represented simplicity, integrity, and security—it was the hallmark of a vanished golden age of rural wholesomeness, family cooperation, and domestic stability. The standard of self-sufficiency was, however, not only introduced in a context of nostalgia and regret. In the case of America, it became part of a political metaphor of democratic independence: for example, Benjamin Franklin mused in 1772 about "the happiness of New England, where every man is a freeholder, has a vote in public affairs, lives in a tidy warm house, has plenty of good food and fuel, with whole clothes from head to foot, the manufacture perhaps of his own family."[1]

In Ireland, on the other hand, perceived reliance on self-sufficiency became synonymous with economic retardation: for example, the observation, made in 1936, that Irish farmers "mainly produce for their own needs, but send their surplus products to markets which link them with the world markets of capitalism"[2] led one writer to remark that the "Ulster rural economy [lay] at an intermediate stage between primitive and developed economies."[3] If one enjoyed self-sufficiency in America, one was emancipated and materially secure; if one endured it in Ulster, one was poor and structurally underdeveloped.

The extent to which early rural households functioned as self-sufficient islands has been energetically reviewed in recent years. Some of the most successful challenges have come from American historians employing a vast range of quantitative material to construct a picture of everyday life in the colonial countryside substantially different from that popularly assumed and contemporaneously argued.[4] Careful analysis of probate records, tax inventories, import and export data, demographic sources, and so on has created estimates of production and consumption that clearly indicate a high degree of integration between local, national, and international markets. This position is strengthened by new evaluations of the level of capital investment, technical knowledge, and human energy required to sustain comfortable, commercial independence. For example, in an article bristling with common sense, Carol Shammas argued convincingly that the costs of even the most basic self-sufficiency—about £145 sterling for raw material in the shape of land, livestock, seeds, and agricultural and craft tools, never mind the wealth of time and talent needed to turn this raw material to serviceable ends—would have far outstripped the resources of the average colonial family.[5]

Belief in what one writer has christened "the mythic vision of near-total independence"[6] has, in the case of America, been severely shaken by scholarly investigation. This demolition process has had some extremely positive results. By working at both the macro and the micro levels, American historians have created analyses of the rural economy that richly combine the general process with the individual experience. In doing so, moreover, they have critically reinstated culture and personality as key variables in the dynamics of rural development.

Their interpretations fall into several distinct categories. The first sees the farmer as an entrepreneur whose aspirations to a secure living were realized by maximizing production to meet a rational assessment of market opportunities. This argument underpins Robert D. Mitchell's study of economic development in the Shenandoah Valley,[7] a region in which commercial agriculture emerged as the focus rather than the outcome of expansion. His early settlers were far from self-sufficient but sought to remedy this situation not by extending their range of enterprise but by establishing specialized external trading exchanges, first in butter and then in tobacco. Other economic activities were certainly exploited at preliminary levels, but these remained supplementary to, or at most temporarily competitive with, the creation and maintenance of an active, commercially oriented agricultural base.

The second category sees the farmer as a household provider who sought to sustain economic well-being through an ample sufficiency and a subsequent cushion of exchangeable surpluses. In certain aspects, this farmer appeared as the central character in James T. Lemon's *The Best Poor Man's Country*, practicing "extensive farming . . . to produce enough for his family and to be able to sell a surplus in the market place."[8] Elaboration of this analysis has prompted some historians to argue for the existence of a specific rural *mentalité*, which instilled a "desire for competency"[9] rather than an ambition for commercialism. "Competent" farmers did not shun the marketplace entirely, just as entrepreneurial farmers did not sell everything they produced. But they regarded it as an adjunct to or a support for functional independence, rather than their primary objective.

A third and subtly different interpretation sees the colonial farmer as incumbent in an enforcing commercial structure: "integrated economically as well as socially and culturally . . . [in] local networks of exchange involving all sorts of goods and services and with labour as the principal item of exchange within that economy."[10] This analysis assumes that basic self-sufficiency was unattainable, either as a short-term strategy or as a long-term goal. Some form of contractual arrangement was, therefore, a fundamental component of the household economy, with farmers responding to opportunity and need with an expedient, commercially directed mixture of subsistence activity and market enterprise. At the same time, by seeking to establish whether commercially framed behavior was an intrinsic and unavoidable part of the everyday life of everyday people, this analysis also provides an essential first platform for the later imposition of those more complex assessments that seek to establish why members of preindustrial rural societies acted in the commercial manner that they did. As such, it is the one whose application to eighteenth-century Ulster seems most appropriate at this stage of the historical study of the region.

The first element to be considered is the extent to which the general tenor of life in the Ulster countryside of this period was shaped by market forces. Although our knowledge of the precise pattern of development in Ireland as a whole during the seventeenth century is far from complete, the situation in Ulster is sufficiently well documented to suggest that it was very much a place of growing commercialism.[11] In many respects, the region represented an early modern enterprise zone, where incoming undertakers were promised generous grants of potentially productive land, together with tax relief on designated exports and export sites, in return for the economic energy they would bring to an under-developed locality. They in turn parceled out their estates to tenant farmers, initiated a boom of private and public building programs, established key processing sites, and created a network of fairs and markets to promote and sustain internal commerce and communications. Both the substantial increase in the importation of highly taxed goods, particularly after 1650, and the expansion of overseas trade in cattle and cattle products, wool, and grain are confirmation of the commercial dynamism of the latter half of the seventeenth century.

The century ended, moreover, on an extremely high note when bumper harvests in Ulster coincided with general harvest failure throughout Britain and Ireland. This gave local farmers large surpluses to sell in hungry export markets—an exceptional event in terms of pre-industrial rural economies and one that was of enormous significance in expanding still further the commercial framework of the Ulster economy. Not only did it "enrich the ploughman, who hithertofore sold his corn to pay his rent,"[12] but it also attracted a new wave of tenant settlement: an estimated 50,000 Scottish migrants arrived in the region after 1691. If, as Louis Cullen has suggested, these immigrants brought with them an average of just £10 each,[13] then this migration by itself represented a considerably sharp increase in rural purchasing power and money supply.

Ulster's contemporary reputation as the most heavily populated of Irish provinces[14] was due in no small part to this late influx of new settlers. It is clear, nevertheless, that the region was well populated in comparative rather than absolute terms and that large tracts remained undersettled to the point of emptiness.[15] This scarcity of population, particularly of nonagricultural population, had profound consequences. It is clear that the need to secure tenants from a comparatively small pool of prospective renters persuaded many landlords to set first leases at extremely attractive, long, cheap terms, thus creating for a time a market for land that was biased toward the tenant. But the establishment of rented tenure throughout the region placed landholding firmly and irrevocably on a competitive, commercial base, ensuring that those who lived on the land inevitably had to find from it enough saleable commodities to meet at least the cost of remaining on it. At the same time, low levels of local and internal demand ensured that the commercial success of farming was ultimately dependent on the sale of produce in overseas markets. This is not to deny the existence of local networks of trade in agricultural items. It is instead to stress that, for most items, local demand was by itself too inelastic to secure the levels of return generally necessary to pay the rent and buy essential goods and services.

Dependence on overseas trade rendered the early rural economy, and those who lived within it, open to threat from a range of "modern" commercial and fiscal pressures,[16] as well as the more traditional preindustrial rural hazards of bad weather, crop failure, and livestock mortality. The need to maintain a basic level of commercial stability amid this sea of financial and ecological insecurity stimulated a high degree of development in rural domestic industry and a wide diversification in agricultural pursuit. By the early 1700s even the most marginal of Ulster counties displayed considerable signs of growth. For all his desire to convey to his patron a story of high-mountain strangeness and wilderness, William Henry's account of Fermanagh in the 1730s[17] describes a region where tillage was widespread; where experiments with various types of soil improvers, such as sand, lime, and marble, had been tried; where stock had been improved through the importation of large cattle from "the choicest herds in England";[18] and where hay was cultivated and stored for winter fodder.

Significant efforts had been made to extend communications within and without the locality. Enniskillen, the principal town, was served by a network of roads offering access to many places: to Sligo and thence to the sea and Connaught; to Benburb, the nearest major linen market; to Ballyshannon and thence Donegal and the north; to Dublin via Newtownbutler; and to Clogher, Omagh, and "several others."[19] But one of Henry's innocently most revealing tales concerned a strange whirlwind, which lifted a field of drying flax and carried it for two miles before dropping it on top of a mountain where it was found and kept by an enterprising neighbor. The flax belonged to a woman "noted amongst her neighbors for cheating with false count in her dozens of yarn,"[20] and the word was passed round that it was in punishment of this that the devil and a troop of his fairies had come in person to steal away her crop. Commercial markets did more than just exist in south Fermanagh; they were held in such regard that to treat them dishonestly was considered worthy of supernatural intervention.

The dynamics of development in border regions of Ulster in the eighteenth century are made plain in O'Hara's contemporary diary of the economy of County Sligo. According to O'Hara, in the early 1700s the whole area was "covered with cottage tenants who, having no foreign demand for the produce of their farms, mostly paid their rent in kind, in duties and in work, the only money brought among us was by means of the army and some very few lean cattle sold to the Leinster graziers."[21] During the next ten years, however, increasing demand for salt beef stimulated fat-cattle farming in the Irish midlands and, by extension, demand for "store" cattle—that is, cattle sold live to be fattened for sale as beef elsewhere—from the north and west. At the same time, the first steps in local textile production were taken with the manufacture in Sligo of coarse frieze for local purposes. Linen, however, continued to be bought from Scottish and northern peddlers until about 1717, when landlords introduced flax cultivation and made their tenants' wives spin it into yarn for their own use. Soon "even the lower sort of people" followed suit in "having their linens made at home."[22]

Production of yarn specifically for sale took off in the mid-1720s, when the continuing expansion of the cattle trade persuaded landlords to raise rents in an effort to clear areas for grazing. Helped by the Irish Linen Board, which supplied seed, wheels, and reels on public account, tenant farmers began to sell yarn in northern and English markets to meet the new cost of land. Production for these markets was indirectly responsible for a further expansion in local trade in the 1730s, when buyers traveling to Sligo for yarn also bought wool, beef, mutton, and flannels to sell in poorly supplied northern markets. In the 1740s the provisions trade expanded yet again to include the sale of live cattle of varying ages and types to markets in Ireland, Ulster, England, and Scotland, as well as the sale of beasts for slaughter in the beef trade.

It was, however, the sustained increase in demand for yarn, rather than the expansion of commercial agriculture, which enabled Sligo cotters to become "bidders for land."[23] O'Hara's remarks on the effect this ability had on local land markets are as pertinent for Ulster as they are for Sligo, with the qualification that, in more eastern regions of the province, a similar chain of events may have been set in motion up to thirty years previously. In brief, he saw the "wonderful" rise in land prices in the 1730s and 1740s as the result of spiraling competition between those who supported themselves primarily by textile production and "regular" farmers who bid high for land, knowing that if they were unable to pay for it by farming they could set it "to lower people who [make] their rents by labour and industry."[24] Thus, he concluded, "the price of land [has become] far beyond what the people are able to make of it either by grazing or by their manner of farming. . . . One is now to consider the rents in some degree as the price paid by manufacturers for ground sufficient to subsist them—not that they make their rents of the ground but of the yarn or linen wrought upon it."[25]

The tendency for Ulster's rural population to support itself by textile production and a measure of subsistence farming should not be exaggerated. Although in 1776 Arthur Young noted that in linen districts in Armagh "scarce any of [the weavers] have potatoes or oats to feed their families [and] great importations [are brought] from Louth, Meath, Cavan, and Tyrone,"[26] the landscape he described was one that remained heavily committed to the commercial production of food. In fact, as the above quotation indicates, the expansion of rural industry, particularly male domestic industry in the shape of weaving, worked to sharpen demand for purchased agricultural produce in the countryside itself, thus extending still further the commercial base and commercial orientation of Ulster farming.

It should be stressed at this stage that these developments did not occur evenly but took the form of marked internal variations in the nature and direction of market activity. Some areas, such as the famous "linen triangle" of east Ulster—comprising adjoining sections of Counties Down, Antrim, and Armagh—became important for textile production; others, for example, north Down, evolved as centers for market gardening. Some regions, like west Tyrone, concentrated on beef production; others, such as the Lecale in maritime southeast County Down, were key grain producers. The degree to which these specializations became pronounced signifies the deepening penetration of exchange economies throughout Ulster as a whole in the eighteenth century. But they say very little about the extent to which the growing commercialization of the countryside was expressed in the lives and living conditions of tenant farmers and even less about the basis on which tenant farmers formulated their strategies for material survival. It is to this aspect of the rural economy that we now return.

The assessment of the economic perspective of everyday life depends on an awareness both of people's needs and of the arrangements by which these needs are met. To the outside observer, information concerning these related elements is most clearly expressed in detailed property inventories: for example, the type and quantity of food found in a house often reveals a great deal more about the occupants than the size of their appetites. Unfortunately, one of the major sources of information to American historians researching household economies—the vast bank of probate inventories—is not available for the study of Irish lifestyles. As Alan Gailey noted, inventories as a whole "are rare in Ulster and inventories of the belongings of ordinary farmers . . . almost unknown."[27] Indeed, apart from the twenty-five that formed the basis for his survey of Quaker life in Ballyhagan, he found only two others relating to the eighteenth century, both of which concerned well-to-do households.[28] But there is another, more general problem with inventory-based studies of household production and consumption. As lists of the gathered possessions of individual household members at the time of their deaths, these inventories provide but a dim reflection of the daily patterns of family getting and spending—a static, singular interpretation of what was surely a progressive, combined process. Even now there is a profound unreality to wills as documents of life and the living.

This chapter focuses, therefore, on farm accounts and, in particular, on accounts of farm labor, in the attempt to elucidate the extent to which the domestic needs of "ordinary" Ulster people were met by a commercially based strategy. Several such records exist for the eighteenth century, and most have the advantage of including the detailed transactions of a great many years. Two of these long documents deserve special attention: one pertains to the Orr family of Glassdrummond on the coast of County Down and dates from 1730 to circa 1845;[29] the other concerns the Holmes family of Moyar near Benburb in south Tyrone and covers the approximate period 1753–1818.[30]

The Orrs were small farmers whose holding was assessed in 1753 as containing thirty-three acres, one rood, and thirty perches. Very little of their routine farming activity can be gleaned from their records, which deal primarily with servants' accounts. We know, however, that they kept sheep, grew barley and flax, and practiced some level of commercial dairying. They also dealt in nets—presumably hempen herring nets—and by 1745 had apparently sublet several small parcels of land. From 1730 to 1788, records were kept on a total of thirty-eight individual hired servants, of whom thirteen were women and twenty-five were men. The accounts of the Holmes family, on the other hand, are far more extensive in terms of the range of commercial farming activity they describe. Itemized work sheets of the men they employed indicate precisely a mixture of tillage farming, and the inclusion of breeding records for both cattle and horses suggests a healthy interest in livestock management. Holmes also participated in local moneylending, dealing in notes, bonds, and coin; bought and sold beef and linen yarn; and had considerable income from subletting agreements. From 1778 to 1818 he kept accounts on twenty-two hired servants, of which nine were women; in addition, work records indicate the existence of nine "tied" laborers, all men, and accounts against individuals identify the existence of a further five women servants and one male servant. The latter accounts date from 1799.

There was a significant difference in the organization of hired service and what may be termed "tied" labor. Hired servants were contracted to work from the employer's house for a set period, usually six months, from May to November and from November to May—a winter half year and a summer half year. They were paid a set sum for this period, plus, in Orr's case at least, a commodity (shoes, a length of linen, a measure of flax or butter, and so on) and a penny in "arles," or earnest money, when the contract was agreed. In contrast to this, tied laborers worked from their own homes at a daily rate for days worked—an arrangement that figured prominently in Nat Holmes's accounts. There was, however, still a general emphasis within his records of the year being divided into a summer and a winter reckoning, regardless of the particular system that bound a particular worker: for example, Holmes employed William Melly in 1778 at a rate of 7 pence per day and calculated his earnings over the year in terms of "summer" and "winter" wages; likewise, Hugh Tool began to work "days" on November 8, 1818, with his first "toll" ending on May 8, 1819. It is also worth noting that Holmes as a contemporary employer also saw a clear distinction between hired service and tied labor when he employed Thomas McCall "old stile" for £1 in 1810.

Examining the custom of reckoning money owed and money obligated over a period of six months or so opens a window into the material world of the rural laborer. What items of expenditure did hired servants, who received subsistence from their employer, set against wages? Food, household utilities, and the employment of other people featured in a surprising number of accounts. Against Frank Orr, hired for 18 shillings in 1744, Orr counted meat, wheat, and potatoes; in 1751 his reckoning with Molly O'Neal for the winter half year included apples, butter, a toothed hook, flax seed, and a quill wheel. Against Francis Mallone's agreed wages in 1751 Holmes deducted seven bushels of potatoes and later one stone of flax seed; meanwhile Egret Hughes's account included 6 pence to Ezekiel Evans for harrowing. Meal, pork, fish, seeds, nails, locks, candles, hemp, boxes, labels, spinning wheels, parts of wheels, and wheel mending are other named items that fall into this category.

A second category consisted of payments for professional services and taxes. These included money futured on weddings, burials, christenings, priest's devotions, pilgrimages, doctor's services, physics, and cess, tithe, and hearth taxes. A third category consisted simply of cash. Although the number of times money was deducted in amounts of $6^{1}/_{2}$ pence or multiples thereof gives the impression that these sums may have represented money lost in terms of days absent as much as they signified money gained from days worked, it is clear that workers demanded and received as a matter of course numerous cash "subs" from their employers. Other cash advances were nominated as sums to named individuals, presumably for services rendered or goods obtained outside the employer-employee nexus. It was also common for family members—usually but not always a mother or father—to receive sums of cash on account. Cash was also regularly advanced for local fair days and holidays, sometimes in relatively large sums but often in pennies. And some individuals "spent" very little during their terms of service, leaving themselves with quite substantial cash sums to collect when their contracts expired.

Luxury goods formed a further sizable category. These included the two staples of extravagance—brandy and tobacco—as well as rum, hair ribbons, sweetmeats, books, and tea. But the most money-exhausting category by far was clothing and shoes. These items were generally reckoned in terms of cost of materials and cost of making: for example, Orr's accounts with one of his female servants included 12s. 3d. for stuff and silk for a cloak, stuff for a petticoat, drugget for an apron, and $13^{1}/_{2}$ yards of tape, plus 8 pence for making. The range of cloth acquired reveals a high proportion of fine and imported materials—muslin, white linen, saloon, cambric, and chenille—as well as the more serviceable stuff, plaiden, drugget, frieze, and serge. The cost of finished items also indicates a high standard of dress—gowns often cost 12 shillings and more in terms of materials alone, while the ubiquitous handkerchief (in actuality, a type of neck square) generally cost more than 3 shillings. Pumps and britches cost James Wooden half a guinea in 1799; later in the same year he spent a further 11s. 11d. on a coat and waistcoat. The cost of shoes varied considerably, with pumps standing 1–2 shillings and brogues 1–3 shillings. More shoes were mended than bought: half soles, top pieces, heel pieces, and leather nails appear often, together with the expense of putting them on or in.

Although the existence (and exploitation) of both secondhand and homemade clothes must be assumed, the central feature of clothing acquisition and maintenance, as measured in both the Holmes and the Orr accounts, is that of tailor making and mending. And whereas Holmes paid named individuals for shirts and britches for his own family—at, incidentally, a price which paralleled that paid by his farm laborers—and Orr paid outside workers even to knit stockings, the number of transactions involving apparel at fairs and in nearby urban centers clearly indicates that clothes and shoes were commonly obtained from central suppliers in open markets.

Although some mention is made of personal purchases involving apparel, consumption patterns among the Orr and Holmes families themselves are not well recorded in their farm accounts. Nevertheless, even the few entries regarding Orr's dealings with local craftsmen and merchants are revealing in their meticulousness. His accounts with the local innkeeper often note not only cost and type of alcohol purchased but also the occasion and company in which it was imbibed. His blacksmith's accounts consist of credits for metal and old implements he provided to the smith against charges for made items, calculated on a basis of 1 pence granted per pound of metal supplied against, for example, 1 pence each as the cost of made horseshoes. Direct exchange of items did occur, as in the case of Thomas Watterson, who got one hundredweight of butter less $6^{1}/_{2}$ pounds in return for 26 pounds of iron and a bottle of brandy. In the same entry Orr also accounted Watterson with 9 pence for drink taken with two companions and 13 pence for two pairs of soles. There is no doubt, judging by even these meager sources, that tenant farmers, like their farm laborers, were clients in a complex network of supply and service controlled in the main by the market value of commodities exchanged within it and conducted overwhelmingly in the medium of cash or cash credit.

A further aspect of the extent to which exchange networks functioned on a monetary basis is revealed in Holmes's detailed records of subletting agreements. These lets—for small plots of potato and flax ground, houses, and gardens—were arranged in cash terms and redeemed by cash payments, by the cash value of farm labor, and, to a lesser degree, by goods. It is clear from a number of the agreements made with Holmes that labor was an integral component of the tenancy. For example, Alexander Simpson agreed to pay £2 5s. 6d. for a house and garden and to work "when called" for $6^{1}/_{2}$ pence per day. These accounts read together give a strong impression that, as time went on, Holmes met the labor requirements on his farm by substituting the tied employment of subtenants for the hired service of male servants. At the same time, the number of days worked by subtenants varied considerably. While Robert Bustard, a tied laborer and renter, put in only seventy-three days work in 1812 to offset a rental of £6 13s. 4d. (leaving a balance of more than £4 to be found by other means), James McVay worked 239 days in 1816 to secure a cash "profit" of 7s. 7d. In addition, some of those named as holding sublet ground provided no goods or services against their rent, suggesting that the entire sum was paid in full and on time in cash.

It was not only ground that subtenants received from Holmes. They also obtained both the flax seed and the seed potatoes to plant it. In addition, quantities of meal, acquired presumably during the "hungry" months of late spring and early summer, appear in almost all accounts. Money owed for turf figures in a number of cases, as do debts for various cash sums and money owed for items such as tools and implements, tobacco, livestock (generally a pig or a cow), hay, corn, tithe dues, and so on. Holmes also leased looms, at a six-month rental of first an accounted 10 shillings and then the cash equivalent of 11s. 4d. There is, however, no reference of these debts to him being paid in finished cloth, and very few indicating he received yarn in respect of rent or other obligations. Neither did Holmes accept kind against the above liabilities. The fruits of independent tenant labor, in spinning and weaving or growing and raising, were realized in open markets, and the proceeds boosted the household's ability to meet cash demands.

It is likely that both Holmes and Orr were in positions of potential self-sufficiency. At the same time, it is clear that neither reached or even attempted to reach independence from the market. Holmes's work records indicate that, although he supplied quantities of flax seed, he neither grew nor processed flax itself. Neither did he shear sheep. His wool and linen were, therefore, necessarily obtained through outside agencies. Orr's ventures into net knitting and supply, flax and wool production, and his growing tendency, like Holmes, to sublet plots from his comparatively small acreage, suggest either that he regarded his farming activities as by themselves insufficient to meet the everyday requirements of his household, or, perhaps, that the commercial opportunities he saw around him proved irresistible to his entrepreneurial leanings. At the same time, however, the amount of paid farm labor employed by both men stresses that both regarded commercial agriculture as the bedrock of their economic success.

Evidence relating to cottiers and laborers shows more precisely the extent to which the lives of this group were measured in the marketplace. Lacking the capacity for the barest self-sufficiency, even with the support of gardens and potato ground, we cannot expect them to have attained anything like commercial independence. Nevertheless, the acquisition of imported and bought textiles in tailormade clothes, the acquisition of various kinds of foodstuffs and luxury consumables, and the acquisition even by live-in farm laborers of craft tools, agricultural implements, and the material for cash crops suggest a much higher degree of commercial integration and consumer power than is popularly supposed to have existed among this section of society.

This is not to suggest that Ulster's tenant farmers and cottiers were full-fledged participants in the market economy as we understand and experience it today. It is clear that economic relationships were far from straightforward at the local level; in many cases the impact of central market forces was deflected by the existence of a complex network of duty and supply that paid scant lip service to cold commercial considerations. The existence of this intricate combination of formal and informal economic arrangements was not confined to eighteenth-century Ulster. Mick Reed, in an important recent article, criticized the adoption "implicitly or otherwise, by almost all historians of the period,"[31] of George Dalton's view of the extent to which the nineteenth-century British rural economy was framed by entrepreneurial considerations—a perspective that regarded markets as "ubiquitous, dominant, integrating all production nationally: that is interlocking markets in a national purchase and sale network at money price. . . . Practically all farm output was sold for cash. All factors of production, land, labour, tools, transport, artificial fertilizers, were available on national markets for purchase at money price."[32] On the contrary, Reed pointed out, research has demonstrated the survival in England and Wales during the nineteenth century and well into the twentieth of "a numerically significant group of household producers, or 'peasants' . . . [who were] actively concerned with obtaining a living, rather than maximizing profit . . . [and whose] main interest was subsistence."[33] However, because very few members of this group were in a position to attain this objective independently, "exchange was always necessary and production had to be directed to this end to some degree." Drawing heavily on analyses of economic development in rural North America, Reed presented an interpretation of the British rural economy, contending that, though the strategy of "small farmers and [rural] tradespeople"[34] was to gear production in a combination of directions—"for direct consumption, for exchange within neighborhood networks and for exchange through the market"[35]—the networks of exchange through which essential goods and services passed to and from these people did not constitute "a 'market' in any meaningful sense"[36] but were instead part of "a system of reciprocal personal obligations."[37]

Of course, there were aspects of the organization of rural life in eighteenth-century Ulster that may be defined in terms of accepted (and expected) neighborly responsibilities. The same holds true in rural communities today, where freely extended human helpfulness in the shape of sharing time, energy, and equipment is often a key resource of everyday life. At the same time, it is equally clear—then as now—that the image of self-contained rural communities peopled by self-sufficient, small landholders is a myth. On the broad scale, the rural economy of Ulster, with its emphasis on the interchange of raw and finished materials for the domestic linen industry, was tightly annexed to external and interregional trade and underpinned by the commercial rather than the productive value of land. At the personal level, the record books of the Orrs and the Holmeses reveal a pattern of individual survival maintained by a combination of farming and merchant activities and crucially dependent on the cash value of goods and services exchanged in open markets. And the men and women who contributed with their work to the material well-being of the Holmeses and the Orrs were also part of the commercial framework of the Ulster countryside. They too paid rent and taxes, bought the goods and services of local traders and craftsmen, and spent money at local fairs and markets.

To point out that the market's penetration of everyday life was neither complete nor straightforward in no way denies the evidence that rural society in eighteenth- and early nineteenth-century Ulster was, in fact, much more commercialized than is commonly accepted. Reed's central objective in arguing against the existence of a golden age of rural self-sufficiency was to stress the need to develop both a greater awareness of the various ways in which people in rural areas planned their economic strategy and a greater insight into the considerations that informed different types of economic response. His closing insistence that "economic relationships were . . . not always compatible with the preconceptions of 'agricultural history' "[38] is of relevance and importance to all involved in teasing out the complexities of economic behavior and its social and cultural contexts. While the record books of the Orrs and the Holmeses reveal a pattern of survival crucially dependent on the cash value of goods and services exchanged in open markets, a great deal more work needs to be done before we can discuss in confident detail the economic experiences of ordinary people in Ulster in the eighteenth and early nineteenth centuries.

Such investigation can only increase our understanding of the effects and implications of emigration on the development of social and economic structures in America and in Ulster and, by extension, our appreciation of the mechanisms underpinning the material framework of life in the two countries. Individuals from both the Orr and the Holmes families emigrated—James Orr (a son?) in 1743 and William Holmes (a nephew?) in 1772. And all other household and farm accounts I have consulted to date contain references to the emigration of close family members. People who emigrated from Ulster were not unusual or unique. They took a course of action that became more and more of a household event as the number of emigrants, and in turn the number of kin, friends, and neighbors of emigrants, became greater and greater. Was there, as increasingly seems to have been the case, a continuum of cultural and economic behavior stretching across the Atlantic? Or did material goals and the strategies by which these goals were achieved change with the new circumstances of the New World? There are a number of apparently significant parallels in the social and economic climates of early rural Ulster and early rural North America. But we need to know much more about the wider ordinariness of everyday life in these two countries before we can start to define with any accuracy the uncommon features of migrant society and emigrant history.

6 Ulster Emigration to North America, 1680–1720

Graeme Kirkham[1]

In November 1718 Archbishop King of Dublin complained of an "unaccountable humor that has possessed the generality of the people through a great part of Ireland of going to the plantations in America."[2] The exodus to which King referred has been generally acknowledged as marking the beginning of large-scale emigration from Ulster to North America, a movement that continued for perhaps a century as one of the primary regional contributions to the settlement of the New World prior to the mass European migrations of the nineteenth century. The emigration surge of the late 1710s undoubtedly saw the largest short-term flow of migrants from Ulster that had yet occurred, but the origins of significant emigration from the province may be identified a generation or so earlier. This chapter reviews the evidence for emigration from the north of Ireland for the earlier period and presents a considerable body of new data on the major exodus of 1717–19.

English-speaking households in Ulster probably first became aware of the American continent as a potential place of settlement in the early 1680s, largely as a consequence of efforts to entice settlers made by the colonies and their proprietors. Pamphlets and letters promoting the new Quaker colony of Pennsylvania circulated in Ireland soon after its founding and attracted a number of Irish migrants in the early years of settlement, including at least thirteen adults from two County Armagh meetings in 1682.[3] The Scottish Quaker promoters of East New Jersey—first settled in the period 1683–85—also published promotional literature and, in addition, appointed an agent in Belfast to recruit for the new colony; two Ulstermen were among its original proprietors.[4] South Carolina also attempted to attract immigrants during this period, and a settlement scheme promoted by a group of Covenanter merchants and gentlemen in southwest Scotland provided a specific focus for potential migrants in Ulster.[5] In July 1683 Viscount Mountjoy reported from

Newtownstewart, County Tyrone, that local Dissenters "complain much to one another of the great persecution their brethren are under in Scotland, and seem to apprehend the like here, which makes them talk much of going in great numbers to Carolina." The following month, however, Mountjoy reported that "for all the great noise these people made of going in great numbers to Carolina and their keeping a great ship at Derry to transport them, yet, now the time is come, not one man goes, and the ship is forced to alter her voyage."[6] There were also contacts with the northern colonies. A gentleman from Ireland was reported in Connecticut in 1684, seeking land on which to settle 100 families, informing a prospective landlord that many would come over if they could be assured of religious freedom, their views being "much of the same stamp" as those in New England.[7]

These accounts suggest a close link between religious and political discrimination and the awakening of a propensity for emigration during this period. The difficulties perceived by the dissenting population coincided, however, with the beginning of a decade or more of economic and social dislocation. The early 1680s saw outbreaks of epidemic disease and of banditry in Ulster, and a severe winter in 1683–84 threatened the pastoral economic base of much of the north.[8] The complexity of factors motivating potential emigrants at this period is demonstrated by Mountjoy's report from County Tyrone early in 1684, after the introduction of official measures against Presbyterian worship: some Dissenters had been brought to conform, but "others threaten to go to Carolina. Thither, I believe, some may go, but the noise of it is chiefly raised by such as think to make their landlords more indulgent to them from the apprehension of having their lands laid waste. We have had a very hard winter."[9] In the same year a number of ministers from the suppressed Laggan Presbytery announced their intention to emigrate, citing not only "persecutions" and the lack of access to their ministry but also the "general poverty abounding in these parts."[10]

The accession of James II in 1685 and the subsequent progress toward Catholicization of the Irish state increased political and economic uncertainty. An official in Dublin Castle noted in July 1686 the "great consternation upon the minds of the people; no trade, nor traffic; all rents fall; the tenants are not able to pay their rents because the rich men keep up their money, being fearful to lay out their estates in cattle or take farms, apprehending I know not what ruin. And those who can fly out of the country, either to Pennsylvania, Virginia or other places, hasten away."[11] The effects of the economic and social dislocation of this period, succeeded by the depredations of the Williamite War, persisted in some areas of Ulster until well into the 1690s.[12]

Trade restrictions between Ireland and North America lapsed in 1680, resulting in a substantial increase in Irish involvement in transatlantic commerce. Ulster ports built a considerable trade with the Caribbean and the American mainland, and this was maintained even after the reimposition of legal curbs on direct trade in 1685.[13] The focus of mercantile interest on the tobacco colonies provided the means for what was probably the most significant flow of migration from Ulster prior to the late 1710s. Shipping records for this period are limited, but two vessels sailed from Belfast to Havre de Grace, at the head of the Chesapeake, early in 1683, and at least twelve arrived in Virginia and Maryland from Ulster ports from 1688 through 1703.[14] Some of these ships certainly carried servants, and the fact that they sailed directly to the Chesapeake (rather than via the Caribbean) suggests that a human cargo was the primary enterprise on the westward voyage.[15] In addition, some voyages to the Chesapeake from British ports such as Beaumaris, Whitehaven, and Liverpool also called at Irish harbors en route to embark passengers. For example, the *Loyalty* in 1701 and the *Lawrell* in 1703 both arrived in Virginia from Liverpool and Belfast.[16] This traffic from Ulster paralleled the established trade in servants from southern Irish ports, but the movement from the north also included a significant proportion of unbound migrants. In 1680 the Laggan Presbytery received a request for a minister from a Maryland landowner, and a number of dissenting clergy from northwest Ulster can be identified in the eastern Chesapeake in subsequent years.[17] These, however, were the most visible members of a considerably larger flow. A promotional volume for East New Jersey in the mid–1680s reported from an Ulster gentleman recently settled in Maryland: "the account he sends of that country is so encouraging that I hear a great many of his acquaintances are making for that voyage."[18] Edward Randolph observed in 1692 that Somerset County, Maryland, was "a place pestred with Scotch and Irish. About 200 families have within these 2 years arrived from Ireland and settled in that county besides some hundreds of families there before."[19]

Influential individuals in the area had extended credit for the newcomers' first tobacco crops and were thus able to "govern the whole trade on the eastern shore"; legal exports of tobacco had declined, the trade having been seized by "nigh 30 sail of Scotch Irish and New England men." Randolph also noted that the immigrants had established a "linen manufacture," and three years later another commentator reported that in Dorchester and Somerset Counties, "where the Scotch Irish are most numerous, they almost clothe themselves by their linen and woollen manufactures and plant little tobacco, which learning from one another, they leave off planting."[20] Commercial linen manufacture was not widespread in Ulster at the end of the seventeenth century, being most prevalent in a small area of north Armagh and the Lagan Valley hinterland of Belfast. It is possible, therefore, that a proposal made in 1703 to transport to Virginia or Maryland a colony of 500 "inhabitants about Belfast, many of them farmers of some substance," was founded on ties with previous migrants to the region.[21]

The scale of emigration during the two decades before the outbreak of the War of the Spanish Succession (1702–14) remains unclear. Nonetheless, it is evident that a movement from Ulster to North America was established well before the end of the seventeenth century and that the numbers involved, while not great, were by no means negligible. Dickson has suggested that Ulster emigrants prior to 1718 "could probably be numbered in hundreds," yet Randolph's previously quoted comments suggest that at least 2,000 individuals may have arrived in the eastern Chesapeake alone during a few years before 1692.[22] It is also evident that the range of motivating factors involved was complex, encompassing not only religious, political, and economic elements but also the activities of colonial proprietors and governments and changes in the structure of maritime commerce. All of these elements foreshadowed patterns that became more clearly drawn in the succeeding period.

Ulster ports continued to trade across the Atlantic throughout the War of the Spanish Succession. Customs records show exports to the "Plantations" in every year from Belfast and Derry, as well as occasional ventures from other northern ports, including Donaghadee, Dundalk (including Newry), Killybegs (including Ballyshannon), and Sligo.[23] There are few references to shipping arrivals from Ireland in the American press during the war, and it seems likely that much of this trade was with the West Indies or to the Chesapeake, for which newspaper coverage of maritime activity was poor. References to migrants during these years are sparse: a handful of Ulster Quakers arrived in Philadelphia, and a group of Donegal Presbyterians were apparently newly settled at Newcastle-on-Delaware in 1706; a few individuals also appeared in New

England.[24] It seems likely that relatively good harvests combined with the risks of travel in wartime may have suppressed emigration, despite acute recession in the Irish economy. Only in 1711, the year in which the British government effectively withdrew from the war, do specific references to emigrant voyages from Ireland reappear (see Appendix at end of chapter).

Again, the scale of the outflow seems small. Two vessels that had called at Belfast en route from Liverpool arrived in Philadelphia and New York in 1712, but a total of only five voyages from Ulster has been identified for the following four years. Sailings from Dublin and some of the arrivals reported only as from "Ireland" may also have carried northern migrants, but firm conclusions on the scale of emigration at this period are made difficult by the lack of evidence concerning the Chesapeake. Belfast merchants had continued to trade with Virginia during the War of the Spanish Succession, but it seems probable that the occupation of accessible settlement land and increasing use of slave labor in the region had reduced its appeal as an emigrant destination.[25] However, an isolated source recording trade from Belfast in 1715 includes eleven vessels leaving Belfast for Virginia, compared with only two heading to Boston.[26] Of ten voyages from southern Irish ports to Virginia and Maryland identified in the period 1713–26, at least four carried passengers or servants, and vessels from British ports continued to take on Irish servants for Virginia into the 1720s.[27] It is possible, therefore, that migration to the region from Ulster, and from Ireland as a whole, represented a significant additional element in the movement of this period.

The major surge in emigration of the late 1710s began in 1717. Early in 1718 Archbishop King reported that "last year some thousands of families are gone to the West Indies." There is no evidence for a major migration to the Caribbean at this point, and King (and others) appear to have used the term "West Indies" as a general reference for transatlantic destinations. (On another occasion he referred to contemporary emigrants as sailing for Cape Breton.)[28] King's indication of the scale of the movement was undoubtedly exaggerated. Twelve voyages from Irish ports have been identified for 1717, of which only three were from Ulster (Table 6.1). The number of northern emigrants may, however, have been greater than this figure suggests. In late October 1717 the Philadelphia merchant Jonathan Dickinson reported the arrival of immigrants at the port, including "from the north of Ireland many hundreds."[29] The only arrivals reported for Delaware River ports in the pre-ceding weeks were four vessels from Dublin and Cork, three of which were noted as carrying passengers; an unnamed vessel arrived from the "North of Ireland" with "near 200 passengers" a few days later. Some northern migrants may have traveled via Dublin, but it is also possible that some of these voyages had called at an Ulster port en route. In September 1717 the *Friends Goodwill* was reported as having arrived at Boston direct from Dublin: only in the accompanying accounts of the horrific eighteen-week voyage that the fifty-two crew, passengers, and servants had endured was reference made to an additional call at Larne (Appendix).

The peak of the exodus came in the following two years, during which there were at least thirty voyages to North America originating from or calling at Ulster ports (Table 6.1). A further six vessels arrived from "Ireland"—some of which may have originated from Ulster—and eight came from Dublin. Again, the data certainly underestimate the real numbers. Newspaper sources listed only seven vessels from Ulster ports arriving in the Delaware during 1719, yet Jonathan Dickinson re-ported from Philadelphia in November that "this summer [we] have had about 12 or 13 sail of ships from the North of Ireland with a swarm of people . . . being well nigh 2000 and more a coming."[30] Other voyages may have arrived unrecorded at minor ports.

The historical focus on New England as the primary destination for Ulster emigration during this period has concealed the scale of the movement. In fact, during the years 1717–19, northeastern ports saw the arrival of only about one-third of the voyages identified from Ulster (Table 6.2). Eighteen other sailings on which Ulster migrants may have traveled—nine from "Ireland" and a further nine from Dublin—arrived in New England during these years, compared with only four such voy-ages elsewhere. Yet, at the most conservative estimate—setting aside the question of continuing migration to the Chesapeake—it is still likely that the number of sailings to other American ports at least matched those to the northeast. The outflow to South Carolina—eight vessels in three years—has not been recognized as a significant element in the movement from Ulster at this time. It was short-lived, however, and emigrants did not take this route again in any numbers until the 1730s. More important is the conclusion that the emergence of the Delaware as a major gateway for Ulster migrants, usually dated to the late 1720s, in fact took place a decade earlier. Emigration directed to the Delaware

Table 6.1 Departures from Irish Ports for North American Destinations, 1711–1720

	1711	1712	1713	1714	1715	1716	1717	1718	1719	1720	Total
Belfast/Larne	0	2	0	1	1	2	2	5/6	3	0	16/17
Coleraine	0	0	0	0	0	0	0	2/3	0	0	2/3
Derry	0	0	0	1	0	0	0	6	13	3	23
Unidentified Ulster Ports	0	0	0	0	0	0	1	0	1	0	2
Total for Ulster	0	2	0	2	1	2	3	14	16	3	43
"Ireland"	1	0	1	3	2	0	4	2	4	3	20
Dublin	3	0	1	0	3	4	4	4	4	4	27
Cork	1	2	3	6	2	3	2	2	2	1	24
Waterford	0	0	0	0	0	2	0	2	1	0	5
All Ireland	5	4	5	11	8	10	12	24	27	10	116

SOURCE: Appendix to chapter 6.

NOTE: Voyages that departed from two Irish ports (e.g., Dublin and Waterford, Belfast, and Derry) are counted separately in the figures for each port. Annual totals, however, indicate the actual number of voyages. These figures include vessels that sailed from British ports and called at Ireland en route.

Table 6.2 North American Destinations for Sailings from Ulster, Dublin, and "Ireland," 1717–1719

	1717			1718			1719			Totals		
	Ulster	Dublin	"Ireland"	Ulster	Dublin	"Ireland"	Ulster	Dublin	"Ireland"	Ulster	Dublin	"Ireland"
New England	1[a]	2[a]	3	7	3	2	4	4	4	12	9	9
Delaware	1	2	1	1	1	0	7	0	0	9	3	1
New York / Amboy	0	0	0	2	0	0	2	0	0	4	0	0
South Carolina	1	0	0	4	0	0	3	0	0	8	0	0
Total	3	4	4	14	4	2	16	4	4	33	12	10

SOURCE: Appendix to chapter 6.

NOTE: In 1719 two vessels sailed from Derry to Newcastle-on-Delaware and then proceeded to Boston; it is not known whether these voyages carried passengers to Boston, and they have not been counted in the New England total for that year.

[a] The voyage of the *Friends Goodwill* from Dublin and Larne in 1717 has been counted in both the Ulster and Dublin totals for that year.

developed in parallel with the flow to New England rather than in succession to it.

The data on shipping provide some indication of the regional origins of emigrants within Ulster (Table 6.1). Nineteen of the voyages identified during 1717–19 originated from or called at Derry, serving the relatively lightly populated northwest of the province, compared with only ten or eleven sailings from Belfast (and nearby Larne), the major trading port of Ulster and center of a much larger population hinterland. Coleraine, the only other northern port from which sailings have been identified, saw only two or three departures. Some emigrants probably departed by way of Dublin, which was more accessible than either Belfast or Derry for much of south Ulster and possessed stronger commercial and trade links. The Irish Lords Justices noted that in addition to the information they had received on the departure of emigrants from two northern ports in the summer of 1718, "many others ... have transported themselves from those parts as well as from this port [Dublin]."[31] When the *Prince Frederick* was advertised to sail for New England from Dublin in 1719, prospective passengers and servants were directed either to the vessel's Dublin agent or to the merchant James Arbuckles in Belfast.[32]

Bolton and other historians have seen Tyrone, Derry, Antrim, and Donegal—"the heart of the Scotch Irish country"—as the primary source for emigrants of this period.[33] However, it is clear that emigration was much more widely dispersed. In September 1718, Alexander McCulloch of Ballycopeland, County Down, informed his cousin in Scotland of his own intended departure for America, commenting: "A great many in this country [locality] are going thither (having so great encouragement from their friends that are gone)."[34] This suggests significant movement from this area of north Down before 1718 and is the first indication of the influence of information from migrants already settled in North America in promoting further emigration. The agent on the Barrett estate in County Monaghan reported to his employer in December 1718, "your Honour never saw how many is going for New England out of this country. There is near forty families going out of this parish of Clownis [Clones]."[35] Three months later he announced that "there is a hundred families gone through this town [Clones] this week past for New England," adding that more than fifty tates of land on the neighboring Balfour estate around Lisnaskea, County Fermanagh, were "all waste, the tenants being all gone to New England. I believe we shall have nothing left but Irish at last."[36] The agent for the O'Hara estate in County Sligo noted in November 1718 that "[A]ll the news in this country is that several families in and about Sligo and all over the country are preparing to go to New England."[37]

These accounts indicate that by the latter part of 1718, emigration was in progress from many parts of Ulster and had, in popular perceptions at least, taken on the characteristics of a mass movement. What precipitated this exodus? The older, "Scotch-Irish" orthodoxy, which regarded Presbyterian grievances as a uniquely important cause of emigration, has been to a large extent discarded by more recent studies.[38] As Dickson pointed out, the fact that most northern emigrants were Dissenters does not necessarily prove that they departed because of religious difficulties; emigrants were predominantly drawn from the Protestant population, of which Presbyterians comprised a majority in the north.[39] Emigration was not, in any case, confined to the north; a significant number of vessels left from ports such as Cork and Waterford with no significant local nonconformist population (Table 6.1).

Nonetheless, some contemporary Presbyterian leaders asserted a connection between the specific grievances of Dissenters and emigration, and Presbyterian ministers have been depicted as the major instigators and architects of the movement. This role has undoubtedly been overstated, and it seems probable that most of the ministers who left departed for personal, largely temporal, reasons.[40] Those more closely involved were acting as representatives, responding to popular demand for emigration rather than promoting it. This was certainly the case with William Boyd's mission to Boston in 1718: "Many in that Kingdom having had thoughts of a remove to this part of the world . . . considered him as a person suitably qualified to take a voyage hither and to make enquiry about what encouragement or otherwise they might expect in case they should engage in so weighty and hazardous an undertaking." Boyd, minister of Macosquin, County Derry, arrived in New England on the first of the emigrant vessels of 1718 with a petition for "encouragement" from more than 300 prospective settlers and did not return to Ulster until the following summer; his activities could not therefore have contributed significantly to the emigration of 1718–19. Boyd did not eventually emigrate, and neither did any of the ministers who signed the petition.[41]

Objectively, the situation of Irish Presbyterians improved considerably in the years after the accession of George I in 1714, and by the late

1710s there were hopes for imminent relief from many of their legal disabilities.[42] At the point at which the movement to America reached its peak, therefore, the situation of Dissenters provided little rational stimulus toward emigration in order to seek religious or political freedom elsewhere. Yet the social psychology of popular Presbyterianism at this period remains obscure: the resentment inculcated by petty harassment may have worked with other factors to "tip the balance" in favor of emigration.[43]

In essence, the oppressions suffered on occasion by Presbyterians were founded, not on the differences of religious dogma and forms of worship that defined the parties, but rather on rival claims to the exercise of authority. Repressive actions against Dissenters were the response of individual magistrates and Church of Ireland clergy to the lack of deference of a group that sought to exercise its own forms of social discipline and to usurp or deny many of their functions.[44] Such a conflict was deeply rooted in the social structure of Ulster, for while Presbyterians were numerically superior in many areas, they were perceived by many members of the elite as lacking the "interest" of land, social status, or authority that legitimized their own position.[45] The Reverend Choppin, visiting the north in 1712, noted that many Presbyterian ministers had 1,000–1,800 communicants in their charge, with hundreds attending services, compared with less than ten in most Church of Ireland congregations: "Since I have made these observations I cease to wonder at the jealousy and rage of the clergy in these parts, and of all that they can influence."[46] "Almost all the clergy, and very many of the laity, are more bitter than ever against us, and miss no opportunity of aspersing us, and making us odious to the government," reported a Presbyterian minister in County Down in the same year.[47] Irish Dissenters, wrote Archbishop King in 1716, "make laws for themselves and allow not that the civil magistrate has any right to control them and will be just so far the King's subjects as their lay Elders and Presbyteries will allow them."[48] Three years later he presented the confrontation within Ulster society more succinctly: "The true point between them [Dissenters] and the Gentry is whether the Presbyterian ministers with their Synods, Presbyteries and lay Elders in every parish shall have the greater influence over the people to lead them as they please or [whether] the landlords [shall have the greater influence] over their tenants."[49]

Antipathy between Dissenters and the elite was not universal, and the incidence of harassment depended on local circumstances and personalities. Some landlords were accused of introducing lease covenants that barred meeting houses from their lands; others, however, found it advantageous to encourage Presbyterians on their estates.[50] During the 1690s, for example, a Presbyterian minister received "a valuable lease of a farm" on the Murray of Broughton estate near Donegal town, and in 1715 the agent of a County Monaghan proprietor recommended that a lease be granted on the estate for the site of a meeting house.[51] Lord Massereene interceded with the General Synod in 1712 to oppose the removal of a minister from Antrim; and in 1717–18, perhaps spurred by the prospect of tenants leaving their estates, Lord Blaney offered help in building a meeting house for a congregation on his estate in County Monaghan, Arthur Maxwell of Drumbeg, County Down, offered £1.50 per annum toward the support of a minister, and William Conolly, one of the Lords Justices during the year, asked the Synod to recommend a minister for Limavady, on one of his County Derry estates.[52]

The role of landlords, and of land, in accounting for emigration was crucial to contemporaries such as King. At pains to explain the exodus in the face of increasing political pressure for the repeal of the Sacramental Test Act, he rejected assertions that it was caused by Presbyterian grievances. He recognized that this was a powerful propaganda claim, however, and warned his clergy to avoid overenthusiastic pursuit of Dissenters. "Several thousands . . . all or most of them Dissenters," had already departed, he said, "in so much that many landlords are afraid of having their estates left waste. . . . if it be noised abroad that they [Presbyterians] are to be prosecuted in the Ecclesiastical Courts for mere conformity . . . they will press the landlords either to obtain for them a legal toleration or threaten to leave them, and I am afraid we shall not be able to prevent it [toleration] next parliament, if any colour be given of our inclination to prosecute them."[53] Presbyterians had never been more "easy" in the practice of their religion since the Glorious Revolution, King claimed in June 1719: "Nor do only Dissenters leave us, but proportionally of all sorts, except Papists. The truth of the case is this: after the Revolution most of the Kingdom was waste, and abundance of people destroyed by the war. The landlords therefore were glad to get tenants at any rate and set their lands at very easy rents. This invited abundance of people to come over here, especially from Scotland, and they have lived here very happily ever since, but now their leases are expired and they [are] obliged not only to give what was paid before the Revolution, but in most places double and in many places treble, so that it is impossible for people to live or subsist on their farms."[54] It is not clear whether King's assertion here that emigrants were "proportionally of all sorts," rather than "all or most" Presbyterian, was political expedience or a new assessment of the composition of the emigrant population.

Others also believed that rents were a cause of emigration. A report on the County Derry estates of two of the London companies in 1718 noted that "one reason they give for their going is the raising of the rent of the land to such a high rate that they cannot support their families thereon with the greatest industry."[55] A group of newly arrived immigrants petitioning the Massachusetts House of Representatives in the same year complained specifically of the "severity of rents and taxes."[56] Examples of rent increases can certainly be found for this period. Twenty holdings totaling almost 6,000 acres were relet on the Bath estate in County Monaghan around 1714, with rises of about 16 percent; increases on six smaller farms among these averaged 25 percent.[57] On the Clothworkers estate near Coleraine, County Derry, the rents of seventeen holdings relet in 1717 rose by 17.5 percent, with rents on nine of these predicted to increase by a further 10 percent.[58]

Some increases were considerably greater. In the relatively prosperous area around Lurgan, County Armagh, in which domestic linen manufacture was developing rapidly, the average rent per acre for new lettings on the Brownlow estate rose from approximately £0.12 in the first decade of the century—much the same as it had been since the 1670s—to £0.20 in the period 1710–19, an increase of more than 60 percent.[59] Nineteen leases on the Murray estate in south Donegal were relet in 1720 for a short term of seven years with an overall rise of more than 75 percent. Here, however, the increase on smaller holdings, those probably farmed directly by the tenants, was only 57 percent.[60] In 1718 an emigrant family surrendered the lease on the farm in County Monaghan that they had held since 1693 at an annual rent of £16; the land was relet at £44 per annum, almost three times the former rate.[61]

To what extent such increases were typical of the 1710s, or whether the number of leases falling in then was abnormally large—whether, indeed, there was a significant upset in Ulster landholding during this period—is not known.[62] Rising rent levels were not, in any case, simply a reflection of the demands of landlords. Rents set in the latter part of the seventeenth century were, as King noted, very low—"landlords were then glad to get tenants at any rate"—and the regional economy had changed considerably by the time these leases fell in.[63] Crawford has suggested that the impact of Scottish immigration into Ulster in the 1690s was not reflected in rent levels until about 1715, but there were also other factors encouraging increased land costs: the release of the Irish economy from the long depression it suffered during the War of the Spanish Succession; developments in communications; the spread of domestic industry; and, not least, the improvement of land and increased numbers of households seeking a livelihood from it.[64]

Demand for land was not underpinned by the rapid population growth that marked the second half of the eighteenth century, however, and was sensitive to market conditions and shifts in economic confidence. "I believe if the lands were now out of lease the proportion might be raised about £100 per annum at the rack rent as the times have been for some years past," observed Amos Strettele in a survey of the Vintners' estate in County Derry in 1718. "But the undertenants having as long terms as the immediate tenant has, and markets being uncertain in this Kingdom makes it very doubtful whether it may be raised so much at the expiration of the present lease. . . . most thinking intelligent people are of opinion that lands here must fall soon, chiefly by reason that a great many of the inhabitants and tenants of that part of the country are going off to America and leaving their habitations and lands, which must of necessity reduce the rents very low in all the northern counties."[65]

Rents were not the only financial demand on the landholding population. Tithes, which became a greater issue later in the century, were occasionally commented on during this period. George Pyke noted in 1725 that tithes on the Ironmongers' lands in County Derry were collected "in so rigorous a manner as is not known and scarce would be believed in England."[66] On the Barrett estate, on the Monaghan-Fermanagh border, the proprietor held the tithes on at least some of the lands. His agent reported in March 1719 that, while tenants had emigrated from other local estates, "I hope your Honour's estate will be safe enough for they complain most [that] the hardships of the tithes makes them all go, which is true for the clergy is unreasonable."[67]

Rents and tithes that were supportable in average years became more onerous in harder times, and it is clear that the late 1710s were a period of some distress in Ireland. In 1717 an alteration in the exchange rate between Irish and English currencies raised the price of Irish goods, depressing exports and drawing specie out of the economy.[68] Early the following year, as many emigrants were making their final decisions for departure, Archbishop King complained that "our commodities that used to bring [money] in have failed us these last two years, and [are] like to grow more scarce. . . . our hide[s], tallow and butter come to little by reason of the death of our black cattle, and our grain that used to be transported by our ill harvests will not serve our selves."[69] Exports of butter from northern ports fell by almost a third, from a yearly average of more than 20,000 hundredweight in the period 1710–11 to 1716–17 to only 14,000 hundredweight in 1717–18. Shipments of hides peaked in 1717–18 and 1718–19, suggesting increased mortality in herds or the slaughter of stocks no longer economic to maintain.[70] Domestic industry was also affected. At the end of 1718 the agent for the Conolly estate near Limavady, County Derry, reported that "trade is fallen very much in this country and particularly the yarn."[71] In fact, exports of linen yarn from Ulster ports soared, from an average of 1,700 hundredweight annually from 1712–13 to 1717–18 to more than 2,700 hundredweight in 1718–19, as households attempted to defend their standard of living by increasing production.[72]

There are also indications of deficient harvests. The winters of both 1716–17 and 1717–18 were long and cold, and the summers of 1716, 1718, and 1719 considerably drier than average; harvest seasons were notably wet in 1716 and 1718.[73] Ulster exports of oatmeal, the primary diet constituent of the north, fell from more than 20,000 barrels annually in the years 1714–15 and 1715–16 to a little more than a quarter of that figure in the year ending in the spring of 1717, immediately prior to the first significant upturn in emigration. Shipments from Derry totaled 5,700 barrels in the year ending March 1716; in the following three years they fell to 779, 60, and 137 barrels. Bishop Nicolson traveled from Dublin to Derry in the summer of 1718 and was given a military escort through south Ulster, "a country said to be much infested with a set of barbarous and pilfering Tories. I saw no danger of losing the little money I had, but was under some apprehensions of being starved, having never beheld even in Picardy, Westphalia or Scotland such dismal marks of hunger and want as appeared on the countenances of most of the poor creatures that I met with on the road." The reappearance of banditry in Ulster at this time may in itself be an indication of growing economic difficulties and social dislocation.[74] Some areas experienced substantial rises in mortality: in Magherafelt, County Derry, burials ran at more than twice the normal level in 1718, and even in the relatively prosperous area around Lisburn, County Antrim, the number of interments in the period 1717–19 was 80 percent higher than for the three preceding years.[75] In April 1720 it was reported from south Ulster that "many people died here this spring and money is scarce; nothing gains money well but corn, them that has it"; the following month King reported from Dublin the acute distress of the poor and high mortality from "the ague."[76]

Economic distress, though undoubtedly a major factor in spurring the sudden rise in emigration of this period, does not provide a complete explanation. The difficulties resulting from the severe slump that followed the South Sea Bubble crisis in 1720 and harvest failures in the following years were considerably more acute than those of the late 1710s, yet migration to North America declined sharply after 1719; only nine voyages from northern ports have been specifically identified for the years 1720–23.[77] It is conceivable that by this time the pool of prospective emigrants had been temporarily reduced. It is more probable, however, that, as in the early 1680s, short-lived projects to promote settlement by the American colonies had coincided with a period of difficult conditions in Ireland, offering a prospect of relief to the distressed. In 1716 the South Carolina Assembly enacted legislation to encourage the immigration of white indentured servants and to promote settlement on the frontier; a package of measures, including 300 acres of land for each male settler of military age, was publicized in Ireland.[78] In New England, moves to entice settlers to the undeveloped lands of various proprietors and to defend the frontier grew from circa 1714.[79]

Information on opportunities in the northeast also reached Ulster: a petition to the Massachusetts House of Representatives in October 1718 from a group of immigrants explained that "having heard of the great willingness to encourage any of His Majesty's Protestant and loyal subjects of sober conversation to settle within this province they have this last summer, with their families, undertaken a long and hazardous voyage to the said parts."[80] In August 1718 Thomas Lechmere reported that the immigrants arriving in Boston "are come over hither for no other reason but upon encouragement sent from hence upon notice given them they should have so many acres given them gratis to settle our frontiers as a barrier against the Indians."[81] James Logan, secretary of Pennsylvania, issued an invitation to Ulster settlers in 1717; in 1724 he referred to immigrants who were squatting on the Pennsylvania-Maryland border as "bold and indigent strangers, saying as their excuse when challenged for titles, that we had solicited for colonists and they had come accordingly."[82] The South Carolina legislation encouraging migrants was repealed in 1718 and New England became increasingly hostile to Irish immigration once the impact of the influx of the late 1710s had been perceived.[83] This decline in opportunities seems the most probable cause of the dampening of the movement from the north of Ireland in the period after 1719, until the catastrophic harvests of the late 1720s again spurred a major outflow to the gateway remaining open in Pennsylvania.

The period also saw the emergence of emigration as a commercial enterprise, promoted and facilitated as a branch of mercantile trade. This development may have been prompted in the short-term by the decline in other opportunities for profit. In March 1718 King reported that high prices for Irish goods had rendered them unsaleable in foreign markets, "and I hear several ships go away unfreighted."[84] The fact that a few vessels underwent a series of voyages between Ireland and North America in the late 1710s and early 1720s suggests that some masters, owners, and merchants had begun to specialize in providing passages (Appendix). One example is the Belfast merchant Robert Wilson. In 1714 Wilson carried a petition for a minister to the Presbyterian General Synod from a group of emigrants waiting on board a vessel in Belfast Lough, bound for South Carolina; presumably he was involved in their passage.[85] He chartered vessels in 1717 and 1718 for voyages from Belfast to South Carolina and was part owner of a snow, the *Arthur & Ann*, which arrived in Charleston from Belfast in December 1718.[86] Wilson was also connected with Archibald MacPheadris of Portsmouth, New Hampshire, a substantial shipowner and merchant with kinship links in Ulster. In December 1717 MacPheadris informed an Irish correspondent that he intended to send "several vessels to Cork, Belfast, Dublin and Waterford for the bringing over of servants and good farmers which will settle in our new plantations about 40 miles from this town in as pleasant a place and plentiful as any in the world. And every good farmer that comes, I will give him 100 acres of land for ever at 12d. per acre."[87] MacPheadris may already have made one voyage bringing migrants to New England, for he was reported as master of a vessel that arrived at Piscataqua (Portsmouth, New Hampshire, or Kittery, Maine) from Ireland a few weeks earlier.[88]

One of MacPheadris's ships was probably the *Betty*, reported at Piscataqua from Ireland (probably Belfast) with 178 passengers in June

1718.[89] Robert Wilson had shipped a misjudged cargo of linen, wine, and brandy on this voyage, and MacPheadris wrote to him in August, informing him of the poor market for his goods; he also advised him that he intended to arrive in Belfast with three vessels during the coming months.[90] In the same letter MacPheadris wrote of his plans to set up an iron works and, offering Wilson a share in the venture, asked him to "bespeak five or six good men that understands the making of iron to get their furnaces hammers and every thing necessary for the carrying on that work and that they may be in readiness to come along with me in the month of April next, and by bringing over twenty able servants with these men I hope will render a better account than any other employment I can follow, having everything so convenient, and being the only commodity that is always in demand in this country."[91] Links with the north of Ireland continued after the major surge in migration faded. In July 1722 a vessel from Belfast arrived at Portsmouth under Captain Gilbert MacPhadres, sailing soon afterward for Boston "with upwards of 200 Irish people on board," including an unnamed merchant.[92]

T. M. Truxes has suggested in his recent work on Irish-American trade that MacPheadris's activities were not typical of North American merchants and that the emigration trade was predominantly in the hands of Irish interests.[93] It has been possible to identify the home ports of vessels involved in twenty-nine voyages from Ireland during the years 1717–19, and almost two-thirds of the vessels were Irish owned.[94] A further seven were American, however, and another four were based in English ports. Archbishop King protested in March 1719 that he had been informed of "great numbers" of people preparing to go to America, "the London and Bristol merchants encourage it, send ships on purpose to transport them, and put advertisements in the news papers to invite them." (Advertisements for passages from Dublin to Boston on the Globe Galley and the Prince Frederick had appeared in Dublin newspapers in the weeks preceding King's letter.)[95] American interests certainly sought involvement. The Essex, of Salem, Massachusetts, arrived in Dublin in November 1719 and advertised a sailing to New England in January or February of 1720.[96] The vessel was described as "well accommodated and built on purpose for transportation of passengers." The proposed voyage may have been a speculative venture, however, for prospective passengers were advised to "come and make their agreement between this and Christmas Day, otherwise the vessel will proceed on another design." In late December the owner of the Essex, Benjamin

Marston, reported that "several persons have bespoke a passage with me, and tomorrow morning I shall set out on a journey towards London Derry in order to make up my complement of passengers"; by early March the Essex was ready to sail, "but that I wait for about 30 passengers which I expect on board next week, and at Derry I hope to make up the complement of 100."[97] Marston's enterprise was ill-fated, however. Before the Essex left Dublin, Marston died of smallpox. Then, en route from Dublin, the vessel became stranded, and she did not leave Derry until June 16. A month later she was boarded at sea by two pirate vessels, who robbed the passengers and took nine of the servants on board to crew another prize. The Essex finally reached Salem on August 22.[98]

Who were the emigrants of the late 1710s? This exodus was not necessarily a movement of the poor, for at times of harvest deficiency and depressed markets even relatively prosperous rural households could experience difficulty.[99] Tenants with some years to run on a lease were better situated for emigration, for their "interest" (the right to occupy the land and to negotiate a renewal of the lease with the proprietor) could be sold to underwrite the fare and the cost of setting up in a new home. Patrick Brett reported from the O'Hara estate in County Sligo in 1718 that news of the emigration of several local families, combined with "the sudden fall of our markets, has put the tenants on a project of surrendering their leases, which several of them has offered."[100] Before emigrating from their County Monaghan farm in 1719, the Forster family attempted to sell their lease interest and received offers from several "high bidders."[101] Such sales could raise relatively substantial sums. Early in 1718, William Caldwell obtained £7 for the remaining eleven years of his lease on a small part of the townland of Duncrun, which was on the Gage estate at Magilligan, County Derry; his annual rent previously was probably about £1.50. In April of the same year, the minister of the neighboring parish of Dunboe signed a testimonial for a William Caldwell and his family, they "being designed to go to New England in America."[102] Another tenant on the same estate sold the six years remaining on his lease for £7, having previously paid £1.75 per annum, and a more substantial occupier obtained £23 for the remaining thirteen years on his holding, on which he had paid £8 per annum. The purchasers of the latter subsequently asked 60 guineas for the interest and refused £46.[103]

This potential for raising capital provides a context for Thomas Lechmere's observations on the arrival of one of the first shiploads of Ulster migrants in Boston in July 1718. He evidently expected them to be poor, with many indentured servants among them; instead, he noted, "they are none to be sold, [they] have all paid their passages sterling in Ireland."[104] There were some servants among the immigrants, but they were not a majority. Two weeks later Lechmere cautioned his brother that "whoever tells you that servants are cheaper now than they were, it is a very gross mistake. . . . never were they dearer than they are now, there being such a demand for them, and likewise pray tell him he is much out of the way to think that these Irish are servants, they are generally men of estates."[105]

The emigrants Lechmere observed may have been exceptions; other migrants were clearly poorer. As early as August 1718 the Boston authorities were considering how to secure the town against "charges which may happen to accrue or be imposed on them by reason of the passengers lately arrived here from Ireland"; the following month the Reverend Cotton Mather was finding "many and wondrous objects for my compassions" among the Boston immigrants and intended to donate money anonymously to be distributed among the needy.[106] Leonard Cotton, who traveled to Boston from Dublin in 1719, noted that the "generality" of his fellow passengers were "very poor."[107] Ulster arrivals in the Delaware were described in November 1719 as a "swarm of people, poor and beggarly most of them" and as "mostly poor beggarly idle people and will give trouble to the inhabitants."[108] The agent on an estate in County Derry whose opinion on current emigration was sought in 1718 was concerned only that the authorities in Ireland should "oblige those rogues who goes off to pay their just debts before they go, and then let all go when they please who are inclined to go."[109]

It is clear from the number of references to "families" in contemporary accounts that Ulster migration at this period was dominated by the removal of entire households, perhaps to a greater extent than for much of the rest of the eighteenth century.[110] It is not clear whether there were also significant numbers of unaccompanied migrants, although it is likely that most in this category arrived as indentured servants. Some voyages from Ulster carried servants, but a larger proportion arrived from Dublin and other southern Irish ports.[111] Judging from the skills these immigrants possessed, many of the latter were from urban backgrounds; servants from the *Globe*, for example, which arrived in Boston from Dublin in June 1716, included an anchor- and shipsmith, house carpenters, ship joiners, nailers, locksmiths, a printer, and a silver and gold lace weaver. Some female trades were also listed: milliners, ribbon and lace weavers, housekeepers, washerwomen, and cooks.[112] The few advertisements for servants from Ulster were less specific: a Boston notice that probably refers to the arrival of the *William & Elizabeth* from Derry in July 1718 offered "sundry boys times for years by indentures, young women and girls by the year."[113] Servants were mostly young. Eight of the twelve Irish runaways whose ages were reported in press notices from 1717 to 1722 were twenty-two or under, six of them aged twenty or less. Most of the limited number of Catholic Irish who emigrated at this period probably came as servants: among the runaways were several individuals with distinctively Irish names—Miles Macward, Francis Macnemar, Thomas Shaughnessy, and Dennis Makanultie.[114]

How many Irish emigrants traveled to America during the surge of the late 1710s? Dickson acknowledged some emigration to other American destinations but regarded the flow to New England as the major component of emigrant numbers, estimating that perhaps 1,000 migrants arrived there in 1718, with a maximum of 2,600 arrivals in the three years prior to 1720.[115] This latter total is probably reasonable, but, as has been shown, the movement to New England was only part of a considerably greater exodus. The average number of passengers reported for ten voyages direct from the north of Ireland to North America in 1717–19 was nearly 140 per vessel (Appendix).[116] Thus, for the more than thirty sailings specifically identified from Ulster ports to North American destinations during these years, the number of emigrants may well have exceeded 4,500. To these must be added an unknown number who traveled from Dublin, on vessels recorded only as from "Ireland," and on unidentified voyages from British ports that took on passengers in Ireland. Others arrived unrecorded in the Delaware, at minor ports in New England, and perhaps at ports in Virginia and Maryland. It is within reason to suggest that at least 7,000 emigrants left Ulster during these years.

This is not a large number by the standards of later emigration peaks, and it represented only a small fraction of the total Ulster population of about 500,000. Nonetheless, contemporaries clearly felt that a major movement was in progress. The fact that migrants were predominantly drawn from the Protestant population, which made up about one-third of the Ulster total, meant that the social impact of the exodus was concentrated and, within local communities, highly visible.[117] The geographic distribution of the outflow within Ulster also meant that the model of behavior it provided was widely disseminated. For those faced with difficulties at home, the option of emigration, both psychologically and in terms of information on potential destinations, means of travel, and other key factors, was already established. Although emigration subsided for a few years after 1719, it rose again to new peaks within less than a decade. In 1725 the surveyor of a County Derry estate noted of one townland that the tenants paid "£27.7s.6d. among them and offer but £24.10s. as most of them have agreed to go to New England where many of them do go hence every year."[118] The example set by the emigrants of 1717–19, and those who had preceded them, was not lost on those who remained.

Appendix: Voyages from Ireland to North America 1711–20

Name	Type of Vessel	Master	From	To	Date of Arrival	Reference to Passengers	Sources
1711							
Hope	brigantine	Joshua Pickman	Cork	Boston	`	`	Bos. *N. L.*, Aug. 27–Sept. 3
Silvin Gally	ship	Robert Irwin	Dublin	Boston	`	`	Bos. *N. L.*, Aug. 27–Sept. 3
Brown Galley	`	`	Cork	Pennsylvania	`	pass.	Lockhart, 177
`	ship	Pickering	Liverpool & Ireland	Philadelphia	`	70 pass.	Bos. *N. L.*, Oct. 15–22
`	ship	Edward Ver	Bristol, Mine-head & Cork	Philadelphia	`	`	Bos. *N. L.*, Nov. 19–26
1712							
`	`	`	Bristol & Cork	Philadelphia	`	`	Bos. *N. L.*, May 5–12
`	`	`	Bristol & Cork	Philadelphia	`	`	Bos. *N. L.*, May 5–12

Name	Type of Vessel	Master	From	To	Date of Arrival	Reference to Passengers	Sources
1712 (continued)							
Neptune	-	Smith	Liverpool & Belfast	Philadelphia	July 28	-	Bos. N. L., Aug. 4–11
-	brigantine	Pierson	Liverpool & Belfast	New York	-	-	Bos. N. L., May 19–26
1713							
-	-	Traill	Ireland	Newfoundland & Nantasket	-	-	Bos. N. L., Oct. 12–19
-	ship	Laurence Clifton	Liverpool & Cork	Christeen Creek, Delaware River	-	-	Bos. N. L., Mar. 2–9
-	ship	-	Cork	Philadelphia	before Aug. 17	140 pass. & svts.	Bos. N. L., Aug. 3–10, Aug. 17–24
Laurell	pink	Peirson/Pearson[a]	Dublin	Philadelphia	Nov. 12	75 pass. & svts.	Bos. N. L., Sept. 7–14, Nov. 23–30
Elizabeth	-	Rochdell	[Liverpool? &][b] Cork	Virginia	-	-	Bos. N. L., May 11–18

1714

Name	Type of Vessel	Master	From	To	Date of Arrival	Reference to Passengers	Sources
Greyhound	sloop	Benjamin Elson	Ireland	Boston	`	`	Bos. N. L., Apr. 19–26
Elizabeth & Kathrin	ship	William Robinson	Ireland	Boston	`	pass.	Bos. N. L., May 31–June 7; O'Brien, "Authoritative," 135
Mary Anne	ship	John Macarell	Ireland	Boston	`	`	Bos. N. L., Aug. 2–9
William and Susannah^c	brigantine	Edomiram Collins	Cork	Salem	Sept.	29 svts.	N. O. Returns, 848, f. 121; Truxes, 24
York Merchant	[ship]	John Beach	Cork	Boston	`	svts.	Bos. N. L., Sept. 6–13, 13–20
Thomas & Jane	ship	William Wilson	Derry	Boston	`	pass.	Bos. N. L., Oct. 4–11; Bolton, 82

Name	Type of Vessel	Master	From	To	Date of Arrival	Reference to Passengers	Sources
1714 (*continued*)							
Friendship	pink	-	England & Cork	Baltimore & Philadelphia	-	about 100 pass. from Engl. and Irel.	Bos. N. L., Oct. 4–11
-	-	Pinkethman	Cork	New York	Oct. 26	-	Bos. N. L., Nov. 1–8
Dispatch	-	Joseph Hayes	Liverpool & Cork	Baltimore & New York	-	-	Bos. N. L., Jan. 10–17, 1715
Hopewell	ship	Samuel Hayes	Liverpool & Cork	Baltimore & New York	-	-	Bos. N. L., Jan. 10–17, 1715
-	-	-	Belfast	South Carolina	-	70 pass. & crew	Recs. Gen. Synod, 1:336–37
1715							
Amity	snow	Nathaniel Breed	Ireland	Boston	-	-	Bos. N. L., June 13–20
Swallow	ship	James Cumberford/Comerford	Belfast	Salem	Aug.	-	N. O. Returns, 848, f. 126; Donovan, 64–65

1715 (*continued*)

Name	Type of Vessel	Master	From	To	Date of Arrival	Reference to Passengers	Sources
Mary Ann[e]	ship	James Hamilton	Dublin	Salem	Sept.	ˋ	N. O. Returns, 848, f. 126; *Bos. N. L.,* Sept. 12–19
Mary Anne	ship	Robert Maccarell	Dublin	Boston	ˋ	ˋ	*Bos. N. L.,* Sept. 26–Oct. 3
Happy Entrance	ship/brigantine	Matthew Bell	Dublin	New York	Aug. 29	pass. & svts.	N. O. Returns, 1222, f. 25; *Bos. N. L.,* Aug. 29–Sept. 5
Prince George	ship	Murgatroyd	Liverpool & Cork	New York	ˋ	ˋ	*Bos. N. L.,* Sept. 5–12
ˋ	ˋ	Totterdell	Bristol & Ireland	New York	ˋ	ˋ	*Bos. N. L.,* Sept. 26–Oct. 3
ˋ	ˋ	ˋ	Liverpool & Cork	New York	before Oct. 24	ˋ	*Bos. N. L.,* Oct. 24–31

Name	Type of Vessel	Master	From	To	Date of Arrival	Reference to Passengers	Sources
1716							
Truth & Day-light	~	Robert Campbell	Cork	Boston	'	Pass.	*Bos. N. L.*, May 14–21, June 4–11; Bolton, 318
Globe	~	Nicholas Oursell	[Dublin?]	Boston	'	Svts.	*Bos. N. L.*, June 18–25; June 25–July 2
Mary Anne	~	Robert Maccarell	Dublin	Boston	'	Pass.	*Bos. N. L.*, June 18–25; Bolton, 318
—	~	Montgomery	Waterford	Piscataqua	'	-	*Bos. N. L.*, July 2–9
America	~	-	Lisburn	Boston	July 3	-	O'Brien, "Irish Immigrants," 179
Cezer [*Sizargh*]ᵈ	ship	Matthew Cowman	Dublin & Waterford	Philadelphia	'	"70-odd" pass.	*Bos. N. L.*, July 30–Aug. 6
Mary	~	Cumpthy	Chester & Dublin	Philadelphia	'	-	*Bos. N. L.*, Oct. 15–22

Name	Type of Vessel	Master	From	To	Date of Arrival	Reference to Passengers	Sources
1716 (*continued*)							
-	-	Parr	Cork	New York	before June 4	-	*Bos. N. L.,* June 4–11
Endeavour	hoy	Jeremiah Donovan	Baltimore (Ireland)	Virginia & New York	Oct. 31	-	N. O. Returns, 1222, f. 86
Upton	pink	Patrick Trayle	Bristol & Belfast	Charleston	Jan.–Feb. 1717	-	N. O. Returns, 508, f. 12
1717							
-	-	-	Ireland	Boston	June	pass.	Bolton, 318
Globe	-	Alexander Dowglase	Dublin	Boston	-	svts.	*Bos. N. L.,* August 12–19; Bolton, 318
William	snow	Robert Montgomery	Ireland	Boston	-	-	*Bos. N. L.,* Sept. 2–9; Sept. 16–23

1717 (*continued*)

Name	Type of Vessel	Master	From	To	Date of Arrival	Reference to Passengers	Sources
Friends Goodwill	ship	Edward Goodwin/Goodin g	Dublin & Larne	Boston	-	52 pass., svts. & crew	*Bos. N. L.*, Sept. 9–16, Sept. 23–30; Bolton, 319
-	-	Archibald Mac Pheaderies[e]	Ireland	Piscataqua	Sept. 27	-	*Bos. N. L.*, Sept. 23–30
-	ship	Ball	Cork	Philadelphia	Aug. 30	130 & a minister	*Bos. N. L.*, Sept. 2–9
[*Sizargh*]	-	Cowman	Dublin	Philadelphia	-	"about 100" pass.	*Bos. N. L.*, Sept. 9–16
-	-	Clayton	Liverpool & Cork	Philadelphia	-	-	*Bos. N. L.*, Oct. 14–21
-	-	Codd	Liverpool & Dublin	Philadelphia	Oct. 24	150 pass.	*Bos. N. L.*, Nov. 4–11
-	-	Joseph Travers	"North of Ireland"	Philadelphia	-	"near 200" pass.	*Bos. N. L.*, Nov. 11–18

Name	Type of Vessel	Master	From	To	Date of Arrival	Reference to Passengers	Sources
1717 *(continued)*							
Dove	ship	Gough	Ireland	Philadelphia	`	pass.	Bos. N. L., Nov. 18–25
Hanover	brigantine	James Wires	Belfast	Charleston	Sept. 26	`	N. O. Returns, 508, f. 32
1718							
`	`	Gibbs	Dublin	Marblehead	`	"Irish & Scotch" svts.	Bos. N. L., May 12–19
`	`	John Hayes	Cork	Piscataqua	`	`	Bos. N. L., May 12–19
[Betty]	`	Caldwell	Ireland [Belfast?]	Piscataqua	June 27	178 pass.	Bos. N. L., June 23–30; MacPheadris
William & Mary	snow	James Montgomery	Coleraine	Boston	July 29	pass.	N. O. Returns, 848, f. 113; Bos. N. L., July 21–28

Name	Type of Vessel	Master	From	To	Date of Arrival	Reference to Passengers	Sources
1718 (*continued*)							
William & Elizabeth	ship	John Wilson	Derry	Boston	July 29	pass.	N. O. Returns, 848, f. 113; *Bos. N. L.*, July 28–Aug. 1
William	ship/snow	Archibald Hunter	Belfast &/or Coleraine	Boston	Aug. 5	132 pass.	N. O. Returns, 848, f. 113; *Bos. N. L.*, Aug. 4–11
Robert	brigantine	James Ferguson	Glasgow & Belfast	Boston [& Casco?]	-	pass. & svts.	*Bos. N. L.*, Aug. 4–11; Bolton, 146, 149
Mary Anne	ship	Andrew Watt	Dublin	Boston	Aug. 7	svts.	N. O. Returns, 848, f. 113; *Bos. N. L.*, Aug. 4–11
Dolphin	ship/pink	John Makay/ Mackay	Dublin	Boston	Sept. 1	34 svts.	N. O. Returns, 848, f. 114; *Bos. N. L.*, Aug. 25– Sept. 1, Sept. 1–8

1718 (*continued*)

Name	Type of Vessel	Master	From	To	Date of Arrival	Reference to Passengers	Sources
McCullom/ MacCalum	ship	James Law	Derry	Boston [& Kennebec River]	Sept. 2	100 pass.	N. O. Returns, 848, f. 114; Bos. N. L., Sept. 1–8; Bolton, 142–43
—	—	—	Ireland [Derry?]	Casco	—	"several passengers and a Minister" ("above 160 persons")	Bos. N. L., Sept. 22–29; Bolton, 225
Mary & Elizabeth	ship	Alexander Miller	Derry	Boston	Oct. 20	100 pass.	N. O. Returns, 848, f. 115; Bos. N. L., Oct. 20–27
Beginning	sloop	John Rogers	Waterford	Boston	Oct. 27	pass. & svts.	N. O. Returns, 848, f. 115; Bos. N. L., Oct. 27–Nov. 3

1718 *(continued)*

Name	Type of Vessel	Master	From	To	Date of Arrival	Reference to Passengers	Sources
'	'	Epps	Ireland	[Rhode Island or Boston]	'	'	Bos. N. L., Dec. 29, 1718–Jan. 5, 1719
'	'	Spofford	Cork	Philadelphia	'	"about 50" pass.	Bos. N. L., April 7–14
Elizabeth & Margaret	ship	John Beeby	Dublin	Philadelphia	'	160 pass.	Bos. N. L., Aug. 11–18
Brunswick	ship	Maclista/ Maclester	Derry	Philadelphia	'	80 pass.	Bos. N. L., Sept. 15–22
Dispatch	'	John Cleaveland	Liverpool & Waterford	New York	'	'	Bos. N. L., Oct. 6–13
Hart	ship	Samuel Gorden	Derry	New York	Oct. 29	"about 100" pass.	N. O. Returns, 1222, f. 189; Bos. N. L., Oct. 27–Nov. 3
Friends Adventure	ship/pink	John Riede/Read	Derry	New York	Nov. 4	pass.	N. O. Returns, 1222, f. 189; Bos. N. L., Nov. 10–17

Name	Type of Vessel	Master	From	To	Date of Arrival	Reference to Passengers	Sources
1718 (*continued*)							
Upton	pink	Patrick Trayle	Belfast	Charleston	March 10	`	*N. O. Returns,* 508, f. 44
Friendship	`	John Galt	Belfast	Charleston	March 17	`	*N. O. Returns,* 508, f. 45
Arthur & Ann	snow	Hugh Hoods	Belfast	Charleston	Dec. 2	`	*N. O. Returns,* 508, f. 71
Lettice	ship	Hugh Mackelelan	Coleraine	Charleston	Jan. 3, 1719	`	*N. O. Returns,* 508, f. 79
1719							
`	`	Yoa	Waterford	Piscataqua	`	`	*Bos. N. L.,* May 11–18
Prince Frederick	`	John Hicks	[Bristol? &] Dublin	Boston	`	pass.	Dublin *Courant,* Feb. 10, Apr. 6; *Bos. N. L.,* June 8–15

1719 (*continued*)

Name	Type of Vessel	Master	From	To	Date of Arrival	Reference to Passengers	Sources
Jane	~	John MacArthur/MacMaster	Glasgow & Belfast	Boston	June 9	pass.	*Bos. N. L.*, June 8–15; Bolton, 321
Return	schooner	Joseph Newall	Dublin	Boston	~	~	*Bos. N. L.*, July 13–20
Globe Galley	[ship?]	John Mackey/Makey	Dublin	Boston	~	pass. & svts.	*Dublin Intelligence*, Jan. 6–May 2; *Bos. N. L.*, Aug. 3–10, Aug. 10–17
St. Joseph	[ship]	Philip Bass	Derry	Kennebec River	Aug. 21	"about 200" pass.	*Bos. N. L.*, Aug. 17–24
Joseph	~	Samuel Harris	Ireland	Boston	~	svts.	*Bos. N. L.*, Aug. 31–Sept. 7
Mary	schooner	Philip Rawlings	Dublin	Boston	~	~	*Bos. N. L.*, Sept. 21–28

1719 (continued)

Name	Type of Vessel	Master	From	To	Date of Arrival	Reference to Passengers	Sources
Amsterdam	~	John Wakefield	Ireland	Boston	~	~	Bos. N. L., Oct. 12–19
Mary & Elizabeth	~	William Grubb	Derry	Boston	before Nov. 3	~	Bos. N. L., Nov. 2–9
Elizabeth	~	Robert Homes	Ireland [Ulster?]	Boston	before Nov. 3	about 150 pass.	O'Brien, "Authoritative," 138; Bolton, 321.
~	~	Dennis	Ireland [Dublin?]	Boston	~	"sundry" pass.	O'Brien, "Authoritative," 138; Bolton, 322; Cotton
Greyhound	~	William Lea	Ireland	Boston	~	~	Bos. N. L., Nov. 16–23
William	snow	James Clark	[Belfast? &] Derry	Philadelphia	Aug. 20	"149 souls on board"	Bos. N. L., Aug. 24–31; Spaight
George	snow	John Welland/ Grashinham Salter	Derry	Newcastle-on-Delaware & Boston	before Sept. 24	pass.	Bos. N. L., Sept. 28– Oct. 5, Nov. 2–9

1719 (continued)

Name	Type of Vessel	Master	From	To	Date of Arrival	Reference to Passengers	Sources
Joseph & Mary	ship	Ebenezer Allan/ Alexander Macklester	Derry	Newcastle-on-Delaware & Boston	before Oct. 1	pass. & svts.	Bos. N. L., Oct. 5–12, Nov. 2–9
-	ship	Vance	Derry	Philadelphia	before Oct. 8	pass. & svts.	Bos. N. L., Oct. 12–19
McColum	-	Linn	Derry	Philadelphia	before Oct. 15	pass. & svts.	Bos. N. L., Oct. 19–26
Prosperity	-	Brown	Derry	Philadelphia	before Oct. 15	pass. & svts.	Bos. N. L., Oct. 19–26
Mary Galley	-	Liston	Derry	Philadelphia	before Oct. 22	pass.	Bos. N. L., Oct. 26–Nov. 2
Exchange	brigantine	John Parsons	Cork	Philadelphia	-	pass.	AWM, Dec. 29
-	-	Hayes	Liverpool & Cork	New York	May 30	-	Bos. N. L., June 1–8
-	pink/ship	-	Derry	Amboy, NJ	after Nov. 9	pass.	Bos. N. L., Nov. 9–16

Name	Type of Vessel	Master	From	To	Date of Arrival	Reference to Passengers	Sources
1719 (continued)							
-	brigantine	-	Derry	Amboy, NJ	-	pass.	Bos. N. L., Nov. 9–16, 16–23
Friendship	-	James Watson	Derry	Charleston	April	-	N. O. Returns, 508, f. 97
Young Lenox	-	William Wilson	Derry	Charleston	April	-	N. O. Returns, 508, f. 98
Friendship	-	John Maine	Belfast	Charleston	April 24	-	N. O. Returns, 508, f. 98
1720							
Amity	-	James Goodman	Cork	Boston	-	-	Bos. N. L., Apr. 25–May 2
Margaret	-	Luke Stafford	Dublin	Marblehead	Aug. 4	-	Bos. N. L., Aug. 1–8

Name	Type of Vessel	Master	From	To	Date of Arrival	Reference to Passengers	Sources
1720 *(continued)*							
Essex	brigantine	Robert Peale	Dublin & Derry	Salem	Aug. 27	100 pass. & svts.	*Dublin Courant,* Nov. 16, 1719; *Bos. Gaz.,* Aug. 22–29; *Bos. N.L.,* Aug. 1–8; *AWM,* Sept. 8; Donovan, 79–80
'	'	Nathaniel Jarvis	Ireland	Boston	'	'	*Bos. Gaz.,* Aug. 29–Sept. 5
Return	brigantine	Joseph Newell	Dublin	Boston	'	'	*Bos. N.L.,* Sept. 5–12
St. Joseph	ship	Philip Bass	Ireland	Boston	Oct. 16	'	*Bos. Gaz.,* Oct. 10–17
Prosperity	'	Josiah Carver	Dublin	Boston	'	'	*Bos. N.L.,* Nov. 21–28
Experiment/ Experience	ship	George Read	Derry	Boston	'	'	*Bos. N.L.,* Dec. 5–12; *Bos. Gaz.,* Dec. 5–12

Name	Type of Vessel	Master	From	To	Date of Arrival	Reference to Passengers	Sources
1720 (continued)							
Mary	ship	William Beran/ Bevan	Ireland	Philadelphia	May 19	-	AWM, May 19
-	brigantine	-	Derry	Philadelphia	-	about 90 pass.	AWM, Oct. 27
Laurel	ship	John Coppel	Liverpool & Cork	Philadelphia	Aug. 30	"240-odd Palatines"	AWM, Sept. 1

Sources: *American Weekly Mercury*; C. K. Bolton, *Scotch Irish Pioneers in Ulster and America* (Boston, 1910); *Boston Gazette*; *Boston News Letter*; R. J. Hunter, "Dublin-Boston, 1719," *Éire-Ireland* (1971): 2; G. F. Donovan, *The Pre-Revolutionary Irish in Massachusetts, 1620–1775* (Menasha, WI: 1932; reprint, Ann Arbor, MI: University Microfilms, 1981); *Dublin Courant*; *Dublin Intelligence*; Audrey Lockhart, *Some Aspects of Emigration from Ireland to the North American Colonies Between 1660 and 1775* (New York: Arno Press, 1976); Archibald MacPhaedris, Portsmouth, [NH], to Messrs. Robert Wilson & Co., Belfast, August 28, 1718, Baker Library, Harvard Business School, MSS. 766, F-7-168; Naval Office Returns, PRO, Kew, London, CO 5; M. J. O'Brien, "An Authoritative Account of the Earliest Irish Pioneers in New England," *Journal of the American Irish Historical Society* 18 (1919); M. J. O'Brien, "Irish Immigrants to New England," *Journal of the American Irish Historical Society* 13 (1913–14); James Spaight, Carrickfergus, to George Macartney, April 18, 1719, PRONI, T.519, Transcripts, State Papers, Ireland, 1717–19, f. 137–38; *Records of the General Synod of Ulster from 1691–1820* (Belfast: Synod of the Presbyterian Church, vol. 1); T. M. Truxes, *Irish-American Trade, 1660–1783* (Cambridge: Cambridge University Press, 1988).

(sources continued)

NOTE ON METHOD: The data in the appendix were compiled from a comprehensive search of American newspaper records and the limited number of Naval Office Returns for American ports for this period, and from a variety of other sources. I am particularly grateful to the library of the John F. Kennedy Institut für Nordamerikastudien, Freie Universität, Berlin, for the loan of microfilm files of the relevant newspapers.

Voyages have been included only where there were sufficient substantive detail to identify them unambiguously; thus, for example, there are no entries for five or six additional voyages implied by Jonathan Dickinson's report of twelve or thirteen vessels arriving in the Delaware in 1719 (see chapter 6, note 30). In many cases no specific reference to emigrants has been found for particular voyages. These instances have been included partly for the sake of completeness but also because it is apparent that the reporting of this information in the press and in Naval Office Returns was haphazard; the absence of a reference to passengers or servants in these sources does not indicate that none were aboard, and in a number of cases confirmation that emigrants did travel on a voyage has come from other sources (e.g., references from Bolton and O'Brien to New England records). It seems probable that similar supplementary information for many more of these voyages could be identified in local archives in the United States.

[a] A slash indicates that different names are cited in different sources.
[b] Brackets are used wherever there is a strong inference that the information contained within is correct, although it is not entirely proven.
A question mark indicates a greater degree of doubt.
[c] Given only as the *Susannah* in one source.
[d] Given as *Cezar*, though *Sizargh* is the correct name.
[e] This is the spelling used in the source cited. The correct spelling is "MacPhaedris."

7 Philadelphia Here I Come: A Study of the Letters of Ulster Immigrants in Pennsylvania, 1750–1875

Trevor Parkhill

People with a family advanced in life find great difficulties in emigration but the young men of Ireland who wish to be free and happy should leave it and come here as quickly as possible. There is no place in the world where a man meets so rich a reward for good conduct and industry as in America.

—John Dunlap

John Dunlap wrote these words in a letter he sent from Philadelphia to his brother-in-law in Strabane, County Tyrone, nine years after he had printed the American Declaration of Independence, and one year after he had established the *Pennsylvania Packet,* the first daily newspaper printed in the United States. Dunlap was born in Strabane in 1746, the son of a saddler, and emigrated at an early age to America, where he settled in Philadelphia and clearly reveled in the opportunities to develop his professional skills. The political connotations of the "wish to be free" that he referred to in his letter were particularly manifest in his associations with the Philadelphia Convention and later in his work for the American Congress. Elsewhere in this letter he mentions that "my brother James left this [town] for Kentucky a few weeks ago. I expect him back in the summer, then perhaps he may take a trip to Ireland. The account he gives of the soil is pleasing but the difficulty of going to it from this place is great indeed as the distance is not less than a thousand miles. I was there last year and must confess that although the journey is a difficult one I did not begrudge the time and labour it cost me."[1] Dunlap eventually owned large estates in Kentucky and in Virginia.

It would be ambitious to argue simply on the basis of this letter that Dunlap was a typical Ulster-Scot immigrant, but it would be fair to view his letter as representative of the observations, aspirations, and advice that to a large extent are characteristic of letters from emigrants until the last quarter of the nineteenth century. One task uppermost in the mind of those researching emigrants' letters is gauging to what extent can they be regarded as exemplary and to what extent should they be looked on as interesting but atypical. Dunlap's letter is a striking case in point: the defiant liberalism of the eighteenth-century Ulster-Scot is apparent in his emphasis on the freedom and independence to be found in the New World, for which he could personally vouch. Though there can be no denying that Dunlap's success was exceptional, the general tenor of his letter is reiterated in many similar communications, from Pennsylvania as well as other states. This chapter aims to distill from the letters of Ulster settlers in Pennsylvania their experiences as immigrants on the land and in cities and, at the same time, to evaluate the extent to which the letters and the personal example of the emigrants themselves facilitated the channels of emigration and helped the emigration movement maintain its own momentum.

One of the more fundamental insights that arises from a scrutiny of the range of sources available for the study of emigration in the eighteenth century is the extent to which there was a greater flow of human traffic to and fro across the Atlantic than has traditionally been believed. The custom of the emigrant wake, signifying the irretrievable removal to another world of integral members of a community in Ireland, derives mainly from the Famine period. It is especially common in the frequent representations of affective scenes in publications such as the *Illustrated London News* and in the many emigrant songs from that time. Collections of eighteenth-century emigrant letters, especially those describing commercial associations with the New World, indicate that many so-called emigrants might more accurately be described as travelers who returned to Ulster after a relatively short stay in North America.

Job Johnston, writing in 1767 from Oxford Township, Pennsylvania, confessed, "I was fully determined to agone home this fall, but I could not get ready in time, therefore I continue in the above township where I have now been two and half years teaching a very large school . . . if God permits the days I intend to come home not with any other view than through the regard I have to see you all once more and to settle my affairs there and so to return (God willing) here agin."[2] Later in the letter he offers an interesting viewpoint on the part played by the return of other, earlier emigrants to his native area in encouraging him to follow their example and emigrate: "The only encouragement that I had to come away was because many go to America worth nothing yet some of them servants and to hear or see them come back again in two or three years worth more than they would have been by staying at home while they lived, and yet they would not content themselves at home but went back again which was sufficient to convince anyone that the country was good."[3]

The visit home, even as early as the 1760s, was unlikely to be as permanent a move as was settlement in America. Job Johnston is clear in his own mind about the certainty of his decision when he says:

> And I do not know one that has come here that desires to be in Ireland [presumably permanently] again, for to live there, and I have often wondered at our countryfolk that was hard of belief in regard of what was said of their county, and would rather live in slavery and work all the year round and not be threepence the better at the year's end than stir out of chimney corner and transport themselves to a place where, with the like pains, in two or three years, they might know better things. . . . For my part I would never had the least thought of returning home only through regard of seeing you all again. I would here write more particularly to each of you concerning us both but seeing, god willing, I shall so suddenly follow this epistle in person, let these suffice.[4]

Often these prematurely returning "Yankees" were entrusted with letters intended for the Ulster families of emigrants living in, particularly, Philadelphia—the port of departure for so many ships bound for Ulster. One other way of conveying letters back across the Atlantic was to send an acknowledgement with the ship on which the emigrant had just arrived in America, for the regularity of trade often meant the vessel would be returning to Ulster, if not that same year then early the following spring. This letter appeared in the *Belfast Newsletter* on November 20, 1771:

> You will confer a singular obligation on those of your countrymen that went as passengers to Philadelphia in America from Belfast last May by giving the following a place in your useful paper. We think

that we would deservedly incur the censure of the judicious and impartial should we omit thus publicly mentioning the conduct of our captain, Mr James Malcom, whose every action was calculated for the advantage, convenience and pleasure of his passengers. With a liberality not generally practised, he distributed a greater variety of provisions than was promised; which, with his human[e] usage, helped much to the rendering the voyage unhurtful and agreeable. The friends of the passengers, some of whom, by a diversity of accidents may hear no account for a considerable time will, we believe, be glad to know that we all arrived, vigorous and healthy. From no other motive than a grateful acknowledgement of the captain's kind, social, benevolent and friendly behaviour, do we whose names are underwritten desire this to be made public; and, that those of our friends who desire to become adventurers to this land of milk and honey, may know where to find a man who is particularly adapted for the trade in which he is employed.[5]

The language used in these public newspaper letters, especially the unequivocal praise for the captain's treatment of the passengers, is generally fulsome enough to raise immediate suspicion. The fact remains, however, that such letters were clearly an effective way for immigrants to let their families in Ulster know that their arrival had been a safe one. For that reason alone they may have been glad enough to put their names to such commercial rhetoric. The letters' reliability as evidence is further enhanced because the ships were, in many cases, set to return to Ulster and take on passengers the following year. This applies particularly to the years immediately prior to the outbreak of the War of Independence, during which a number of laudatory letters accompanied by passengers' names appeared in the *Belfast Newsletter*.[6] This period, the early 1770s, was characterized by a recession in the linen industry that provided a regular annual quota of emigrants, estimated at 10,000 per annum,[7] for ships returning to Philadelphia and Baltimore, though of course the competition among ships' masters for passengers may well have encouraged a rhetorical flourish or two.

From the researcher's point of view, these newspaper letters have two additional merits. First, they are one of the few sources that provide the names of emigrants in the eighteenth century. Compensating for the absolute dearth of ship manifests—which, if they did exist, have not survived—they at least name individual emigrants, including females, although lack of additional information on ages, occupations, or relationships with others of the same surname—male and female with the same surname could be husband and wife or blood relatives—makes it difficult to make more substantive deductions from them. Second, they provide details of the conditions of the voyage itself. All describe the availability of provisions; some specify the length of journey—usually forty to fifty days—and others refer to "the distribution of medicines and other necessaries to every person who had occasion for them as well as doing many acts of benevolence in order to alleviate the many distresses ever attended on persons not used to the sea."[8]

It is possible to check in the private letters of emigrants for independent corroboration of the potentially questionable claims found in the newspapers regarding treatment of passengers. Generally they support the claims made about shipboard conditions and treatment, all this at least a half century before parliamentary legislation to ensure a minimum standard of conditions had been introduced. The emigrants' private letters are, however, more forthcoming about the hazards and difficulties that the published letters do not mention. In James Horner's first letter home from Philadelphia to his parents in Bovevagh, County Londonderry, in August 1801, he describes the setbacks and delays that most emigrants encountered on their journey:

> Dear father and mother, I have taken this opportunity in letting you know that I am well at present thanks be to God for his mercies towards me. I am well and happy since I left you; I was very bad for three weeks at first for we had very rough weather that time but I soon got better and was able to eat some of my sea store; we had nine weeks passage sailing besides two weeks at Innashone and a week at Newcastle. We had some little tribute to pay. We had 2s 2d to pay for a permit to get our wearing apparel . . . they have annexed a law that every passenger must pay a dollar for a certificate or pass; they put down our names and age and occupation and where you intend to reside.[9]

The waiting time at both ends of the voyage and the additional charges were normal hazards of the emigrant journey. Although in a few, relatively rare cases, emigrant ships foundered, often the main threat came not from the weather or the vagaries of captain or crew but from fellow passengers. As Robert Smith, emigrating to Philadelphia from Londonderry in the early 1830s, described it, "there was scarcely a day without a fight or a night without a robbery."[10] Disease, even before the rampant contagion suffered on emigrant ships during the Famine period, was a dreaded fear often realized. James Horner, in his letter of August 1801, wrote, "I will let you know a little of our passage. We had 30 children died with the smallpox and measles; we had one old woman that died. I got grosser when I was on sea than ever I was. I sold spirits at 7s 7d per quart and sugar at $7^1/_2$d, teas and some other articles; we had plenty of water; we got plenty of our allowance every day; we had no scarcity of victuals."[11] And then, at the end of the letter, Horner includes an interesting comment about the effort required in writing letters followed by a hint suggesting the importance of the option of returning home as a strong psychological force, as well as an occasional practical one, motivating eighteenth-century emigrants: "Pray excuse me for my bad handwriting for I had but $1^1/_2$, hours to write [a letter of some 750 words, obviously a considerable physical effort]. I was not going to write to the fall but I thought best to let you know I am as well as ever in my life. Dear mother, do not fret for me being away from you but think that this time will soon be over, that you will see me once more. I believe it was my fortune to come here to a strange land."[12]

Of particular interest for Ulster settlement in Pennsylvania is the extent to which the city of Philadelphia and its environs served as a base from which immigrants undertook journeys, to find work or land, elsewhere in America. The attractions of land and, more important, owner-occupancy, were throughout the eighteenth century the most consistent magnetic forces attracting prospective emigrants. David Lindsey wrote in 1758 from County Tyrone to his cousin in Pennsylvania, "The good bargains of your land in that country do greatly encourage me to pluck up my spirit and make ready for the journey."[13] And what made land in America even more irresistible is revealed in the comparison David Lindsey made between his own lot in Ireland with that of his correspondents: "We are now oppressed with our lands at 8s per acre and other improvements, cutting our lands into two acres parts, and quicking, and only two years' time for doing it all . . . yea, we cannot stand more."[14] Lindsey seemed to be protesting against the introduction of agricultural improvements, such as the development of a more economic field system and the spread of hedging, features that were to help put agriculture in Ulster in an ideal position to meet the demands of a growing population, in particular during the Napoleonic Wars, when Ulster and Ireland became the granary of England. These protests were voiced at a time when there were other factors just as likely to be agents of propulsion from the land in Ulster, ranging from increasing fines for renewal of leases to hardy annuals such as the tithe due the Church of Ireland. Whatever the validity of Lindsey's grounds for complaint, when the farmer in Ulster compared his lot with the experiences that friends and relatives described in their letters from America, the contrast surely played a large part in deciding in the minds of those who dithered that emigration was not only practically feasible but would give the independent-spirited Ulster tenant farmer the control over his own destiny that he dreamed of but could not often find.

But it was not simply the attraction of land in Pennsylvania that comes across in emigrants' letters, at least not at the beginning of their time in America. For it was unlikely that, in the period from 1770 to 1815, tenant farmers, even if they could raise the capital, would readily undertake a root and branch family migration when, on the whole, Ulster agriculture had never had it so good, certainly as far as prices for products were concerned. A rapid increase in population was, however, a corollary of this prosperity. John Kerr, writing from south Tyrone in 1806, commented that "as . . . population increaseth every necessary of life increaseth in proportion, for land at present is become remarkably high and still seems to increase in price and in demand, so that very few are capable of entering on farms, which occasion numbers of our Inhabitants to transport themselves to America."[15] It was the younger sons of Ulster families, many of them skilled tradesmen, whose letters from Pennsylvania are available to us. They indicate that not only was there a wide range of skills among the 5,000 Irish-born who were to be found in the Philadelphia city and county population in 1800 but that there was also a zestful mobility in their attempts to find work that would help them to become established either in business or, ultimately, on the land. Joseph Wilson wrote to his uncle from New York in 1774: "I have begun the copper business in Wilmington, a town about 28 miles from Philadelphia and 5 from Newcastle. I have so far met with pirty good encouragement. . . . I sold my pewterer's tools in Philadelphia . . . the pewter business is very much on the decline here as well as in Europe. They import all the plates and dishes from England."[16] It was, in all probability, the same English competition that had prompted Wilson to emigrate in the first place, as it had many young tradesmen who were engaged in the manufacturing of better quality durable goods.

Joseph Wilson's letter was sent to Thomas Greer of Dungannon,

County Tyrone, a Quaker linen draper whose business dealings with Pennsylvania customers, all of them Quakers, are recorded in the family's extensive business archive of some 1,000 items covering the period 1764–75.[17] Greer came to the linen export market in 1769 when the merchants of Philadelphia agreed not to import goods in protest against the Revenue Acts. Faced with the loss of this market, Greer and other linen merchants filled their empty cargo space with emigrants, many of whom made the voyage as indentured servants. Thomas Wright, in his letter to Thomas Greer of June 15, 1774, from Bucks County, Pennsylvania, said that he had arranged with merchants in Philadelphia that "Charles Thompson (master of the ship *Liberty*) was to take on board said ship at Newry as many apprentices as my friends could procure."[18] Samuel Brown, who emigrated from Belfast to Philadelphia in 1793, met numerous Ulster acquaintances after his arrival: "Andrew Sproule, carpenter, and William Gamble Moore, cutler, and Medoloe [McDowell?] the baker and Robert the plummer and John Morrow, cabinet-maker."[19] Brown himself was a glazier: "I am glazing a house at present for this employer and for priming and putty and workmanship."[20] It is important to remember Rodney Green's caveat "of the imperfect nature of emigrant letters as a sample. The unskilled are obviously badly under-represented, as are failures."[21] Nevertheless, the picture that emerges from the evidence available before 1815 is one of skills acquired by craftsmen apprenticed to their trade in Ulster. Such artisans were generally welcomed, and this reception gave them an excellent opportunity to become established in the New World.

What the evidence does not permit is even a general assessment of how many, having obtained work, eventually progressed to the eighteenth-century emigrant's dream of settling on the land. As Rodney Green wrote, "In the eighteenth century, the aim of most immigrants no doubt was to take up farming where land was cheap and abundant and free of rent and tithe. Unfortunately the number of letters which have survived from this time is too small to hazard any generalisation" about the number of emigrants who eventually took up farming. There are, however, more letters from emigrants available now than when Green conducted his research in the mid-1960s, mainly due to Kerby Miller's research in the Public Record Office of Northern Ireland.[22] For example, John Denison is at least one example of an Ulster emigrant who, benefiting from the craft skills he carried with him to America, graduated to install his family on a farm in Pennsylvania: "Dear brother, you wanted to know what I follow here and my first employment in the contery was weaving . . . I now live upon the waters of Juniata provience of Pensylvania Huntingon county franklin township about one hundred and fifty miles from Baltimoar and I follow farming now. Land can be purchased here for twenty shillings a acre which is then free only paying the tax."[23]

Even by the 1790s, prospective settlers on the land looked beyond western Pennsylvania. John Dunlap noted in his letter that his brother was based in Kentucky, where Dunlap himself eventually bought land. But it was not until 1857 that H. Riddle, a friend of the Anderson family whose letters will be considered later, wrote from Pittsburgh, "Lands in Pennsylvania and Ohio have advanced beyond the reach of the new emigrant. There is however an alternative to the hardy enterprising emigrant for he can wind his way into a new territory where he can buy land."[24] Until the 1850s, the lure of land in Pennsylvania remained not only a strong attraction but a practical possibility. Many continued to see it as their ultimate goal after a series of jobs that enabled them to accumulate enough capital to finance a deposit on a parcel of land.

James Wray reported from Spruce Creek on October 1, 1818, "We live about 90 miles from Pittsburg. The land here is cheap. You will get unimproved land for 2 dollars per acre. There is a farm to be sold here, with improvements, at 5 dollars per acres, which we are in some notion to purchase. They want a third of the money in hand and the rest in 2 or 3 years."[25] Wray and his two brothers had individually emigrated from County Londonderry to Pennsylvania and New York State at various times from 1818 to 1821 and found employment at a variety of jobs. Their letters, and those of most other immigrants to Pennsylvania in the post-Napoleonic period, reveal a continuing preoccupation with land. But they also show a growing adaptability and mobility in the employment patterns of immigrants.

Among the jobs the Wrays performed was teaching, particularly when they could find no alternative employment. The propensity with which Ulster emigrants turned to teaching as stopgap employment figures frequently in their letters home. Indeed, their general level of education, which allowed them to teach apparently at will, is not unrelated to the level of educational attainment throughout Ulster. The 1826–27 Irish Education Inquiry showed Ulster to have the highest ratio of schools to pupils in Ireland before the national system of schooling was introduced in the 1830s.[26] Even young men whose employment history was confined to manual work could lay claim to teaching posts. John Kerr, writing in 1843 from Upper St. Clair, Allegheny County, Pennsylvania, described this phenomenon in an honest fashion. Having catalogued the schools where he had taught, he wrote:

> You may wonder that the schools are so numerous and teachers so scarce that it is so easy getting a school, but neither of these are the case. There are schools sufficient for the number of inhabitants and teachers as plenty as you chose but the half of them are bunglers. Every human being who can write his own name and read a newspaper goes to teaching when he can do no better . . . but what is the reason schools are so easily got? The answer is the extreme fickleness of the American. The whole power over everything is in the hands of the people and although men are elected for the transaction of any public thing, still it is left in the hand of the people. This is here styled democracy, but is fast verging to anarchy.[27]

A more likely explanation is the large numbers of children in a young and rapidly growing population. The city and county of Philadelphia was an excellent example of thriving population growth, rising in the period Kerr comments on from 258,037 in 1840 to 408,762 in 1850; of those counted in 1850, 72,321 were Irish-born, some 18 percent of the population.

Denis Clark has commented on the extent to which Ulster men and women figured in the Irish population of the city of Philadelphia: "The representation of Ulster names in Philadelphia was notable as can be seen in McElroy's Philadelphia Directory for 1850–65. . . . The immigrants came from both the north and west of Ireland and were mostly young and single."[28] This is a surprising summary of the marital status of Ulster immigrants in the mid-nineteenth century and runs counter to the generally accepted notion that Irish immigrants, particularly those found in cities on the eastern seaboard of the United States, were by the time of the Famine arriving predominantly in family units. W. F. Adams, in his seminal work on pre-Famine emigration published in 1932, averred that "the Irish preferred to emigrate in families when they could,"[29] but the evidence of letters from immigrants to Pennsylvania, and especially from the city of Philadelphia, supports the recent revisionist findings of Denis Clark, Deirdre Mageean, Cormac Ó Gráda, and Kerby Miller that the pre-Famine emigration movement was dominated by single young people. Ó Gráda's study of the passenger lists for Boston and New York in the early years of the nineteenth century found that "even in 1803–06 almost seventy percent of all emigrants left singly, or in parties of two or three people."[30] For the half century before the Famine, Miller is even more assertive: "during the entire pre-famine period most emigrants from farming background left singly or accompanied by only a sibling or a cousin."[31]

What the letters of emigrants from Ulster do show is the extended emigration process by which families *did* emigrate, but in a gradual and piecemeal fashion. This process involved, primarily, the establishment of a base that could serve as a reception point for subsequent immigrant members of the same family. In this process, letters home from first-phase settlers were crucial in the timing, arranging, and, perhaps most important, financing of the journeys of other members of the family. This is a recurring theme in the letters of both the eighteenth and nineteenth centuries, from rural and from urban environments. For example, John Denison, who ultimately settled on a farm in Pennsylvania, wrote to his brother in 1789, "I have given a small account of the country to you and if you thought it answered you to come I would be fond to see you here. But I cannot take it upon me to advise you. But if you ware hear you might doo well and if you ware heare and settled nigh to me I would not see you want untill you would have time [to] fix yourself."[32]

Evidence for the role of family support in assisting emigration is even more frequently encountered in the nineteenth century. Joseph Anderson wrote in 1840 from West Salem, Mercer County:

> I am arrived safe with my relations. . . . I rested two weeks with John and David. I then set out to work about 30 miles distance from John's brother. Robert and I works for the one man. Our pay is 16 dollars per month all found. John and David is living on their farm. A young man can do better here than in Ireland . . . but a man that has got a large family is [not?] well situated unless he has got £100 sterling to [purchase with?] when he comes here. A man, once he gets a start in this country in the farming way, can get along pritty well—great deal better than in Ireland. Once they get the deed of their place they are safe. No rents at all and every man here is Lord of his own soil.[33]

In this case, Joseph Anderson's family had clearly been settled on farms in the western Pennsylvania–Ohio border country for close on a generation. The flow of letters confirms this family to be an example of gradual emigration aided by practical assistance in the form of money and a welcoming base on arrival. Joseph Anderson had settled on his brother's farm as soon as he disembarked, and Joseph remained there while looking for employment. The rest of the family correspondence witnesses a series of removals, both from Ireland and from within Pennsylvania and Ohio. And it was in Pennsylvania more than any other state that the features of extended family emigration were described in the immigrants' letters.

By the mid-nineteenth century, the system of assisting passages to Pennsylvania had reached a new level of sophistication with the introduction of a prepaid passage scheme. Using this system, an immigrant paid money into the hands of a shipping agent in Philadelphia, who then notified his associate agent in Ulster that the passage money had been received. The beneficiaries—the Ulster members of the immigrant's family who were waiting to join him—were then notified that the money had been paid on their behalf and their passage arranged. One of the agents in Philadelphia was Robert Taylor, who worked in cooperation with shipping and emigration agents in the port of Londonderry. The close links between these two ports had been well established as early as the middle of the eighteenth century. Of the 236 ships that arrived in Philadelphia from Ulster in the period 1750–75, 42 percent originated in the port of Londonderry, a figure not much less than the combined share of the other two main Ulster ports: Belfast and Newry.

William Smyth wrote in March 1837 to his nephew Robert in Moycraig, near Ballymoney, County Antrim, "You wish to come to this country and say that your mother thinks you too young. But, if you want to come, you are old enough. The sooner the better. You are not coming to strangers . . . you will come to the best home you ever had and if you are coming I wish you to come in the first vessel that will sail from Londonderry belonging to James Corscadden as I have paid your passage and sent you two pounds for pocket money which James Corscadden will pay you on presenting this letter to him."[34] This system continued until direct sailings from Londonderry to Philadelphia ceased in the 1860s. There is in the Public Record Office of Northern Ireland a series of volumes recording the names of people in the area of Donegal, Tyrone, and Londonderry—generally northwest Ulster—whose passages had been prepaid in Philadelphia and were to be arranged through J. & J. Cooke, a shipping and emigration agent in Londonderry.[35]

The immigrant on arrival in Pennsylvania was likely to feel reassured by more than the presence of members of his family. The presence of Ulster faces and accents would have been a striking feature of any immigrant's first experience and is frequently mentioned in their early letters home, particularly those from the city of Philadelphia. Herbert Gans's study of the Italian immigrant community in Boston's North End in the mid-twentieth century developed the idea of an immigrant "urban village" where the characteristics of Italian family and culture were preserved in a modern American city by the closeness of the community.[36] Ulster settlers in Philadelphia were never a truly homogeneous, closely knit community, but the frequency of passenger traffic from Ulster to Philadelphia was so constant that, from the 1770s, letters list acquaintances whom the writer has met, or has heard of, and who were known to those who received the letter and their associates in Ulster.

Samuel Brown emigrated to Philadelphia from Belfast in 1793, and his first letter mentions people who were clearly known to the community from which he had just come. Belfast in the 1790s was a compact market and manufacturing town of less than 20,000. So Samuel Brown's letter would have had an altogether greater poignancy when it was received: "I came to this city on the 7 of November which was nearly the ending of the sickness, when I got the account of so many of my acquaintances being dead shocked me very much. Amongst these was Mr Faulkner and Andrew Sproule, carpenter, and William Gamble Moore, cutler . . . John Morrow, the cabinet-maker . . . and a great number too numerous to mention. The number in whole died from the first of August to the 15 November is concluded to be 6,500 people."[37] And in the 1830s Robert Smyth, whose passage was paid by his uncle, in his first letter home identified the people he had met in Philadelphia who would be known to the local community in the parish of Billy in north Antrim: "Let Daniel Crawford know that his son is well and John Stewart and John Anderson is well and living in the country. John Brown is well. He is living with one MacFeren in the country; and all the McKinney boys is well. James McCain is well and is living next door to us. He and Samuel Woodside has a bottling establishment."[38] There is more than a hint here of a north Antrim community in Philadelphia, just as there is a strong sense of an expatriate Belfast community in the Brown letters.

The initiative for William Smyth to pay for Robert's passage came from his brother James, whose letter of December 4, 1836, is one example of what Rodney Green originally called "reverse" emigrant letters:

letters written by family members in Ulster to their kin overseas. James wrote, "Robert expresses a strong desire to go to America in the spring and indeed I am sorry to say that I am not fit to send him at that time . . . and we were thinking . . . that you could be so far a friend to him as answer his passage . . . until such times as he would earn it and repay you and if you had employment for him yourself he would repay you with great cheerfulness." This letter indicates the extent to which prospective immigrants without means in Ulster depended on financial assistance from family members who had managed to break clear from the increasingly difficult social and economic circumstances in pre-Famine Ulster. But it also shows why the small number of "reverse" emigrant letters are more likely than letters from America to answer the perennial question, Why did people emigrate? In the same letter written from Ulster by James Smyth there is an echo of the problems facing small landholders with sizeable families in a period of dwindling incomes and employment opportunities in agriculture and domestic industries, shortened leases, rising rents, and poor harvests. Smyth wrote with some feeling, "I met with great losses since I came to this place [Moycraig, parish of Billy, County Antrim] . . . in summer, my horse died and I have not yet got another. This has been the severest season ever I experienced in my life. Our summer was almost like winter and our harvest in November. And this 4th day December a great deal of grain in the fields and likewise a poor crop of potatoes, which have the appearance of a hard summer in Ireland." He laments the size of his family "which is in number ten."[39]

Even in the relatively more prosperous late eighteenth century, local difficulties of poor harvests and wet seasons combined with turbulent political events to induce friends of previous emigrants to express a desire to follow their example. Henry Johnston wrote a series of letters from Loughbrickland, County Down, to his brother Moses in Northumberland County, Pennsylvania, throughout the 1780s and 1790s. In them he described poor harvests, agrarian unrest and, in his final letter in May 1800, a culmination of all the trouble he had been predicting: "My dear wife departed this life in December 1795. Since that time there is nothing but disturbance, confusion and in many places rebellion . . . the dreadful consequence arising from so much disturbance was a great check to agriculture together with . . . a very wet and scanty harvest. . . . I have reason to hope from what I hear from America and what I see here that you left this in good time."[40]

By the late 1840s the economic impact of the potato blight, even though Ulster was comparatively less affected than the rest of Ireland, was such that Henry Keenan's letter from the parish of Ballyscullion, near Lough Neagh, exemplifies the dependence of the cottier class on the prospect of emigration. It also illustrates the reliance on communications from members of the family already in America for advice on how best to prepare to emigrate: "I have seven sons at the fireside with me yet. Times, indeed, are becoming worse every day here. There is no appearance of the potatoes recovering. I wish you to inform me in your next letter what trades I am to put my boys to in order to go or send them to that country. It is very difficult here to hold land at any price. If I could get anything for my land I would yet go myself and take the family."[41]

The frequency of written communications across the Atlantic suggests that emigrants strongly maintained their ties with Ireland. Though it is true that they kept up contact with family and friends in their region of origin, their sense of national identity was somewhat less durable, however. The letters of those who settled in the United States indicate a positive eagerness to be seen as American, not only by their neighbors and work colleagues in America but by their families in Ulster. This, in fact, is a very consistent theme in the evidence left by Ulster settlers in America in the eighteenth and nineteenth centuries. In 1774 Margaret Duncan, writing from Philadelphia to a merchant in County Tyrone, said:

> No doubt you understand we have great confusions in trade with us, but the English parliament represent it wrong in saying we refuse to pay taxes . . . it is not the tax but the mode of taxing we dispute . . . the inhabitants here lament Ireland and did not want to stop trade with it but it was thought it would have [been] a cover to bring goods from England. We lament our difference with England and are determined to give their troops no offence but if they are commanded to cut us off we must defend our lives as far as we can . . . if ministers and congregation would rise and come out here they might in a short time be settled out of the power of landlords and tithe-masters.[42]

Andrew Greenlees wrote to his brother from Dayton, Ohio, in 1863, "I am a citizen of this country. All my interests are here. I look upon this as my country which I love with a true patriotic heart and although it would be very hard for me to leave my family . . . yet should the [Civil

War] draft name me . . . I will seek no substitute, no creep hole, but march at once to fight and if need be to die for my country."[43]

The letters of the Ulster emigrants to Pennsylvania are valuable in enabling us to view the experiences of individuals and families. Yet the question remains, To what extent can generalizations about emigration from Ulster between 1750 and 1875 be drawn from them? Each collection of letters is as unique and as personal as the experience of each individual immigrant. But in a number of ways the letters can justifiably be regarded as broadly representative. The general picture to emerge is of a young single male with a passable level of literacy and working skills prompted by economic circumstances in Ireland and encouraged by the example of friends and relatives who themselves have recently emigrated. Their relative success, rehearsed in their letters home, often provided him with some financial assistance for the passage and, at the very least, with a welcoming base on arrival in the New World. The immigrant could undertake a variety of short-term clerical or semiskilled jobs, often on a peripatetic basis, as a means of accumulating some capital. The letters leave some gaps: for example, there are few Roman Catholic letters in the pre-Famine period, and only occasionally are there glimpses of how Protestants aligned themselves with churches in their locale. As with all evidence the gaps may be in themselves significant. Most consistent of all, the letters reveal a preoccupation with personal advancement balanced by a conscious or unconscious message of example and advice for prospective emigrants.

Only the reverse emigrant letters have anything direct to say about causes of emigration. In this regard, the almost traditional explanation for eighteenth-century emigration, the lure of land, bears up until well into the nineteenth century. On the subject of who emigrated, the consensus of recent historiography appears to be faithfully represented in the letters from young single males—in search of a range of jobs—whose irrepressible tone has been aptly summarized by the title of Brian Friel's play *Philadelphia Here I Come*.[44]

8 The Scotch-Irish and Immigrant Culture on Amherst Island, Ontario

Catharine Anne Wilson[1]

The Scotch-Irish who migrated to North America have been characterized as "frontiersmen *par excellence*."[2] Described as self-assertive, rational individualists, they were supposedly inspired by the possibility of
personal gain and eagerly left their homeland in the hopes of "cashing
in" abroad. They were considered to be "energetic adventurers, ruthless
land grabbers, and a highly speculative, grasping, rural middle-class,"
always on the edge of the frontier and always moving away from European influence, social inequality, and the rule of the privileged class.[3]
Recently we have seen this characterization in Rory Fitzpatrick's aptly
titled *God's Frontiersmen* and in Kerby Miller's *Emigrants and Exiles*,
where the Scotch-Irish stand in sharp contrast to the emotional, fatalistic, and communal Catholic Irish, who viewed emigration as exile and
doom.[4] This characterization of the Scotch-Irish, first applied by historians to the frontier of colonial America, has been carried over to the
rural Irish of nineteenth-century Canada. For example, R. Cole Harris,
Pauline Roulston, and Chris de Freitas, in their study of the Protestant
Irish in an Ontario township, have argued that by living on isolated
farms along the concession lines, where material progress was the only
means to success, Irish Protestants became even more individualistic
and materialistic.[5]

This chapter examines 105 Scotch-Irish families who settled the
frontier, but not as "God's frontiersmen." They emigrated from 1820 to
1860 from the United Parish of St. Andrews in Northern Ireland to
Amherst Island (near Kingston), Ontario, Canada. St. Andrews, the
community of departure, was a parish on the Ards Peninsula, on the
northeast coast of Ireland, just east of Belfast.[6] Because of its proximity
to Scotland, the first Scottish settlers began arriving there as early as

1606 from the Scottish border counties of Ayr, Renfrew, Wigton, and Lanark.[7] Two centuries later their descendants contemplated migration to America, and so began the exodus of the Bailies, Boyds, Gibsons, Kilpatricks, McKees, McMullans, McMasters, McCormicks, Watsons, and many more families to Amherst Island.[8] Since we are accustomed to associating the Scotch-Irish with colonial America, to label these immigrants Scotch-Irish may be to push the term beyond validity. I have chosen, however, to follow the example of Maldwyn Jones, who defines the Scotch-Irish as the descendants of Presbyterian Lowland Scots who settled in Ulster and later, in the seventeenth century, began emigrating to North America and continued doing so right up into the twentieth century. Indeed, he argues that the peak period of Scotch-Irish immigration was in the early years of the nineteenth century, a period he classifies as the nonheroic era of Scotch-Irish migration.[9]

Perhaps the use of atomistic land records, and an emphasis among researchers on the geographic relationship of families and land, has tended to exaggerate the individualism and materialism of the Scotch-Irish in Canada. This study, though it uses traditional sources such as land records, is based on genealogical profiles and the tracing of individuals through time. From an examination of the common experience of migration, the relationships between people, settlement patterns, and landholding experience, it is clear that these particular families were not the individualistic Scotch-Irish immigrants of the stereotype but were in fact cautious, familial, and communal.

Economic opportunity was the prime motivating factor for their migration. By 1820 the population of St. Andrews had reached the uncomfortable level of 398 people per square mile, and land was becoming scarce.[10] Agricultural prices were declining, and employment in farm labor was increasingly uncertain.[11] Nonagricultural employment was also in decline. At the turn of the century, a woman could get 1 shilling or more for a hank of linen yarn, and linen weavers, usually men, earned 10 shillings per week. By 1836, one hank of yarn fetched only 4–5 pence, and linen weavers earned only 6 shillings per week.[12] The problem of nonagricultural and supplementary income was compounded when the herring, a migratory fish that made a yearly circle around the Irish Sea, stayed out in the deeper waters where Ards fishermen were not equipped to go.[13] In addition, the expiration of old, underrated leases created a juncture at which tenants—whether farmers, fishermen, or weavers—considered emigrating instead of paying double their previous rent.[14] Thus, the young—from the ranks of middling and small tenant farmers, fishermen, sailors, and tradesmen—left for Canada in search of prosperity and security.

In many ways their circumstances were similar to those of earlier Scotch-Irish who crossed the Atlantic. Some left prosperous, fertile areas where opportunities for further settlement were limited; others left communities where the economy was characterized by proto-industrialization, where rapid socioeconomic change was restructuring society, and where households were particularly vulnerable to the fluctuations of internal and external markets. Believing that comparative advantage could be had by emigrating, migrants were attracted by the economic potential of North America, which contrasted sharply with the economic vulnerability and rising rents in Ulster.[15]

Certainly economic opportunity was the prime motivating factor for families leaving St. Andrews. But if we can judge from their activities, individual gain was not their only objective. The nature of their emigration and settlement shows that familial and local loyalties were just as important, and sometimes more so, than individual gain. They left as much to provide a secure environment in which to establish the next generation as to better themselves individually. Three characteristics of their migration stream demonstrate how family and community shaped their experience. First, the vast majority of migrants traveled not as individuals but within families. Only twenty people journeyed to Amherst Island as unaccompanied single adults. The other 382 emigrants (95 percent) traveled within family groups that themselves formed links in a continuing chain of extended families and communities that chose emigration. For example, Sam Pentland and Mary Jane Finnegan left Ballyobegan with their newborn son in 1824. Eight years later they were joined by more Pentland and Finnegan relatives, who brought with them the McWaters, the Flemings, the Girvins, and the McFaddens.[16]

Second, the decision to migrate was closely associated with creating a new family unit. Most groups bound for Amherst Island consisted of newly formed families or young adults of marriageable age—people who had reached a transition point in the family life cycle. Sixty-six emigrant families consisted of couples recently married and still childless, couples with only one child, or siblings of marriageable age who were traveling together. Fifteen families were headed by parents over the age of fifty whose children were of an age to marry and set up households of their own. The fact that so many migrants were of marriageable age illustrates that, for most, emigration was an integral part of setting up a new family. All the predisposing factors—such as the fall in agricultural income, the expiration of old leases, and the decline of supplementary nonagricultural income—encouraged people to consider emigration, but the final decision often awaited some transition point in the family life cycle. Marriage was obviously one such transition, an appropriate time to start anew. The young had very little invested in St. Andrews. It was easier for them to set up house in the New World, especially when economic prospects were dim at home, than it was for their parents' generation, who had more invested financially and personally in St. Andrews. It is quite likely that many newlyweds used dowry or inheritance money to emigrate. Marriage, with its new beginnings, thereby created an appropriate time for departing. John McQuoid and Elizabeth King, for example, eventually headed for Amherst Island following their wedding in Kircubbin, on November 3, 1823.[17] Thomas McDonnel, a sailor, and Elizabeth McCormick left Newcastle soon after their marriage in 1846.[18] Likewise, Hugh McCormick, a farmer in Ballyhalbert, and Ann Reid departed within a few weeks of their marriage at Glastry Presbyterian Church in 1856.[19]

Finally, their migration stream was shaped not only by familial ties but also by communal ties. Families bound for Amherst Island traveled as part of a larger community network. In fact, the locational bias of these migrants is quite remarkable. The bulk of them came from within five miles of each other, and once on Amherst Island they settled together. Of the 105 families whose origins were the Ards Peninsula, 85 families came from the United Parish of St. Andrews, 16 from the neighboring parishes to the south known as Ardkeen and Castleboy, and 4 from parishes still farther south, known as Slanes and Ballytrustan. Half of those St. Andrews families came from a particular crossroads known as Ballymullen, which subsequently became deserted and disappeared from the maps. No doubt the reticence to sail across the ocean was partially overcome by this network of emigrating neighbors and other forms of community support.

Since 1775 emigrant ships had left from Portaferry, six miles south of St. Andrews. It is quite likely that some of the sailors who manned these ships were relatives of the families sailing from St. Andrews and circulated stories of Canada throughout the community.[20] Besides these firsthand accounts, emigrants sent letters and passage money home. After deciding to emigrate, a family raffled its possessions to neighbors, who paid high prices as a way of wishing the family well. The community then escorted the family to the port.[21] Family and community, therefore, played an important role in deciding to emigrate, collecting information, and preparing for and executing the move.

So effective was this system that even after Amherst Island was completely settled and it became necessary for the next generation to relocate, families traveled to secondary settlements together, thereby repeating the process of kin and community migration once again. In the early 1840s, when land in the northern townships of Huron County, Ontario, came on the market, tenants Thomas Anderson and Alexander Pentland traveled north to "spy out the land" and report back to Amherst Island. Over the next few years, twenty-five families from Amherst Island settled there, in and around the towns of Goderich and Dungannon.[22] Group migration was obviously one way of reducing the hazards and loneliness of migration.

In settling on Amherst Island, these immigrants from St. Andrews were clearly trying to minimize risk. Exactly why they chose Amherst Island as their destination is still a mystery, but for Irish families who had faced the problems of low wages, underemployment, and competition for land, all of Upper Canada must have offered an attractive alternative. On Amherst Island itself, wages were five times higher than they were in St. Andrews, and rent was only one-thirtieth the cost.[23] Land was cheap to purchase, and markets were nearby. Particularly important was the fact that Amherst Island's economy was so similar to that of St. Andrews. In many respects Amherst Island in the 1820s and 1830s was an economic replica of the Ards Peninsula. Owned by Irish landlords, the island was a coastal community with a mixed economy and easy water access to larger urban markets. Migrating families had left an Irish peninsula where they had made a living from farming, fishing, sailing, and shipbuilding and resettled on a Canadian island where they could pursue these same occupations. The fact that the island was owned by an absentee Irish landlord with no connections to this migrant stream made the form of land tenure familiar as well.

Once on Amherst Island family and fraternal obligations continued. Most important, the growing community of transplanted families gave newcomers a lifeline to food, shelter, credit, and local contacts, not to mention moral support during the setting-up process. Those who were already settled housed newcomers until they found accommodations of their own. There were cases of families getting jobs for newly arrived relatives and even taking in children who had been orphaned on the journey.[24]

Soon after arriving, immigrants were integrated into a complex local money market. Thomas Polley, like several other successful immigrants, found that after a few decades he was able to finance personal loans and farm mortgages for other more recent immigrants.[25] The money network that evolved was quite complex, with debtors being creditors as well. For example, William Allen, a debtor of the local merchant, the land agent, and another farmer, loaned money to farmer William Filson.[26] Perhaps the case of farmer J. C. Murray best illustrates the complexity of the financial network: Murray borrowed from Mulvena and Chown to pay back what he had previously borrowed from Moutray to repay the money he owed in the first place to Neilson, Pringle, and Filson.[27] Save for the rare exception, this web of indebtedness was not ruinous but was a necessary means of operating in a cash-poor economy.

The lifeline of financial aid extended back to Ireland as well, although such efforts were not entirely without risk. It happened that on Amherst Island, the Hill brothers, who were saving their money to bring their parents over, stashed their coins in old Mrs. Patterson's trunk. Their hoard was nearly stolen when the pirate Bill Johnson raided Mrs. Patterson's home during the Upper Canada rebellions of 1837–38. When Johnson and his men came dangerously close to the shrouded hiding place, old Mrs. Patterson intervened, crying, "Ah, sure and yez wouldn't take a poor body's died clothes." Luckily the intruders left the money undisturbed, and within a few years the Hill brothers financed their parents' passage to Amherst Island.[28]

Alexander Caughey offers an interesting case of how the financial lifeline extended across the ocean in both directions. Alexander left Ballymullen in 1848, following the death of his wife in childbirth. He took with him his three eldest children, all under the age of ten, and left his newborn son to be raised by grandparents. Alexander then sent money back home to help raise his son. When the son reached old age and died, he in turn left his estate to his brothers in Canada.[29]

When it came to acquiring land in the New World, these immigrants from St. Andrews were rational pioneers. But they did not fit the Scotch-Irish stereotype—that of the ruthless land grabber, always on the edge of the frontier, moving away from European influence, social inequality, and the rule of the privileged class. Instead, behaving with prudence and caution, they chose to rent land in Upper Canada from an Irish landowner, close to kin, community, and good markets. These choices are easily explained by the fact that most came on the advice of relatives and friends already settled on Amherst Island who wrote that prospects were better there than in St. Andrews.

The popularity of renting in Canada seems especially understandable when examined from an economic viewpoint. Tenancy in North America could operate as one rung on an agricultural ladder. It was possible to climb this ladder from farmer's son or recent immigrant to laborer, then tenant, and finally owner, as one acquired skills and capital. Tenancy, moreover, made economic sense as a means of learning about frontier farming, of becoming familiar with an area before buying, of cashing in on good crop prices with a minimum of outlay, and of saving money that could be put toward machinery or cattle.[30] Generally it was suggested that newcomers rent before buying. Even as late as 1870 an agricultural expert responded to the query, "Can tenant farmers from the old country live and thrive in Canada?" by saying that he was absolutely certain that they could, but that "It is necessary to 'commence economically' remembering that their small capital is all they have and if nearly all invested in a freehold farm it will not be so available as it was in the Old Country where they rented and could invest their money in stock and other effects to produce an immediate return, turning over their capital in part or in whole twice a year."[31] Settlers on Amherst Island were not the only immigrants to take advantage of the safe start and opportunities tenancy provided. In 1848, 45 percent of the occupiers of land in Upper Canada were tenants.[32]

On the frontier, where land was readily available or tenancy had to compete with freehold, rental terms could be very attractive. Compared to Ireland, renting in Canada was a good deal: abundant land and scarce population translated into low rents for farm lots. Whereas the average farm size in St. Andrews in the 1830s was 20 acres and many people were landless, on Amherst Island immigrants went directly onto 50–100-acre farms. Upon arriving on the island, they called at the house of the agent, who received them on behalf of the landlord and showed them the lots available.

In St. Andrews, from 1815 until the Famine, tenants paid a rent of 15–28 shillings per statute acre under old leases and 26–39 shillings per statute acre for newly let land.[33] In contrast, rents on Amherst Island were 1 shilling per acre from 1823 to 1835, then 3 shillings per acre until the 1860s.[34] Besides the much lower rents on Amherst Island, leases were longer, making tenure more secure. In St. Andrews most tenants held at will, and the rent could be raised every year, increasing the possibility of arrears and eviction. On Amherst Island, leases were for 15–20 years, during which time the rents remained the same.[35] Islanders also enjoyed less stringent rental regulations. They did not have to patronize the landlord's mill, labor on his property, or pay additional renewal fines, drivers' fees, and receiver fees as they did on the Ards. Moreover, land could be purchased on Amherst Island for £3 per acre at a time when it cost £8–40 per acre to buy only the leasehold of land in St. Andrews.[36] Thus on Amherst Island, covenants were reasonable and eviction was rare.

Furthermore, rent levels on Amherst Island did not keep pace with the rising cost of land. For example, throughout the years 1835–55 rents remained at an annual £15 for a 100-acre farm, while the sale value increased eightfold, from £100 to £800.[37] This gave rise to a practice known as "tenant right," which greatly increased the tenant's interest in his property. In Ireland, tenant right (or the "Ulster Custom") was the money an incoming tenant paid to the outgoing tenant. The practice was often a clandestine arrangement, and whether anything was actually being sold was often unclear.[38] On Amherst Island, tenant right represented the growing discrepancy between the actual rent paid and what the landlord might have demanded if rents were in accordance with rising land values. Tenants quickly took advantage of this discrepancy, or "uncollected rent," and sold it to incoming tenants. The surviving cases of tenant right show that the sum exchanged could be as much as 94 percent of the assessed value.[39] Renting therefore made economic sense, for it was profitable.

Frequent sales of tenant right indicate that some tenants on Amherst Island viewed renting as a speculative transitional condition; they waited until their property rose in value, then sold their interest and left to do the same again elsewhere or perhaps to buy.[40] Others considered tenancy as an end in itself; as long as it fulfilled their economic expectations of a stable farm experience, they continued to rent even when they could afford to buy. The number of persistent tenant families is worthy of note: between the rent rolls of 1855 and 1871, over half (53.2 percent) of the tenants were persisters.[41] One suspects that so many families continued to rent on the island because they preferred the stability of dense local connections to buying land in unfamiliar territory.

The opportunity for social mobility also existed. From 1855 to 1871, nearly half (44.9 percent) of the persistent tenant families improved their standing by either acquiring more land or becoming freeholders.[42] Alexander Glenn, for example, who was born and raised in Ballywalter, left for Amherst Island in 1863 to join his uncle Sam, who had emigrated in 1827, and his uncle Hugh, who had gone in the 1840s. A few years after arriving on the island, he rented 50 acres and sailed the Great Lakes. By 1873, he had enough money saved to buy a farm.[43] As long as rents were low, prospering tenants seemed to prefer to rent additional land rather than to buy. The majority of families (twenty-five) that expanded their rented acreage increased their farm size from 50 acres to around 150 acres, and some even as high as 250 acres. Surely families that could afford a rental of this magnitude would have had sufficient means to mortgage a smaller farm. When the landlord decided to sell lots, the only way he could induce tenants to buy was to raise rents and to lower the purchase price.[44]

Instead of rejecting European influence or social inequality, tenants seemed content with the transplanted, Old World landlord-tenant system. Benign lease terms on Amherst Island permitted individual improvement and created a relatively peaceful society. No collective or individual protest, no boycotts of rent, and no tenant associations developed. In other words, no tenant class-consciousness of the degree exhibited in Ireland emerged. Old World etiquette, however, continued to surround the relationship of landlord and tenant. As they had in Ireland, tenants continued to hold grand dinners in honor of their proprietors, gave illuminated addresses of gratitude to their agents, and, in a few cases, even named their children after the resident land agent.[45]

Certainly there was a material imperative behind many of their actions, from group migration, to loans, to renting. But as materialists go, these Scotch-Irish seem to have behaved in a timid, cautious manner, stressing family and community ties and shunning risky undertakings in unfamiliar places. In short, they placed security before riches. There is even a sense that although content and relatively successful in their new Canadian homes, they yearned for people and places back in Ireland. Some young men returned to St. Andrews to marry. Samuel Girvin, who had emigrated with his parents to Amherst Island in 1832, returned to Ireland five years later to marry Eliza Gray in Kircubbin and then immediately sailed for Amherst Island to raise his family.[46] Robert Curren, who had emigrated in the 1820s, returned to marry Jane

Reid of Ballyhalbert, and when their children reached marriageable age, the whole family moved back to Amherst.[47] Adam Miller returned to Ballyhalbert twice to visit his parents and might have made the trip again had he not been crippled for life when he was shipwrecked off the coast of Ireland.[48] Others, such as Alexander McGrattan, returned to Ireland in spirit. McGrattan put his heart on paper in a very lengthy poem, which is excerpted here:

> I have come through place of every kind
> As I rolled from East to West,
> But a pretty place I left behind
> I will always mind the best.
> And that place lies in Erin Isle
> And the Ards and County Down,
> Conspicuous, only three miles
> From Portaferry town.
>
> . . . .
>
> Now seventy years have passed and gone
> And I'm both old and blind;
> But in lonely hours I think upon
> That youthful happy time.
> And though five thousand miles away
> And an ocean lies between,
> I remember still and always will
> My school days at Ardkeen.[49]

Particularly moving is the story, passed down through various lines of the family, of David McGrattan (Alexander's brother) and his family. A testimony to the strength of family ties that stretch across the Atlantic, it also depicts the tension many felt between leaving to provide security for the next generation and leaving the old generation behind. David McGrattan and his wife came to Amherst soon after the birth of their second child. Because their baby daughter was too young to travel, they left her with her grandmother. In Canada, David was a sailor on the Great Lakes. Coming home from one of his trips, he decided that he would sail over to Ireland, retrieve his daughter, and surprise his wife, who missed her terribly. Off the coast of Cork a violent storm shipwrecked him, and his body was washed ashore. Meanwhile his wife, not knowing where he was or what could be keeping him, kept a candle burning in the window for a year hoping he would find his way home. Eventually she received news of his death. When the daughter was fourteen years of age she rejoined her mother on Amherst Island. The grandmother, whose life had centered on the child as the last of her kin to remain in Ireland, is said to have died of a broken heart.[50]

This modified image of the Scotch-Irish as frontier people who were not as individualistic or adventurous as their eighteenth-century counterparts raises a number of questions. Were nineteenth-century settlers less familiar with frontier existence than their forebears who settled colonial America? Did they thus feel a greater need to proceed cautiously and surround themselves with the safety net of familiar institutions, kin, and community? What other factors differentiated nineteenth-century migrants and their situations from previous pioneers from Ulster? Or were they really that different? In our search for the heroic and melodramatic, have we sometimes overlooked the less heroic, more mundane aspects of migration and settlement, and thereby distorted the experience of the Scotch-Irish? In our search for praiseworthy (sometimes outrageous) racial characteristics, have we ignored the values and behavior that the Scotch-Irish shared with a larger immigrant culture? Until more studies are done using family reconstruction and individual level tracing, we will not know to what extent these 105 families might be representative of other Scotch-Irish immigrants.

In many respects the people examined in this study were typical of millions of nineteenth-century migrants from the British Isles and Europe. They left from proto-industrialized rural areas where supplementary income, especially from linen, was in jeopardy and where commercialized farming was resulting in an extremely unequal distribution of land.[51] Several recent detailed studies trace the experiences of young families who, concerned primarily about security and family survival, left Ireland, Lowland Scotland, Holland, Scandinavia, Switzerland, and Germany for America.[52] The original pathfinders sent information back home encouraging others to follow, and soon clusters of what John Bodnar has called "transplanted" villages emerged. Walter D. Kamphoefner, drawing from an array of case studies on chain migration to North America, concluded that chain migrants, unlike individual migrants, quickly gained security. Sometimes they sacrificed a degree of upward mobility to maintain the bonds of kinship and community, but they nevertheless attained wealth and security superior to what they had had in Europe.[53]

The behavior and success of the Scotch-Irish families studied here cannot be attributed to the qualities usually associated with the Scotch-Irish but rather to their cautious, rational, and family-based approach to the migration process, an approach that they shared with the larger immigrant culture of their day.

9 Scotch-Irish Landscapes in the Ozarks

Russel L. Gerlach

The body of geographic literature concerned with America's rural ethnic heritage is, to say the least, substantial. Geographers have filled many volumes detailing with great intricacy the geographic attributes of every imaginable group on whom the label "ethnic" can be placed. Yet, in the hundreds of American ethnic studies done by geographers, the Scotch-Irish appear only in occasional references. They have not been the subject of serious inquiry by the profession. The record of scholars in other disciplines is only slightly better than that of geography. Colonel A. K. McClure, speaking in 1889 before the first Scotch-Irish Congress in Columbia, Tennessee, summed up the state of research on the Scotch-Irish in these words: "There is not a single connected history of the Scotch-Irish in American literature. . . . If you were to spend an evening in a New England library, you would find not only scores but hundreds of volumes telling of Puritan deeds and if you were to study them, the natural inference would be that the only people that have existed and have achieved any thing in this land were the Puritans. They have not only written about every thing they have done, but they have written more than they have done. The story that they generally omit is their wonderful achievement in the burning of witches."[1] Although something of an overstatement even then, Colonel McClure's concern for the failure of scholars to record and interpret the contributions of America's Scotch-Irish-descended population remains valid to this day, and particularly for those areas west of Appalachia.

The Ozark highland of Missouri and Arkansas was one region west of the Appalachian Mountains that was heavily settled by the Scotch-Irish in the nineteenth century. Yet few sources make any reference to people of Ulster stock in the Ozarks. The Scotch-Irish represent the most nondescript cultural group to settle in the Ozarks, and many if not most of the Ozark Scotch-Irish are themselves only vaguely aware of their Old World origins. Whereas many Scotch-Irish in the Ozarks blended with old-stock Americans, in some large areas they emerged from the old-stock matrix to become the dominant cultural influence, possessing an identifiable "critical mass" of historical culture traits that set them apart from most other groups. This chapter examines the Ulster legacy of the Ozarks, with particular emphasis on the cultural landscapes that evolved.

The evidence confirming the presence of a large Ulster-derived population in the pre–Civil War Ozarks, although inferential, is substantial. The core areas of Scotch-Irish settlement in colonial America were concentrated in southeastern Pennsylvania, the Delaware Valley, and farther south, into the Carolinas (Figure 9.1). By the end of the eighteenth century, however, a noticeable westward shift had occurred in the core areas of Scotch-Irish settlement. In Tidewater districts of North Carolina in 1790, the Scotch-Irish comprised 39–48 percent of the population, whereas in western districts they comprised 63–100 percent. In the counties of western Virginia, Ulsterites made up nearly 80 percent of the 1790 population. At the time of the Whiskey Rebellion in 1794, approximately three-fourths of the population in some western Pennsylvania counties were of Ulster origin.[2] In 1775 the ethnic composition of the population of the Great Valley of Virginia confirmed the forward position of the Scotch-Irish. At the northern end of the valley the Scotch-Irish comprised less than one-third of the total population, but at the southern end their proportion increased to nearly three-fourths.[3] Because of the large number of Scotch-Irish traveling south from Pennsylvania in the late eighteenth century, the valley route soon came to be called simply the "Irish Road."[4]

As the frontier of settlement pushed inland, the Scotch-Irish from the back country of North Carolina and the Great Valley moved west into Tennessee. A corresponding movement of English-descended pioneers traveled west from Virginia into Kentucky.[5] By 1800, the time at which settlement of those areas west of the Mississippi River was beginning, there is little doubt that a substantial proportion of settlers trekking west from the Appalachians, and particularly those on the leading edge of the frontier, were of Scotch-Irish descent. E. Estyn Evans has described the 250,000 people who passed through the Cumberland Gap between 1775 and 1800 as primarily of Ulster stock.[6] Those settlers descending the Ohio River from western Pennsylvania were largely Scotch-Irish who had left the Atlantic seaboard at an earlier date. Kerby

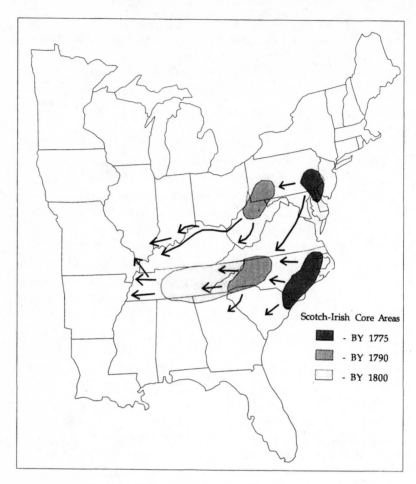

Figure 9.1 Scotch-Irish core areas in the United States, 1775–1800.

Miller's estimate that by 1790 perhaps 50 percent or more of the settlers west of Appalachia were of Ulster lineage would seem reasonable.[7]

The nativity of Missouri's population in 1860 reflected the two dominant cultural influences on the frontier (Figure 9.2). Kentuckians and Virginians, dominated by English stock of Upper South origin, sought out the more productive lands along the Missouri River Valley, the Mississippi River Valley north of St. Louis, and other areas of modest relief. They brought to Missouri a culture very southern in character, including a dependence on slave labor. Eventually, Kentuckians spread over much of the northern part of Missouri, where they were met by large numbers

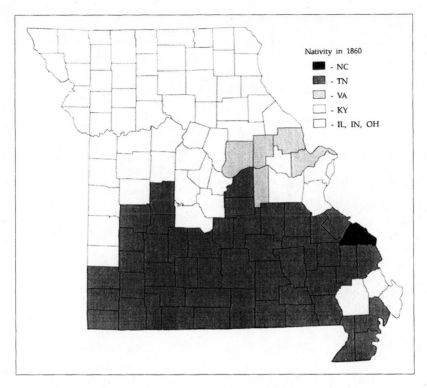

Figure 9.2 Nativity of the old-stock American population of Missouri, 1860.

(From *Manuscript Schedules of Population for Missouri: 1860.*)

of settlers from the prairie states of Iowa, Illinois, Indiana, and Ohio. There were many Ulsterites mixed in among the English-descended Kentuckians. Their importance along both the Missouri and Mississippi rivers in 1850 was evidenced by the presence of large numbers of Presbyterians (Figure 9.3).

The southern part of Missouri, particularly the rougher sections of the Ozarks, was dominated by settlers from Tennessee (Figure 9.4). Floyd Shoemaker said of the Tennesseans, "During the early decades of the nineteenth century the Tennessee settlers spread themselves all over the state of Missouri but later made their homes mainly in our Ozark highlands. Here they occupied almost solidly an area of 31,000 square miles . . . and they still hold it."[8] Carl Sauer added, "It is no rare thing to find some remote valley in the Ozark Center in which every inhabitant is descended from Tennessee stock."[9]

Scotch-Irish Landscapes in the Ozarks 149

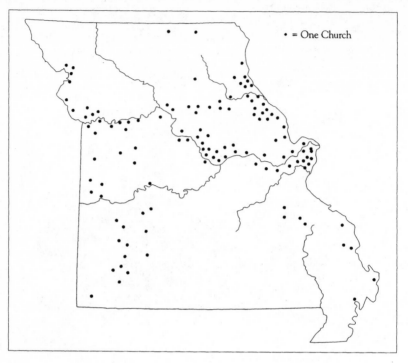

Figure 9.3 Presbyterian churches in Missouri, 1850.
(From the *Seventh Census of the United States: 1850*, 687–88.)

Many, if not most, of the Tennesseans who settled in the Ozarks were of Ulster stock and were more northern than southern in their culture. That many from East Tennessee were of northern origin and had moved down the Great Valley and west through the Cumberland Gap is supported by the presence of Quakers in several Ozark locations.[10] In addition, Pennsylvanians by birth were well represented among the Tennesseans in the central and western Ozarks[11] (Table 9.1)

Harbert Clendenen, retracing the migration routes of more than 650 pioneers who settled in the Ozarks during the years 1820–60, concluded that the primary source region for Ozark settlers was middle Tennessee between the Cumberland and Tennessee Rivers.[12] Writing of the migrants, Clendenen observed, "In their ultimate origins most were Scotch-Irish, but their ethnic or national identity had long been obscured by that all-inclusive name, American."[13]

The ancestry data from the 1980 census provide some useful infor-

150 *Russel L. Gerlach*

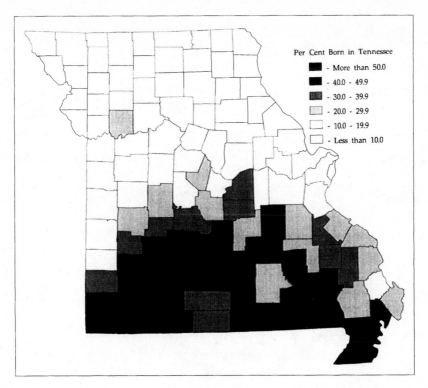

Figure 9.4 Percent of non-native population born in Tennessee in 1860.
(From *Manuscript Schedules of Population for Missouri: 1860.*)

mation relating to the Scotch-Irish. Respondents were permitted to write in any ancestry or combination of ancestries. A number of responses related to the Scotch-Irish, including "Scotch-Irish," "Ulsterman," "Ulster-Scot," and "Ulster."[14] Unfortunately for students of the Scotch-Irish, the Bureau of the Census, apart from a few exceptions, did not publish data on hyphenated ancestries.[15] Therefore, the Scotch-Irish were recorded either as Scottish or as Irish but not as Scotch-Irish. Despite this limitation, the data are of considerable value in assessing the patterns of Scotch-Irish settlement in Missouri.

Except in urban areas and in areas with railroad and mining activity, the Irish in Missouri in 1980 were descended from Protestant Irish stock. As a group, the Catholic Irish were not involved in the frontier phase of settlement in Missouri. By the time of the large-scale Famine emigration from Ireland, the focus in America was shifting from rural

Table 9.1   Nativity of the Population of 1860 Missouri for Those Born in the United States

Missouri	475,246
Kentucky	99,814
Tennessee	73,594
Virginia	53,957
Ohio	35,389
Indiana	30,463
Illinois	30,138
North Carolina	20,259
Pennsylvania	17,929
All other states	69,751
Total	906,540

SOURCE: *Eighth Census of the United States: 1860*, 301.

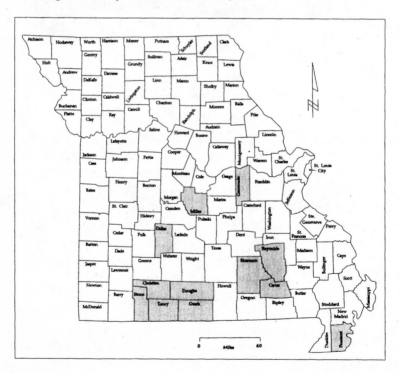

Figure 9.5 Counties in Missouri with sizeable Irish-American population, 1980.

Table 9.2   Irish Population Compared to Total Population
for Selected Missouri Counties, 1890 and 1980

	1890		1980	
County	Irish-Born Population	Total Population	Irish-Ancestry Population	Total Population
Carter	9	4,659	1,130	5,428
Christian	18	14,017	5,663	22,402
Dallas	8	12,647	3,067	12,096
Douglas	2	14,111	2,451	11,594
Gasconade	6	11,706	2,229	13,181
Miller	8	14,162	3,868	18,532
Ozark	8	9,795	1,902	7,961
Pemiscot	2	5,975	4,832	24,987
Reynolds	3	6,803	1,200	7,230
Shannon	9	8,898	2,341	7,885
Stone	3	7,090	3,592	15,587
Taney	3	7,973	5,476	20,467

SOURCES: *Compendium of the Eleventh Census: 1890* and *Ancestry of the Population by State: 1980*.

to urban settlement. In 1860, one-half of the Irish in America were in ten major cities, one of which was St. Louis.[16] A modest 4.1 percent of Missouri's population was Irish-born, and most were in St. Louis.[17] In 1890, there were 41,130 Irish-born in Missouri, with 74.4 percent of these divided between St. Louis, Kansas City, and St. Joseph.[18]

In twelve Ozark counties with a sizable Irish-ancestry population in 1980 (Figure 9.5), the Irish-born component in 1890 was miniscule (Table 9.2). All twelve of these counties were settled by substantial numbers of Scotch-Irish in the first half of the nineteenth century. The Irish were already in these counties by 1890, as the modest change in total population from 1890 to 1980 suggests, but by then they were native born and already several generations removed from their Ulster origins, and so they did not show up as Irish in the 1890 census.

The absence of significant numbers of Catholics in these twelve counties for all time periods, except those counties settled by substantial

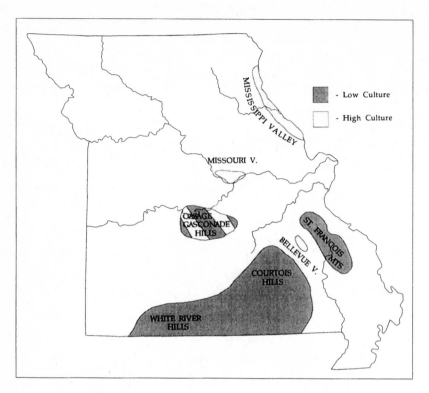

Figure 9.6 Areas of Scotch-Irish influence in Missouri, 1860.

(Adapted from Russel L. Gerlach, *Settlement Patterns in Missouri* [Columbia, 1980]. Wall map.)

numbers of Germans, is further evidence that the Irish in these counties were Protestant. In 1850, the only county with a Catholic church was Gasconade,[19] and it was in the German-settled northern third of the county.[20] By 1890, Catholics were well established in Christian and Miller Counties, in addition to Gasconade;[21] all three counties contained significant German Catholic settlements.[22] By 1980, Catholics composed less than 5 percent of the population in nine of the twelve counties.[23] The exceptions were Gasconade and Miller, representing German settlements, and Taney, a county with a substantial retired population of both mixed and recent origin.

By 1860, several areas in Missouri possessed a strong Scotch-Irish influence (Figure 9.6). High-culture Scotch-Irish, mostly slaveholders, were important early settlers in the middle Missouri Valley and along the Mississippi north of St. Louis, where they formed part of Missouri's emerging plantocracy and, as such, enjoyed an elevated social status denied to later arrivals. High-culture Scotch-Irish were also an important element in the pioneer population of the Osage-Gasconade hills (Miller County) and the Bellevue Valley of Washington and Iron Counties. Robert Flanders described the high-culture Scotch-Irish of the Bellevue Valley and the community of Caledonia in Washington County:

> The Bellevue was the site of the earliest interior agricultural settlement of Americans in Spanish Upper Louisiana. The settlers were "high" Scotch-Irish from the westernmost Carolina Piedmont, the Valley of Virginia, and the more elevated valleys of the upper Tennessee watershed. A relatively cultivated class of clan-related persons, they were early inclined to progressive values: property ownership and accumulation, organized religion, education, village life, and other incipient middle class goals. These respectable yeoman-cum-bourgeois founded the first Presbyterian church and one of the first Methodist churches west of the Mississippi as well as the oldest Masonic lodge continuously organized in Missouri. . . . Caledonia was and has remained a high Scotch-Irish community. . . . Evidence of such continuity is an almost ethnic self-consciousness and celebration of the social and cultural attributes of community values as expressed in its constituent families and institutions.[24]

By the time of the Civil War, the influence of the Scotch-Irish in these areas was on the wane with the exception of the Bellevue Valley and, to a lesser extent, the Osage-Gasconade hills. The effects of the Civil War, especially the abolition of slavery, and continued immigration accelerated the Americanization of the Scotch-Irish in both the Missouri and the Mississippi Valleys.

Large areas of Missouri, in particular the rougher districts of the Ozarks, were settled by low-culture Scotch-Irish in the early to mid-nineteenth century. These settlers represented the underclass of Ulster, pushed early to the frontier in their quest for land. Carl Sauer described the low-culture Scotch-Irish as a "restless frontier type, leading a semi-nomadic life of hunting and farming and removing to newer lands whenever the older region became fairly well settled. In the main, these people formed the advance guard of civilization on the outer margin of the frontier."[25] Expounding their character, Sauer added, "Many of those who came were unable or unwilling to meet the competition of life in more progressive regions. The Ozark Center has held few prizes to stimulate the ambition of its people, most of whom have lived uneventful lives and therefore have made little local history. . . . The paucity of important events, the want of pride in local affairs, and the character of the people all are reflected in the scarcity of written accounts of the history of the region."[26] The areas in Missouri most greatly influenced by the low-culture Scotch-Irish were the St. Francois region, the Courtois hills, the White River hills, and portions of the Osage-Gasconade hills (Figure 9.6). Aside from the Scotch-Irish, few groups showed any interest in settling these areas, and it was in these areas that the cultural legacy of the Scotch-Irish found its fullest expression in Missouri.

That the Scotch-Irish were an important element in the settlement of the nineteenth-century Ozarks has been established. What is not clear is whether the Scotch-Irish who settled in the Ozarks brought with them elements of an ethnic culture. John Blake stated the problem this way: "What happened to the descendents of the Scotch-Irish emigrants of the pre-revolutionary era? Did they still cling to their separate ethnic and cultural identity? Or, were they assimilated into the emerging 'American Society'? Here we enter unknown territory. We simply do not know, because the necessary research has not been undertaken."[27] Restated, the question is this: Was the cultural landscape associated with the frontier and postfrontier Ozarks one where conditions of soil, topography, and access imposed a culture on the pioneers? Or did an ethnic culture, in this case that carried by Ulsterites, produce a landscape that reflected the experiences, traditions, and perceptions, consciously and unconsciously pursued by its members, who were imposing their will on the Ozark environment rather than simply reacting to a difficult set of conditions over which they had little control?

Under normal circumstances, geographers would lean toward the latter interpretation, the former representing a kind of determinism the profession rejected some time back. The problem in the Ozarks is that scholars have never associated the region with a specific and definable culture such as that of the Scotch-Irish. Instead they have focused on processes such as the moving frontier, the semi-arrested frontier, and the perpetuated frontier. Following such reasoning, the people in the Ozarks and their cultural landscapes were the products of these processes, and these processes resulted in a cultural leveling whereby the need to survive in a difficult and unfriendly environment somehow negated the influence of cultural heritage.

By the time of their arrival in the Ozarks, the Scotch-Irish lacked visible identity as an ethnic group. This did not mean, however, that they were not carriers of an ethnic culture. Nor did it mean that their ethnic culture was not a meaningful component in past Ozark landscapes. What was lacking were the overt behavioral manifestations attributable to the original ethnic group, and what remained was an ethnic culture characterized by "cultural traits that are transmitted across generations through family structures and socialization processes, and are often so deeply imbedded in the subconscious fiber of individuals that they are unaware of their existence."[28]

It is an understanding of the Scotch-Irish in the Ozarks as carriers of an ethnic culture, rather than members of an ethnic group, that forms the basis for the analysis of landscapes that follows. In defining the concept of the cultural landscape, Carl Sauer wrote, "Its forms are all the works of man that characterize the landscape. Under this definition we are not concerned in geography with the energy, customs or beliefs of man but with man's record upon the landscape. Forms of population are the phenomena of mass or density in general and of recurrent displacement, as seasonal migration. Housing includes the types of structures man builds and their grouping, either dispersed . . . or agglomerated. Forms of production are the types of land utilization for primary products, farms . . . and those negative areas which he has ignored. The cultural landscape is fashioned from a natural landscape by a culture group. Culture is the agent, the natural area is the medium, the cultural landscape the result."[29]

In addition to the Scotch-Irish, major cultural groups present in the nineteenth-century Ozarks included French, Germans, and old-stock Americans. Any comparisons of these groups, and the cultural landscapes associated with each, must take into account differences in the natural environment. In general, the Germans acquired control of the most productive and most accessible land in the Ozarks, whereas the Scotch-Irish ended up with the region's least productive and least accessible land. The comparison used here is that between the Scotch-Irish and the Germans in the Ozarks. For the most part, these two groups lived separate from one another (Figure 9.7): the Germans dominated the Missouri and Mississippi River borders while the Scotch-Irish dominated in the interior areas.

Excepting James Lemon,[30] the consensus among scholars seems to be that the Scotch-Irish have always been bad farmers. Prior to emigrating from Ulster, their record in agriculture was less than exemplary.[31] In co-

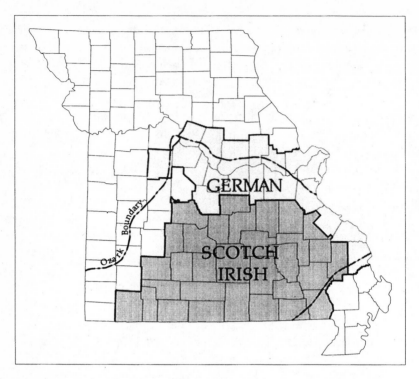

Figure 9.7 Scotch-Irish and German settled counties in the Ozarks, 1860.

lonial America, the story was much the same.[32] It is not that these char-
acterizations lack objective validity; rather the problem has been that
they assume the Ulster Scots were, in fact, farmers. For many, and perhaps a majority, farming was a part-time activity, with linen manufacturing occupying the majority of both time and interest. Arthur Young
said of farmers in the north of Ireland in the late eighteenth century,
"the agriculture of the country is so subservient to the manufacture [of
linen], that they no more deserve the name of farmers than the occupier
of a mere cabbage garden."[33] That large numbers of Ulster emigrants
were not farmers is confirmed by numerous accounts.[34]

These quasi-farmers from Ulster remained quasi-farmers in colonial
America. Those Ulsterites who pushed early to the frontier, and on to
the Ozarks, probably possessed fewer agricultural skills than those who
remained back East. Their style of farming could not pay the rents demanded for top quality land, whether in the Shenandoah Valley[35] or the
Ozarks. On the other hand, since by tradition the Scotch-Irish could

pursue several lines of advantage simultaneously, with farming being only one of them, they were well adapted to settlement on lower-quality land. It was their versatility that permitted them to settle where others would not enter,[36] and it was their experience with extracting a living from marginal lands in Ulster that permitted them some measure of success where others might have failed.

The Germans in the Ozarks were of a single mind in what they considered important in selecting land: they wanted soils capable of supporting the rather intensive crop agriculture that was so much a part of their culture. They sought land to fit their system, and one of their Ozark settlements once fired a land agent who had purchased unsuitable land. The land desired by Germans in the Ozarks was expensive, but they were both willing and able to pay the price. The areas in the Ozarks settled by Germans in the nineteenth century approximated a map of the region's better soils.[37]

The Scotch-Irish had a much broader view of land capability, and they were not locked into any single system of subsistence that restricted their choice of habitat. They made little attempt to compete with the Germans for the better land, and where the Scotch-Irish did manage to acquire better land, they often sold out to incoming Germans at a fair profit. For the Scotch-Irish, land unwanted by the Germans could offer several possibilities for exploitation, including hunting, crop farming, ranching, lumbering, and mining. Several of these activities might be pursued simultaneously, or perhaps consecutively. In the lumbering areas of the interior Ozarks, the Scotch-Irish made a reasonable living felling trees. When the timber was gone, many purchased cutover tracts and began farming. The agricultural economy was largely subsistence in type, and most suffered a reduced standard of living.[38] When agriculture became less profitable, many of the Scotch-Irish simply relocated. Changing from one pursuit to another, and relocating if necessary, were traditions of the Scotch-Irish; they had done both many times before.

The Scotch-Irish faced little competition with others for the land they settled. It was cheap, and this was important to these cash-poor peoples. In the more remote areas, settlers could squat on land for extended periods of time, thus gaining its free use. This practice was greatly restricted in the better areas, where competition for land was intense. Partly for this reason, squatting was a practice little known to Germans but widespread among the Scotch-Irish.[39] The cultural pre-adaptation to squat was suggested by Evans, who noted that "the right to claim land by possession and improvement was arrogantly assumed by colonists who had fought stubbornly for their tenant rights in Ulster."[40]

The German-settled areas were along both the Missouri and Mississippi Rivers and thus offered easy access to market. The Germans, from their beginnings in the Ozarks, were commercial farmers, and for them the market connection was a necessity, particularly for grain exports. The Scotch-Irish, on the other hand, had to adjust to less favorable market access. As pioneers of the interior they were quite capable of living at the subsistence level as they had done in Appalachia[41] and in Ulster.[42] In interior locations they could, and did, stress livestock raising, which was, after all, the mixed farming that they were most familiar with from Ulster.[43] According to the 1850 Census, most Scotch-Irish areas of the Ozarks, and particularly those areas farther west, averaged a per capita value of livestock that indicated a commercial rather than a subsistence economy (Figure 9.8). In the more remote interior and western areas, the ratio of cattle to swine increased,[44] indicating that the Scotch-Irish responded to their limited access to markets, which made it difficult to market pork and grain over substantial distances, by substituting cattle, which could be walked to markets in St. Louis, Memphis, and Little Rock.

The practice of converting grain, and particularly corn, to liquid form to reduce marketing costs in more isolated areas is legendary,[45] but nonetheless it suggests the adaptability of the Scotch-Irish. As isolation broke down, so did the subsistence economy, for the Scotch-Irish quickly turned to more commercial pursuits.

The very structure of Scotch-Irish versus German farms in the Ozarks differed in the nineteenth century. Statistically speaking, the average value of farmland per acre in the Scotch-Irish areas was two to three times as great as in the German areas (Figure 9.9). The ratio of improved land to unimproved land favored the Scotch-Irish areas over the German areas by a factor of between three and ten (Figure 9.10).[46] But these figures are misleading, for Scotch-Irish farms did not, in fact, have a greater value per acre than German farms, nor was the ratio of improved land to unimproved land in favor of the Scotch-Irish, if the total farm unit in both the German and Scotch-Irish areas is examined.

The German farms were "complete" farms in which all land that the farmer used, ranging from good cropland to lower-quality land, the farmer owned. Scotch-Irish farms, on the other hand, consisted of what the farmer owned, which usually included only a few acres of relatively

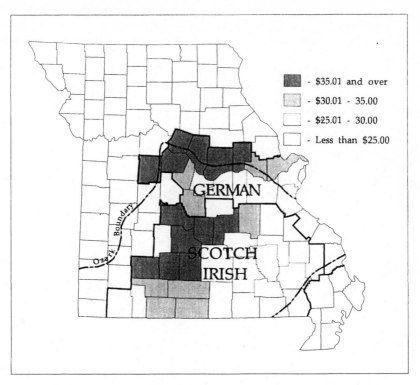

Figure 9.8 Per capita value of livestock in dollars by county, 1850.

(From the *Seventh Census of the United States: 1850*, 555, 676–77.)

good land, and unclaimed land in the public domain that was utilized as open range. The legal basis of open range in Missouri was summarized by Miller and Porter: "Missouri, contrary to states east of the Mississippi River, but in accord with the Great Plains and Western states takes the basic view that owners of animals need not fence them in; instead the landowner must fence them out if he does not want them on his land. This 'free range' law came from the Laws of the Louisiana Territory as adopted in 1808. Under this act, which is almost identical to our present Enclosure Act, all fields are required to be enclosed with a fence of certain specifications. . . . If the landowner does not have a lawful fence as provided in the statute, he cannot recover damages for other people's livestock running upon his land."[47] To alleviate problems associated with the use of open range, the Missouri legislature in 1883 passed a law that handed this issue to the individual counties to regulate. Almost imme-

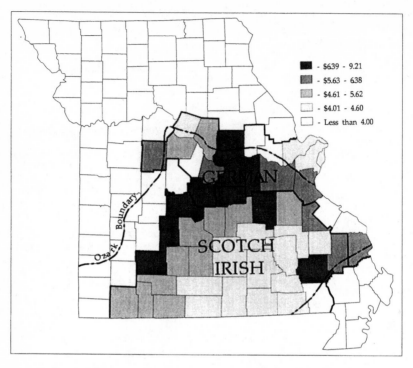

Figure 9.9 Value of farmland in dollars per acre by county, 1850.

(From the *Seventh Census of the United States: 1850*, 554, 675–76.)

diately, free range began to disappear in northern and western Missouri. By 1934–35, free range was permitted in only 25 of the state's 114 counties,[48] and all of those counties were in the Scotch-Irish settled areas of the interior Ozarks (Figure 9.11).

Evidence that the Scotch-Irish had utilized a similar system in Ulster is substantial,[49] and Mogey noted the occasional use of common pasture in Ulster as recently as the 1930s.[50] Whether, in fact, the Scotch-Irish made a sensible adjustment to conditions "where lands are extensive, labor scarce, and transportation facilities minimal"[51] or employed an open-range system drawn from their Ulster antecedents is of secondary importance. The point is that they and not the Germans were culturally preadapted to recognize the option of an open range under the correct conditions. And in the Ozarks, that is exactly what they did. To acquire title to land that they could use under existing free-range laws would hardly have made sense to the Scotch-Irish. The resistance of

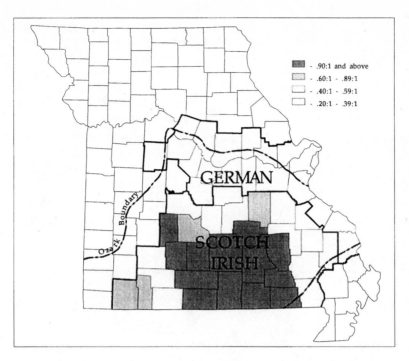

Figure 9.10 Ratio of improved land to unimproved land by county, 1850.
(From the *Seventh Census of the United States: 1850*, 554, 675–76.)

some Scotch-Irish well into the twentieth century to the abandonment
of open range could be viewed, as Evans suggested, as "arrogantly extended tenant rights" from their Ulster past.[52]

Germans in the Ozarks practiced agriculture utilizing a carefully
planned system, characteristic of German farmers, of rotating crops
in permanent fields. The Scotch-Irish, on the other hand, developed
a loosely structured "generalized stockman-farmer-hunter economy,"
characterized by "an extreme adaptability with regard to their commercial crop."[53] In some areas the Scotch-Irish employed a form of shifting
cultivation known as "patch agriculture."[54] Patch agriculture of a similar
type has antecedents in Ulster in association with the Irish outfield system.[55] Practices such as patch agriculture, which required a steady supply
of fresh woodlands, have been instrumental in creating the negative image so often associated with Scotch-Irish agriculture. Yet, as John Fraser
Hart suggested, "the people of Appalachia have been brainwashed by
the economic bigotry of the rest of the nation into feeling that they are

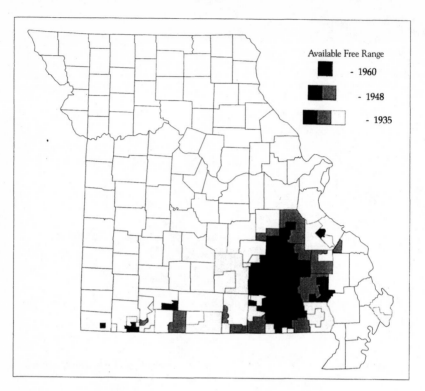

Figure 9.11 Progressive elimination of free livestock range in Missouri, 1935–60.

(From Brohn and Thomas, "Free Livestock Range in Missouri.")

supposed to be ashamed of a farming system based on land rotation because that system has failed to produce an economic surplus. No matter that land rotation is an effective technique for maintaining production and sustaining life in a niggardly environment."[56]

The Germans, from the early days of settlement in the Ozarks, invested heavily in farm improvements, including both land and structures. This is visibly apparent as one travels through Ozark German settlements. Stemming from a tradition of locational stability, substantial investment, much of it long-term, was quite logical. And in fact these Germans have shown tremendous locational stability in the Ozarks.[57]

The Scotch-Irish, with exceptions to be sure, are at the other end of the investment continuum. Improvements directly affecting the land have been minimal. Since the Scotch-Irish depended less on the quality of land for their subsistence than did the Germans, this is not surprising. But there are Ulster antecedents for this pattern as well. The tenant tradition they came from discouraged investment in land, for "fields pass from one hand to another every year."[58] Beyond that, the mobility of the Scotch-Irish—from Scotland, to Ulster, to America, and then within America—led to what Green termed a "frontier mentality"[59] that discouraged investment in permanent structures. In 1945 a Northern Ireland governmental inquiry observed that "most of the lands [in Ulster] were let to tenants in small lots with neither buildings nor fences on them, and the latter were created by tenants out of their own resources. The result in most cases was that the houses built were of a very poor type. . . . Insecurity of tenure was undoubtedly a factor contributing to this want of enterprise."[60] The mobility of the Scotch-Irish became a state of mind. They were less concerned with the future, including the building of dwellings, due to their uncertainty as to how long they would be in a given location. Williams said of Ulster farmers in the 1920s that "the only problem studied by the farmer is the present one."[61] This statement might apply also to the attitudes of the Ozark Scotch-Irish of the 1920s.

Today, Germans in the Ozarks have remained as close to their nineteenth-century agricultural origins as circumstances would allow. They have resisted change and seem reluctant to accept alterations in their rural economy as progress. This resistance, which fits the cultural tradition of rural Germans in America, is seen by many as a virtue. The Scotch-Irish, by contrast, seem so willing to alter their economy that change has become the norm. A chronology of their economies in the Ozarks begins with commercial hunting followed in rough order by crop farming, ranching, mining, lumbering, commercial gardening, and now employment in the service sector and in manufacturing. To those who find virtue in the unchanging rural economy of Ozark Germans, this pattern of continual change among the Ozark Scotch-Irish is seen as an inability to settle down, hence the characterization of the interior Ozarks as a semi-arrested frontier. Yet it is in the nature of the Scotch-Irish to adjust and adapt to meet changing conditions. In a region of limited material resources, such as the Ozarks, this ability to change may be what has permitted the Scotch-Irish to survive, and at times thrive, in an environment no one else wanted.

The case for an Ozark-Ulster connection is strong. The findings presented here suggest that their Ulster antecedents, as much as their frontier experience, produced the cultural patterns manifested by those Scotch-Irish who settled in the interior Ozarks. Further investigation by historians, geographers, sociologists, and anthropologists is needed to determine the depth of the Ulster influence on the Ozark cultural landscapes—past and present.

10 Land, Ethnicity, and Community at the Opequon Settlement, Virginia, 1730–1800

Warren R. Hofstra

> About three miles from Winchester, on the paved road to Staunton, on the western side of the road, near a little village, is a stone building surrounded by a few venerable oaks. That is Opecquon meeting house; and between it and the village is the grave-yard, in which lie the remains of some of the oldest settlers of the valley. . . . Come, let us sit down here, in the shadow of the church and schoolhouse, which always went hand in hand with the Scotch-Irish emigrants, and these old trees, the witnesses of the past and present, and let us gather up some of the memorials of the events and generations passing in a century of years.
>
> —William Henry Foote

In this passage, published in 1856 as a part of *Sketches of Virginia, Historical and Biographical*, the Reverend William Henry Foote began a historical account of his own congregation. Foote's church had been founded 120 years earlier, and the community of Scotch-Irish Presbyterians it served was spread out on surrounding farms. In many ways the church functioned as a center for this community, but Opequon was not a town or village or even a cluster of houses. It was simply a rural area about six miles long and four miles wide. Not indicated on today's maps, it was a place then, a community in the minds of its people.

Opequon had been settled during the 1730s in part by a group of recent immigrants from the north of Ireland. In contrast to conventional images of the Scotch-Irish as restless backwoods strivers, pursuing individual freedom and material self-betterment at the expense of stable and supportive communities, the men and women of Opequon established social patterns that fostered community cohesion for three generations and at least sixty years. They chose marriage partners within their own ethnic group, making it a kin group as well; they seldom conveyed land outside nuclear families and only rarely outside the kin group; and they worshiped together in a single Presbyterian congregation. Only in trade and financial dealings did they enter into relationships with the German, English, and Virginia-born settlers who also inhabited Opequon. Considering the continuum from conservative, peasant-like communalism to liberal, middle-class individualism that has informed recent historical debate on the attitudes and institutions of early Americans, the experience of the people of Opequon falls more within the former than the latter and suggests that family, kin, ethnicity, land, and congregation were factors of utmost importance in sustaining a cohesive community on the eighteenth-century frontier.[1]

The Opequon settlement took its name from Opequon Creek (Figures 10.1 and 10.2). A tributary of the Potomac, the Opequon flows north parallel to the Shenandoah River through a band of shale soils along the center of the lower Shenandoah Valley. Its springs, however, lie in limestone land on the valley's western flanks. The area around these springs is especially appealing, for there the soil is fertile, the land gently rolling, and water plentiful.

At this spot Samuel Glass made his home in the early 1730s. Glass had recently arrived in the English colonies from Banbridge, County Down, in Ulster. He was among the first Europeans to settle in the Shenandoah Valley, but he was not alone at Opequon. William Henry Foote provided a good account of his company:

> Samuel Glass took his residence at the head-spring of the Opecquon. . . . A son-in-law, [John] Becket, was seated between Mr. Glass and North Mountain; his son David took his residence a little below his father, on the Opecquon, at Cherry Mead . . . ; his son Robert was placed a little further down at Long Meadows, now in possession of his grand-son Robert. . . . Next down the creek was Joseph Colvin and family. . . . Then came John Wilson and the Marquis family, with whom he was connected. . . . Next were the M'Auleys, within sight of the church here; and then William Hoge had his residence on that little rising ground near by us to the west. He gave this parcel of land for a burying-ground, a site for a church and a schoolhouse. Adjoining these to the south were the Allen family. . . . A little beyond the village, on the other side of the paved road, lived

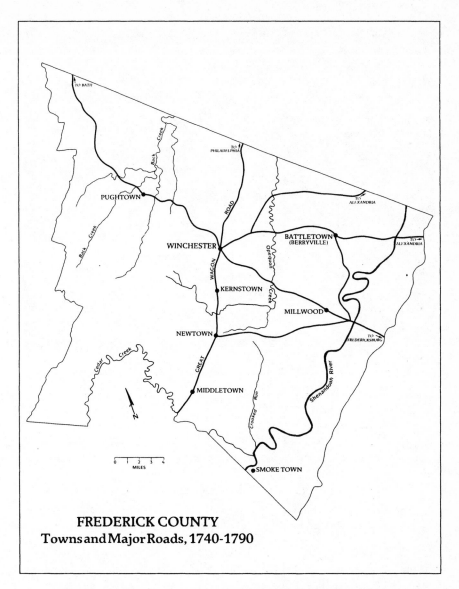

FREDERICK COUNTY
Towns and Major Roads, 1740-1790

Figure 10.1 The Opequon Community, roughly six miles long and four
miles wide, lay along Opequon Creek between Kernstown and Newtown.

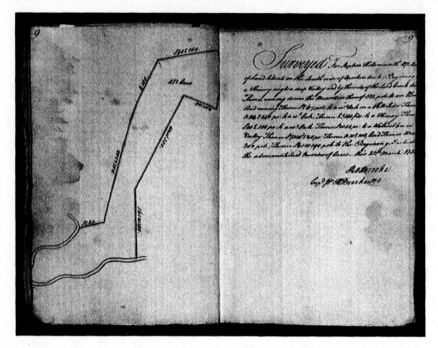

Figure 10.2 Robert Brooke surveyed 472 acres on the south side of
Opequon Creek for Stephen Hollensworth in March 1733.

(Robert Brooke Survey Book, courtesy of the Virginia Historical Society.)

Robert Wilson. . . . A little further down the stream lived James
Vance, son-in-law of Samuel Glass, and ancestor of a numerous race,
most of whom are to be found west of the Alleghenies. These were
all here as early as 1736, or '37. Other families gathered around
these, and on Cedar Creek, charmed with a country abounding
with prairie and pea vines, and buffaloe and deer.[2]

All of these men had recently arrived from Ulster.[3] Collectively they,
their families, and their descendants provide the focus of this chapter,
but other settlers played a role at Opequon as well. Nearly every Scotch-
Irish settler had a German neighbor. Samuel Glass, Jr., and John
Schnepf, Jr.; Joseph Colvill (Colvin) and Abraham Weissmann;
Thomas Wilson, John and Robert Wilson's brother, and Stephen
Hotsinpiller; Robert Allen and Peter Mauk; William Reid, Robert
Allen's brother-in-law, and John Bucher—all owned adjoining proper-
ties. The most significant fact about the settlement pattern these people

created was the absence of geographically defined ethnic neighborhoods. Germans and Scotch-Irish were spatially intermixed, as were the few native-born Virginians and recent arrivals from England.[4]

What brought this colony of mixed nationality to the isolation of the Virginia frontier? Most of the first settlers in the Shenandoah Valley had entered from the north, but the centers of population in Pennsylvania were several hundred miles distant. No roads traversed the Blue Ridge to connect the valley to closer Virginia towns. In fact, much of Virginia's Piedmont had not yet been settled.[5] Were the Scotch-Irish then fulfilling that traditional image of restless backwoods pioneers, fleeing civilization in preference for the primitive economy of the frontier, where one lived poorly but independently? Were they seeking the life of the hunter and herder over that of the settled farmer in a stable community?[6] No. Although isolated by distance and geographic barriers from the people who governed their colony, they in fact had taken up land on the frontiers of Virginia as part of a carefully developed program of western settlement.

All of the Scotch-Irish at Opequon acquired land in one of three ways: by patent from the colony of Virginia through the explicit powers which that government granted to men such as German immigrant Jost Hite to find settlers for the frontier; by deed from land Hite had patented for himself under his powers; or by grant from Thomas, sixth Lord Fairfax, proprietor of the Northern Neck.[7] In no case were Scotch-Irish at Opequon squatters.

Hite acted as a kind of land agent for the colony. William Gooch, lieutenant governor of Virginia, 1727–49, had two purposes in mind when he empowered Hite by virtue of orders of Council, October 21, 1731, to distribute up to 100,000 acres of valley land in the area surrounding Opequon (Figure 10.3). First, Gooch was acting on an imperative that had lain at the base of Virginia's land policy since the first years of the eighteenth century—that is, to establish a buffer zone of settlement against French interests and Native American inhabitants in the Ohio Valley. Hence Gooch wanted not speculation but settlement on small farms by families intent on actually working the land and developing the valley economy so as to provide a first line of defense for the Tidewater. Consequently he imposed on Hite the requirement to fix one settler on the land for every 1,000 acres stipulated in the order. Second, Gooch wanted settlement in the Shenandoah Valley, even though it was far from the economic centers of Virginia, because he needed to

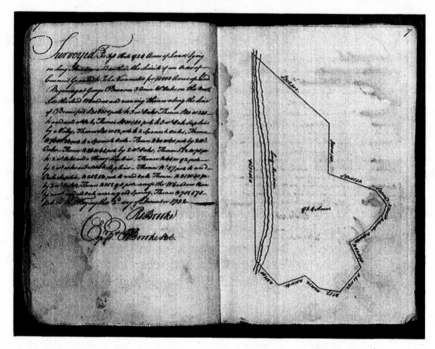

Figure 10.3 By virtue of orders of council issued October 21, 1731,
Lieutenant Governor William Gooch empowered German immigrant
Jost Hite to distribute up to 100,000 acres of valley land in the area
surrounding Opequon. On December 2 of the following year, Robert
Brooke surveyed 924 acres for Hite on Long Meadow Creek.

(Robert Brooke Survey Book, courtesy of the Virginia Historical Society.)

assert the claims of the colony to this valuable region against the coun-
terclaims of Lord Fairfax, who believed it lay within his Northern Neck
proprietary. Because Fairfax was pushing his cause before the Privy
Council in England, Gooch had to act quickly. Consequently he gave
Hite only two years to establish a settlement.[8]

Thus the Scotch-Irish were drawn to the Opequon, not through
wanderlust but through the active recruiting efforts of Jost Hite. Instead
of escaping settled forms of community life, they became an element in
a design for stable frontier communities. Ironically, Gooch lost his struggle with Fairfax in 1745, but by then the colony's settlement pattern
of small farms was already imprinted on the land. Fairfax realized that
Hite's settlers, as inhabitants of the land, not speculators, would actually

pay the quitrents that would make a handsome living for him. Accordingly he chose to continue the colony's land policy.

The Scotch-Irish came to Opequon for land, and they came to develop that land. The way they took up their tracts destroys another popular view of Scotch-Irish frontier settlers—that they gravitated to poor, often infertile hill land. They did so, according to this stereotype, partly as a result of meager means but also because of inclination. They sought out inferior uplands supposedly in reminiscence of the landscape of northern Ireland or in response to an "instinctive" preference for herding livestock over settled farming.[9] In contradiction of this image, Samuel Glass went directly to the springs of the Opequon, where fertile soil and ample water made his land some of the agriculturally richest in the Shenandoah Valley. Those who came with Glass forsook security and comfort in a fort or town to disperse throughout most of the Opequon's limestone watershed. Their behavior suggests that they reckoned the value of their land in terms of its commercial potential: its pasturage and crop yields.[10]

That these Scotch-Irish came to the Virginia frontier under a program of incentives for western settlement and took advantage of that program to acquire some of the best land in the Shenandoah Valley raises a question. In seeking opportunity, were these men and women, in James T. Lemon's terms, "liberal, middle-class" "individualists" who placed "individual freedom and material gain over that of public interest, . . . ready in spirit to conquer the limitless continent, to subdue the land"? Were they people who "planned for themselves much more than they did for their communities"? Did they think that "communities, like governments, were necessary evils to support individual fulfillment"? Was, then, the mutual support and assurance of community only a passing convenience or a necessary expedient for liberal-minded, ambitious people seeking, in truth, their own individual opportunity for financial gain or social advancement on the Virginia frontier?[11] Or—and these are James A. Henretta's words—was "the 'calculus of advantage' for these men and women . . . not mere pecuniary gain, but . . . a much wider range of social and cultural goals"? Did they seek to create a web of support and reciprocity along the Opequon in response to a "felt need to maintain a linguistic or religious identity"? Was this identity "as important a consideration as the fertility of the soil or the price of the land in determining where a family would settle"? Was family itself the "prism" through which they viewed the world?[12]

The answer—as a choice between the alternatives posed by Lemon and Henretta—is not a simple one. The weight of evidence, however, initially supports Henretta's position. Although the Scotch-Irish at Opequon dispersed in the search for good land, a community appeared as a consequence of their "felt need" to maintain ingrained patterns of personal identity and mutual support. The inner workings of the Opequon community were dependent on a complex of interrelated factors: family, kin, ethnicity, land, and congregation. These structures bound the community for the first two generations, but social continuity began to dissolve with the third generation, those who reached maturity during or after the American Revolution. This was a generation presented with economic opportunity on a scale unknown to their parents and grandparents. Confronted with the lure of western lands and a rapidly commercializing local economy, many of this third generation broke out of the physical boundaries of the Opequon community. Strands of community persisted, nonetheless, both for those who left and for those who stayed behind, but only through the development of new forms of social continuity and mutuality in an admittedly more individualistic world.

The people of Opequon in the 1730s were newcomers to Virginia, and they faced a wilderness just as untamed and isolated in the eighteenth century as immigrants to Virginia's Tidewater had confronted in the seventeenth. The Scotch-Irish, however, experienced little of the demographic dislocation that had critically inhibited their predecessors' capacity to form the stable communities so essential to survival.

The problems of Virginia's early Tidewater immigrants can in part be attributed to the demands that a commercial tobacco economy placed on their social organization and on their ability to achieve stability in terms of family and kin. The attraction of high profits in tobacco encouraged immigration by single males and the evolution of various forms of bound labor, namely indentured service and slavery. More men than women in the population meant that a relatively small percentage of people could form families, and for those who did, late marriage, enforced in part by a proscription on marriage by servants, limited the duration of family life in the crucial childbearing years. High rates of mortality attributable largely to a Chesapeake disease environment deadly for Europeans but also to an exploitive social environment further restricted the cohesion of family life and reduced the family's capacity to generate kinship networks. The experience of parental death was commonplace for children coming of age in early Virginia. In Middlesex

County, for example, 67 percent of all children had lost one parent by their eighteenth birthday, and 30 percent were parentless by that age. Combined with the tobacco economy's demand for new sources of labor, high mortality produced a population that grew more by the addition of immigrants than by natural increase and that matured in mixed households of kin, friends, and often strangers. These population dynamics placed serious limitations on continuity in the transmission of property, status, knowledge, and tradition. Thus, weak family institutions, attenuated kin networks, and social discontinuities all inhibited the development of stable community life.[13]

The settlers at Opequon arrived in the 1730s under different social and economic circumstances. Most notably absent in their motives for locating in Virginia was the imperative to grow tobacco—or at least none of the first generation of Opequon settlers left any indication in their estate inventories of tobacco production.[14] Unfamiliarity with tobacco culture and isolation from established tobacco markets discouraged the cultivation of that crop. Some of the first settlers in the valley commented that they found themselves "so far distant from any Settlement . . . that they could scarcely procure any one thing necessary nearer than from Pennsylvania or Fredericksburg." The Great Wagon Road passing through the Shenandoah Valley toward Philadelphia was at first nothing more than an Indian path, and not until the 1750s did roads and ferries link the valley to ports in eastern Virginia.[15] Thus large-scale commercial agriculture did not disrupt society and retard the formation of communities along the Opequon by unbalancing sex ratios or encouraging heavy immigration by laboring classes not free to form families.[16]

Most of the first-generation Scotch-Irish settlers at Opequon arrived in families. In fact, by the time the male members of this generation first appeared in public records, all were married, and ten of these eleven couples had children.[17] Among the second generation, 77 percent of the men married, as did 100 percent of the women. Apparently this generation confronted few demographic barriers to establishing families.

No accurate way exists to measure mortality at Opequon, but parental death was a fact of life. On February 26, 1750, James Vance, for example, made out his will because he was to have "one of my members . . . cut off in a short time." Vance, still a young man less than forty, did not survive the ordeal. He left behind a widow, Elizabeth, and four children: Samuel, William, Mary, and Sarah, aged eight to seventeen. Elizabeth Vance, pregnant at the time with a fifth child, was left with the care and upbringing of this family—a task she managed for the next two decades without remarrying.[18]

Despite the misfortune of the Vance family, parental death was not so widespread as to disrupt social organization. Other families at Opequon were presided over by parents who lived to old age and saw their children mature to establish families of their own. William Hoge, for instance, died in his eighty-eighth year in 1748. His wife, Barbara Hume, whom he met on the voyage to America in 1682, had died only three years earlier. In his will Hoge mentioned eight children. His oldest was already sixty-three and his youngest more than thirty. There were, moreover, twenty-nine grandchildren.[19]

Population at Opequon grew by both immigration and natural increase. The Shenandoah Valley was a rapidly expanding frontier in the middle of the eighteenth century. From only scattered Native American groups in the early 1730s, the population of Frederick, the county where Opequon was located, mushroomed to 4,300 by 1745 and to more than 11,000 by 1763. According to the 1790 federal census, 19,681 people lived in Frederick County, then considerably reduced in geographic size by division to form several new counties.[20] Although the arrival of newcomers was an ever-present source of social flux for the people of Opequon, the population there was also growing by natural increase. The ten families of the first generation with children produced a total of fifty offspring. Able to see their community grow through the addition of their own children, the men and women of early Opequon clearly could transmit both their property and the norms of their society to subsequent generations through the institution of the family.

Not only did family provide the means of population growth and of continuity in the social order, but it also established the basis of broader kinship networks. The Opequon community was for the Scotch-Irish, in fact, a large kin group. Of the eleven families of the first generation, the surnames of both husbands and wives can be determined in eight cases. In six of these eight marriages, men had found wives within other families at Opequon. Through marriage or consanguinity, moreover, every one of the first twenty-two men and women had kin within their own generation. The second generation extended and broadened this network. In nineteen of the twenty-five second-generation marriages for which the last names of the two partners can be determined, both husbands and wives were members of families already at Opequon.[21] Furthermore, eight of nine first-generation families with children who survived to a marriageable age had at least one child marry within the Opequon community, and 75 percent had two or more.[22]

Kinship provided a vital means of support for the people of Opequon, especially in cases of parental death. When James Vance died, he was well entrenched in the Opequon kin group. He had at least six brothers whose marriages allied him to three other Opequon families, including that of William Hoge. His wife, Elizabeth, was a daughter of Samuel Glass, the patriarch of the community. Vance could be assured that his widow and five minor children would be well provided for. As executors of his estate he was able to name his brother William and his wife's brother Robert, an individual he himself affectionately referred to as "brother." Another kinsman, David Vance, became guardian of his children. Symbolic of the continuity kinship brought to disrupted families, James Vance's unborn child was subsequently named James David after both father and guardian.

Kinship also eased the trials Elizabeth Vance faced following her husband's death. Not only did she have three brothers and one sister to turn to, but she was also allied through them to virtually every family at Opequon. To ensure a decent standard of living for his wife, James Vance had directed in his will that their children provide for her as they came of age. Every one of these five children proceeded to marry and remain in the community. With support from kin and children, Elizabeth Vance maintained the cohesiveness of her family. When she died in the early 1780s, she was able to leave property in some form to each of her children. She could also place the management of her estate in the hands of two sons, Samuel and William, and her son-in-law John Gilkeson.[23]

Numbering approximately one hundred individuals by the third quarter of the eighteenth century, the Opequon kin group was bound almost exclusively by ethnic lines. Only one member of the second generation crossed these lines in marriage: Barbara Wilson, the daughter of Robert Wilson, Sr., married Peter Stephens, the grandson of a German compatriot of Jost Hite. This match, however, did not appear to violate community values. To bless their union, Robert Wilson gave his daughter and son-in-law 254 acres of his land in a deed of gift. Perhaps in reciprocation, Barbara and Peter Stephens named their children after her mother and father, who then proceeded to leave these children legacies of £25. Nonetheless, the Stephenses' marriage ended in separation—an act suggestive of the enduring power of ethnic identity.[24]

The experience of Barbara Wilson and Peter Stephens—and even more so of James and Elizabeth Vance—indicated how land bound family and kin in the community. On November 26, 1742, James Vance purchased from Jost Hite 108 acres bordering the Opequon and adjoining the lands of three other members of the Opequon community, including David Vance. In January 1752 Lord Fairfax issued a grant to James Vance for an additional 108 acres on the opposite side of the creek. Vance was dead by this time, but his will indicated that he had previously occupied the tract. He may also have already established a third claim, because in August 1752 Elizabeth Vance received a grant from Fairfax for 338 acres. This grant represented one of the few but significant cases in which women owned land at Opequon. Elizabeth Vance's ability to gain and maintain control of real estate was indicative of the same stability that kin networks brought to the Opequon settlement. It was certainly significant of the way land was interwoven with family and kin as patrimony.[25]

In his will James Vance divided his land between his two sons, Samuel and William, allowing each to choose the tract he preferred. In actuality Samuel ended up with both tracts, and William received his mother's 338 acres in her will. Although James David Vance did not inherit land from his parents, he did purchase land in the Opequon community from his wife's cousin. By their marriages James and Elizabeth Vance's daughters, Sarah and Mary, joined landed families at Opequon. All of James and Elizabeth Vance's offspring subsequently passed their land on to their own children. Thus family, kin, and land wove a web associating three generations of Vances together within the community.[26]

The pattern of family and landholding followed by James and Elizabeth Vance and their descendants reflected a larger pattern that brought stability and continuity to the whole Opequon community for most of the eighteenth century. Nineteen individuals of the first and second generations of settlers initially acquired land in the Opequon area in twenty-five separate tracts, totaling 8,193 acres (Table 10.1). Eighteen of the initial nineteen landowners transferred a total of 7,796.5 acres, or more than 95 percent of the original land, to their own contemporaries or to the next generation. Most of this property passed from fathers to sons or sons-in-law. Thirteen of the initial nineteen devised 6,326.5 acres, or 77 percent of the total, in this way. Another 18 percent of the land was conveyed to brothers or other Scotch-Irish in the community. Surely the commitment of these original landowners to the

Table 10.1 Land Conveyances of the Initial Group of
Opequon Landowners

	Tracts	Landowners	Total Acres	Percent of Total Acres
Land Conveyed to Son or Son-in-law	18	13	6,326.5	77.2
Land Conveyed to Brother	3	3	767.0	9.4
Land Conveyed to Other Members of Opequon Community	3	3	703.0	8.6
Land Conveyed to Individuals outside Opequon Community	1	1	396.5	4.8
Total	25	———[a]	8,193.0	100.0

Source: Frederick County Deed Books.

[a]These twenty-five tracts were held by nineteen individuals. Because some individuals (Thomas Marquis and John Wilson, William and Mary Reid) held land jointly and some individuals (Thomas Wilson, Robert Wilson) with multiple holdings had tracts in more than one of the categories, the total in the landowner column does not represent the total number of individual landowners. This same situation produces discrepancies in the landowner column throughout these tables. For these reasons the distribution of acreage and not tracts or landowners better describes the pattern of land conveyance.

community was neither transitory nor solely self-interested. Land was not a speculative commodity for them but the basis of continuity in both family and society.

As with the institution of marriage, ethnicity determined patterns of land conveyance. In only one instance did a member of the initial group of Scotch-Irish landowners at Opequon convey land in any form to the Germans there, and this case was that of Robert Wilson's deed of gift to his German son-in-law, Peter Stephens. The manner by which fathers transferred landed property to their children further emphasized the integration of land and family. Most fathers elected to convey their land to their children only by will at their own death, thereby prolonging the next generation's economic dependence.[27] Of the land conveyed to sons

Table 10.2 Nature of Conveyance for Land Passed by the
Initial Group of Landowners to Sons or Sons-in-law

	Tracts	Landowners	Total Acres	Percent of Total Acres
Deed of Gift	3	2	902.5	14.3
Sale	1	1	355.0	5.6
Will	9	7	2,157.0	34.1
Will and Sale or Deed of Gift[a]	4	4	2,356.0	37.2
Land Unaccounted For			556.0	8.8
Total			6,326.5	100.0
Total Deed of Gift			1,245.0	19.7
Total Sale			1,410.0	22.3
Total Will			3,115.5	49.2
Land Unaccounted For			556.0	8.8
Total			6,326.5	100.0

SOURCE: Frederick County Deed Books and Will Books.

[a]Some fathers divided their land and gave or sold a portion prior to their death to one son, leaving the remainder to other children by will.

or sons-in-law, 7 percent more passed in this way than by sale or deed of gift prior to death (Table 10.2).

Family, kin, ethnicity, and land, therefore, formed the premise of mutuality for the Scotch-Irish at Opequon. A shared involvement in a single religious body provided a spiritual focus for this community. In one of their first collective acts, the Scotch-Irish at Opequon established a Presbyterian congregation and erected a church. William Hoge played a key role in this development.[28] His own grandson described him as "eminently pious" and attributed him with being "chiefly instrumental in the formation of a religious society which was organized in his neighborhood not long after his settlement in Virginia. His house was the place of resort for those enterprising and laborious clergymen who at an early period visited the frontier parts of that Colony. The church commonly called Opequon, one of the earliest Presbyterian establishments in Virginia, was erected on a portion of his estate which he appropriated for that purpose and for a burying ground."[29] On February 19, 1745, sixteen men of the congregation, nearly all of whom were landowners in the community, signed a deed as trustees accepting two acres from Hoge for the cemetery.[30] Most of the individuals and families described by William Henry Foote in his account of the Opequon settlement were represented in this body.

As early as 1735 Opequon settlers invited the Reverend Samuel Gelston, a member of the Donegal Presbytery in Pennsylvania, to preach at Opequon. Although the following year the presbytery officially appointed him to the charge, the congregation was served by itinerant ministers from Pennsylvania for the next twenty years. In 1755 John Hoge, grandson of William Hoge, became the church's first regular minister. Members of Opequon families then served as pastors to the church well into the nineteenth century. During the religious revivals of the Great Awakening the congregation affiliated with the evangelical New Side Presbyterians. Perhaps the best comment on the strength of both congregation and community was made by an early itinerant minister who on departing in the 1740s reported that he left behind a "numerous, wealthy congregation able to support the Gospel and of credit and reputation in the church."[31]

Family, kin, ethnicity, land, and congregation—the influences described thus far that bound the Scotch-Irish settlers at Opequon into a community—operated through institutions created by members of the community itself. Other bonding influences were also at work. The economic isolation of the Virginia frontier forced the members of the community to rely more on one another for economic support than on market relations outside the settlement. The pattern of small-farm, general agriculture pursued by the Scotch-Irish at Opequon, by diversifying economic activity, tended further to generate networks of local trading relationships that supplemented and reinforced the relationships nurtured by social ties.

The small farm on the Virginia frontier in the middle of the eighteenth century replicated the pattern of agriculture already operative in the more mature economies of rural Pennsylvania. There, on tracts of land averaging 100–200 acres, farmers generally worked about 60 acres in grains and livestock. Fields for wheat, rye, oats, barley, buckwheat, and corn usually took up about half the acreage, while the remainder was devoted to pasture and meadow for cattle, horses, sheep, and swine. Hemp and flax were also grown for manufacture into cordage and textiles. Most small farmers had orchards and gardens. The single most important element of the pattern of small farming as it evolved in Pennsylvania was the diversity of economic activity. Farmers rarely specialized in a single crop, although rising flour prices during the last half of the eighteenth century encouraged surplus production in wheat. Production for family consumption predominated. Local trade enabled each family to make up what it lacked from the minor surpluses of neighbors. Few families were self-sufficient, but local trade made communities largely self-sustaining and their members economically interdependent.[32]

Evidence from estate inventories suggests that the Scotch-Irish brought this pattern of economic life to Opequon. These documents sketch a community of small farmers who engaged in the production of grain and livestock for local and personal consumption and who supplemented agriculture with a variety of domestic enterprises. Inventories spanning the years 1749–97 exist for fifteen of the nineteen individuals who originally took up land along the Opequon. James Vance's estate, inventoried late in 1751, helps illuminate the inhabitants' activities.

Livestock constituted the largest single group of items in Vance's inventory and represented 32 percent of his appraised wealth. Another 13 percent of his net worth was taken up in fields or stores of various grains, including barley, oats, wheat, rye, hay, and "Ingin Corn." Also appearing among his stock of agricultural goods were supplies of flax and hemp. The scale of agricultural activities represented apparently did not generate a large demand for labor, because Vance was appraised for only one male servant. Furthermore, Vance's inventory presents no evidence that he specialized in producing livestock or any particular crop for market. In fact, appraisals for all of his grains and for the flax and hemp were recorded not separately but in groups. No single crop received special attention. Even his servant was enumerated in the same entry as wool cards and books.[33]

Like so many families at Opequon, James Vance mixed domestic industry with agricultural activity. He owned a variety of items related to textile production, including a great wheel, spools, wool cards, pounding tubs, and both woolen yarn and cloth. Listed among his livestock were twelve sheep. Similar entries appeared in thirteen of the fifteen inventories of other original landowners at Opequon. That Vance traded both agricultural commodities and the products of his family's spinning activities with his neighbors can be inferred from the £12 16s. 3d. in book debts on account due his estate. Also due were £8 8s. 1d. in various notes. Against the estate were debts totaling £11 6s. 6d.[34]

Bonds, notes, and book debts were commonplace in Opequon estates. Although no way exists of discerning if these debts were incurred through agricultural, artisan, or merchant activity, the fact that a large number of Opequon settlers were engaged in commercial or financial exchange with each other is certain. For instance, when William Hoge died, he owed money to Robert White, Joseph Colvill, and his own son William, Jr. White and Colvill were also listed as trustees for the land William Hoge deeded to the Opequon church. At the same time that Hoge owed money to Colvill, he held a bond payable to him by Colvill.[35]

Most interesting in Hoge's accounts were debts he owed to John Hite and Stephen Hotsinpiller, two German settlers at Opequon. Even though the Scotch-Irish and the Germans maintained strict separation in the institutions of family, marriage, land, and religion, local trade was common, providing the single greatest vehicle for exchange between these ethnic groups. Stephen Hotsinpiller, for example, arrived from Germany in 1728, married the daughter of a German family in Germanna, Virginia, and settled as a blacksmith at Opequon, where in 1736 he purchased 450 acres from Jost Hite. When he died in 1776, his accounts indicated extensive financial dealings with a large number of individuals. Most were German but many, including Robert Allen, Jr., John Allen, and Robert White, were Scotch-Irish.[36]

Robert and John Allen were sons of Robert Allen, Sr., a member of the first generation of settlers at Opequon and an initial landowner there. He was Hotsinpiller's neighbor and died several years before him. Allen's 1771 inventory indicates that he not only grew wheat and rye but also raised sheep, produced woolen yarn, and distilled liquor in quantities sizeable enough to suggest that this endeavor was commercial. Fifty-one individuals were indebted to him by bond, note, and book account. Aside from his own son, Stephen Hotsinpiller was his largest debtor. Like Hotsinpiller, most of Allen's financial dealings were with members of his own ethnic group, but in addition to Hotsinpiller he also lent money or had accounts with a number of other Germans.[37] Thus the economy of small farms set in commercial isolation on the frontier tended not only to reinforce the bonds of community by generating networks of economic interdependence but also to expand the bounds of community across ethnic lines.

Other factors in addition to its economic setting may have tended to strengthen community cohesion at Opequon. In 1757 Joseph Colvill wrote his will. After providing for sons Joseph and Andrew, he directed that his third son, Samuel, inherit a cash legacy of £40 paid by his brothers. Colvill, however, added the stipulation that Samuel receive only £30 until the "trouble of the times is over."[38] The "trouble" was a result of the devastating and terrifying raids on the Virginia frontier during the French and Indian War. These incursions had touched the area surrounding Opequon and sent numerous outlying settlers fleeing to nearby garrisons. Just as many fathers had chosen to prolong the tutelage of their sons in the community by conferring land on them only by will, so Joseph Colvill delayed his son's legacy until stability returned to Opequon. Thus the French and Indian War may have compelled the men and women at Opequon to rely even more closely on one another for their security. Similarly, the Proclamation of 1763 may have extended the influence of this war by inhibiting western movement and delaying the disruption to the community caused by the departure of younger generations in search of new lands.

After the American Revolution the web of stabilizing forces at Opequon began to break down. The social experience of the Revolution itself may have unsettled the community, but the opening of land in Kentucky, Tennessee, and Ohio after the war certainly began to unravel it. Describing Kentucky as "the finest and most fertile part of America," Lord Fairfax's secretary observed that "the emigration of inhabitants to Kentucky is astonishing." The Shenandoah Valley became a major transportation corridor, and migrants created unprecedented sources of commercial growth. The nearby town of Winchester grew into a staging point for western travelers, and in the eyes of an Italian visitor, Count Luigi Castiglioni, "Winchester for commerce [was] one of the most important towns of Virginia."[39] Winchester merchants developed not only the migrant trade but also the backcountry trade with western peddlers and shopkeepers. The town's importance as a regional market increased further as local farmers produced more and more commercial wheat.

The social flux and economic growth engendered by migration and commercialization had telling effects on the Opequon community—effects demonstrated most clearly by the mobility of the third generation. As William Henry Foote observed, "the reports from the west painted Kentucky as more beautiful in its solitariness, than Opecquon had been to the eyes of the emigrants from Ireland. And the grand-children, like their ancestors, sought a new home among the prairies, beyond the Alleghenies."[40]

The descendants of Samuel Glass provide a good example of these new patterns. His sons, Joseph, Robert, and David, had all established farmsteads near their father's at the head of Opequon Creek. Joseph and David purchased land from their father's original 900 acres, and Robert received a grant from Lord Fairfax. Each had married women from families within the Opequon kin group. David Glass was a trustee of the Opequon church. Thus these men lived out the pattern of community defined by family, kin, ethnicity, land, and congregation. Not so their children. Only seven of the thirty members of the third generation of Glasses married within the group of original Opequon families. Eighteen left for Kentucky. Faced with the departure of their progeny, Joseph, Robert, and David Glass could hardly regard their land as patrimony. With the exception of 200 acres Robert Glass willed to his son Samuel, each father directed that his executors sell his land and divide the proceeds among his children. No longer was land a stable link between generations within a kin group. Instead it became only another form of family wealth convertible into the more fluid means of money needed by a mobile generation to underwrite the costs of migrating and establishing distant households.[41]

The declining capacity of land to act as a vehicle of continuity and stability for the Scotch-Irish at Opequon was also visible in the actions of the group that received the land from its original owners. Whereas the first owners kept 95 percent of their land within the community, those to whom they passed land did so with less than 40 percent of theirs (Tables 10.1 and 10.3). Furthermore, only 32 percent of this property stayed within lineal or collateral families. A smaller proportion of this second group of landowners delayed their sons' economic maturity by devising land in their wills, and some men directed that their tracts be sold to provide cash legacies (Tables 10.2 and 10.4).

Although the pressures of migration and commercialization loosened the social fabric at Opequon, the community by no means disintegrated. Family, kin, ethnicity, land, and congregation still provided for a measure of cohesion for those who stayed behind. The family of James

Table 10.3 Land Conveyances of the Second Group of Opequon Landowners (in acres)

	Actions of Initial Group of Landowners				
	Land Conveyed to Son or Son-in-law	Land Conveyed to Brother	Land Conveyed to Other Members of Opequon Community	Total	Percent of Total Acres
Land Conveyed within Family (to Son, Son-in-law, Brother, Brother-in-law)	2,030	167	316	2,513	32.2
Land Conveyed to Other Members of Opequon Community	350	200	0	550	7.1
Land Conveyed to Individuals outside Opequon Community	2,775.5	400	387	3,562.5	45.7
Land Unaccounted For	1,171	0	0	1,171	15.0
Total	6,326.5	767	703	7,796.5	100.0

SOURCE: Frederick County Deed Books.

NOTE: Only acreage is indicated here because the subdivisions of the land by the second group make reckoning land by tract and landowner complex and confusing.

Vance provides an obvious counterpoint to the experience of the Glasses. All the Vance children married within the Opequon community, and all acquired land there. Each in turn left land to his or her children.

Religion also provided a thread of continuity. When the Opequon congregation built a new church in the 1790s (Figure 10.4), John Gilkeson, James Vance's son-in-law, and William Marquis, a son of original Opequon landowner Thomas Marquis, served as trustees. James David Vance volunteered to collect subscriptions.[42] Furthermore, the spirit of

Table 10.4 Nature of Conveyance for Land Passed by the
Second Group of Landowners to Sons, Sons-in-law, Brothers,
or Brothers-in-law

	Tracts	Landowners	Acres	Percent of Total Acres
Deed of Gift	0	0	0	0.0
Sale	2	2	285	14.0
Will	3	3	794	39.1
Will and Sale or Deed of Gift	0	0	0	0.0
Land Sold by Executors for Legacies	1	1	250	12.3
Land Left to Children in Shares	2	1	216	10.6
Land Unaccounted For	1	1	485	23.9
Total	9	8	2,030	99.9

SOURCE: Frederick County Deed Books and Will Books.

the congregation was no less vital in the 1790s than when itinerant ministers had served the church some fifty years earlier. In addition to their new building, the congregation had a new minister—Nash Legrand, by all accounts a dynamic, evangelical, and effective preacher. According to Foote, Legrand's "ministry was eminently successful. . . . A continued revival filled the church with devoted worshippers."[43]

For those departing for Kentucky, moreover, the power of family, kin, ethnicity, land, and congregation persisted as key elements in a collective experience. As one minister at Opequon recalled, "In 1809 occurred the Exodus from this section to the West headed by the Glasses, David and Robert, and comprising Vances and Allens, Simralls and Newalls, Marquises and Wilsons."[44] While pursuing new opportunity in the West, later generations still set forth from Opequon in an ethnic kin group similar to the one their ancestors had earlier established.

Certainly those who left were "ready in spirit to conquer the limitless continent, to subdue the land." But were they planning "for themselves much more than . . . for their communities"? The record at Opequon

Figure 10.4 Congregation provided one of the bonds of community for the
settlers at Opequon. The ruins of the Presbyterian church, built in the 1790s,
were captured in oils by landscape artist Eva LeConte (1834–1911).

(Courtesy of Opequon Presbyterian Church, Kernstown.)

suggests not. These were men and women who still viewed "the world
through the prism of family values." They were men and women for
whom family, kin, ethnicity, land, and congregation were yet powerful
forces binding them together in a community that was neither a necessary evil "to support individual fulfillment" nor a passing expedient in
conquering the frontier.[45] It was a community that connected them by
mutual support and collective identity, that linked them to place and
past through three or four generations of kin, and that launched them
together into a future of unprecedented opportunity for personal advancement in the open expanse of the American West.

11 The Scotch-Irish Element in Appalachian English: How Broad? How Deep?

Michael B. Montgomery

Within the past few years the idea of tracing different dialects of American English back to regions of the British Isles has aroused renewed interest, particularly with the broadcast of the immensely popular Public Broadcasting Service series "The Story of English" in 1986–87. An early episode of that program, "A Muse of Fire," featured a New Englander visiting an East Anglian pub, purportedly in search of the speech patterns of his Puritan ancestors. A later program, "The Guid Scots Tongue," began by examining the English of Scotland (sometimes called Scots), exemplified by a Scotsman reading from William Lorimer's 1983 version of the New Testament (a translation, host Robert MacNeil tells us, made entirely into Scottish English except for the statements made by the Devil, which are rendered in "London English").[1] In the course of an hour this show argued that the English of seventeenth-century Lowland Scotland, as portrayed from a Scottish pulpit, and eighteenth-century Ulster, as exemplified by farmers at a modern-day sheep auction in the County Antrim town of Ballymena, has evolved into the English of latter-day American descendants of hardy Scotch-Irish frontier folk—not only North Carolina's denizen mountaineers, like the renowned storyteller Ray Hicks, but even long-distance truck drivers using citizens band radio slang along Western interstate highways.

In one form or another the idea of tracing American dialects back to the old country or to earlier times has been around for over a century. For that long popular writers on Appalachia have pointed out similarities between the region's speech and Elizabethan English (e.g., *afeard* or *holp* as the past tense of *help*) and Chaucerian English (e.g., the pronoun *hit* for *it*).[2] This has led to the frequent claim that Appalachian speech is "Shakespearean," that it preserves the "Queen's English"; the latter label has recently been applied to the speech of North Carolina as a whole in a tourist booklet distributed by the Tarheel State's Department of Tourism.[3] A minority of students of Appalachian culture, Cratis Williams for one, have maintained that the region's speech preserves a lode of features with a different source, traceable to settlers not from Southern Britain but from the opposite end of the British Isles: Ulster and Scotland.[4] This case was taken up by "The Guid Scots Tongue," but not very convincingly. Ray Hicks sounds too unlike Ballymena farmers. However enticing it may be to establish a language connection between Appalachia and Ulster-Scotland, and however probable, given our knowledge of settlement history, the program's lack of direct evidence made such a connection seem far-fetched. (In this essay "Ulster" is used rather than "Northern Ireland" because the language patterns associated with Scottish settlers in Ireland spanned the nine-county historical province rather than the six-county modern political entity. Some of the strongest settlements of Ulster Scots were in County Donegal, now part of the Republic of Ireland.)

Writers have applied many labels to the culture of Appalachia, not only "Shakespearean," "Elizabethan," and "Scotch-Irish," but also "British," "English," "Anglo-Saxon," and even "*pure* Anglo-Saxon." In addition to being stimulated by the American yen for finding historical roots, those attempting to connect Appalachian culture to the British Isles have been motivated to provide a specific cultural identity for the people of Appalachia—one linked directly to Old World forebears, perhaps even to famous literary and historical figures—in order to counter a prevailing national perception of Appalachia as a deprived region having little culture and an unflattering, often violent history.

Validating Appalachian culture by identifying its sources was clearly one objective of many commentators who wrote about the region from within, such as John C. Campbell, Josiah Combs, and Cratis Williams.[5] All three men, the last two Appalachian natives, devoted much energy to untangling the early settlement patterns to determine the collective genealogy of the region's inhabitants and to assess the relative proportions of Scotch-Irish, English, and German population groups. Campbell and Combs examined patterns of surnames—Campbell of 1,200 old families from mountain areas of Kentucky, Tennessee, and North Carolina; and Combs of eastern Kentucky schoolchildren. Campbell found equal portions of English and Scotch-Irish, while Combs's smaller sample included predominantly English names. (Although surnames are used to calculate ancestry and place of origin more often than any other trait and represent one of the very few tools available, such assessments are never definitive and their limitations are often not recognized; in the present case one limitation is that many English-derived names have been used in Ireland and Scotland for centuries.) Combs and Campbell had another objective in calculating the national stocks in Appalachia—to temper extravagant, often unqualified statements of popular historians around the turn of the century that the early Scotch-Irish almost single-handedly settled and subdued the frontier, the best-known of such made by Theodore Roosevelt in *The Winning of the West* (1889–96).

Of course, cultural validation has also been the goal of many outsiders, like ballad collectors and folklorists, who have written about Appalachia. For decades hosts of researchers have visited the hills of southern Appalachia to record the natives and to try to capture the echoes of American immigrants in song, story, and voice and to document the survival of Scottish, Irish, and English musical traditions and verbal lore. An early researcher, perhaps the best known of them all, was the Englishman Cecil Sharp, who with his assistant Maud Karpeles found versions of Francis James Child's English and Scottish Popular Ballads in eastern Kentucky in 1916 and 1917, when ballad singing was supposed to be "a lost art."[6] Other researchers, in large numbers, have followed. But whatever specific agenda they may have had, it is well known that scholars in fields other than language, particularly folklorists like Henry Glassie, have made far greater progress in determining how cultural patterns and phenomena spread into Appalachia.[7] It is striking that, with the exception of three brief studies to be discussed below, researchers on Appalachian English have added little to our knowledge of how the region's speech relates to areas of Britain and Ireland and have generated little concrete research into the question.

Beyond Appalachia, the result has been the same. American linguistic scholars have from time to time been interested in the Old World roots of the country's speech, most notably in the early days of the well-known Linguistic Atlas of the United States and Canada Project in the 1930s and 1940s.[8] Prior to identifying these roots, the Atlas Project decided to undertake a nationwide effort to map American dialects into regions by interviewing older, less-traveled, and less-educated speakers. This survey began work in New England in 1931 but has never been completed, and the publication of its findings has been slowed for a variety of reasons. In recent decades Linguistic Atlas researchers have said little about making transatlantic linguistic connections, as it has become apparent that these are much more complicated and difficult to establish than was originally foreseen.[9]

Accounting for the Lack of Research

Thus, there is a general impression (and a fair number of myths) that Appalachian speech preserves relics from a former age and population, but there is a conspicuous lack of concrete information about this, despite the long-standing interest in comparing cultural and language patterns. How do we explain this situation? Is it the case that the research has not been done? Or is it that it cannot be done?

On the one hand, it might simply be that linguists have never sat down to investigate the Scotland-Ulster-Appalachia language connection in a systematic manner. As previously suggested, researchers have severely underestimated the complexities involved in exploring this question. Perhaps they have given up too quickly or have not employed a methodology that can guide them through the pitfalls of comparing speech patterns existing an ocean and several centuries apart. Perhaps they have not looked for evidence in the right places. On the other hand, perhaps the connections are no longer discernible, much less significant, between the language patterns of Ulster and Appalachia. Perhaps too much time has passed to compare Appalachian and Ulster-Scottish English directly using twentieth-century evidence.

Stubborn realities argue against a detectable connection. Speakers on opposite sides of the ocean sound dissimilar today, although this may largely reflect differences in intonation, the pitch and rhythm of the voice, which could mask similar grammar and vocabulary. The Ulster element in Colonial American English, brought by the influx of a quarter-million immigrants in the six decades before the Revolution, may well have faded with the early interaction of the Scotch-Irish with English, German, and other groups. If so, the leveling or disappearance of distinctive language patterns would have accompanied the purported loss of Scotch-Irish cultural identity quite early on (cf. James Leyburn's well-known statement that this had occurred by the time of the American Revolution.)[10] Also arguing for few surviving traces of Ulster and Scottish English in Appalachia is the fact that all varieties of a language, even isolated varieties, change constantly. These difficulties, among others, in comparing twentieth-century Appalachian English with what we will henceforth call Scotch-Irish English[11] are real but not insuperable. This chapter not only traces a range of Appalachian grammatical features to varieties of British and Irish English but also outlines the linguistic processes that account for their preservation in mountain speech. Identifying how features of Scotch-Irish English have evolved into Appalachian English provides a much richer view of the continuing dynamics of Appalachian culture and speech; it also provides important directions for comparing American English to British and Irish English more generally.

Five earlier studies have commented on, or made assessments of, the influence of Ulster and Scottish speech patterns on Appalachian English.[12] In 1931 Josiah Combs cited seven "words of more or less Scottish tincture," including *bonnie, cadgy, fernent, gin* (if), and *needcessity*, but claimed that mountain speech had far more Elizabethan elements. Most recently, historian David Hackett Fischer has argued for considerable similarities between "backcountry [which includes Appalachian] speech ways" and those of the "borders" of the British Isles (which includes northern England, as well as Scotland and Ulster). Three other studies—by Wylene Dial, Alan Crozier, and Michael Ellis, respectively—all of greater depth, require closer attention.

From among the many relics Dial discusses as preserved in West Virginia speech, Table 11.1 lists seventeen words and phrases she identifies as having Scottish counterparts. In making her connections, she relies on published sources like the *English Dialect Dictionary* for Scottish and English items and draws on personal observation for Appalachian items.[13] Since she does not list separately the items she considers Scottish in ancestry, not all of those listed in the table are clearly classified by her as Scottish. The intent of her essay is familiar: to assert, by citing many common Appalachian terms having bona fide Scottish and earlier English sources, that mountain speech has a rich, undervalued heritage.

Crozier's study deals only with items for which there is good evidence of their being brought by Scotch-Irish immigrants from Ulster. Table 11.2 lists the thirty-six items that he discusses. Unlike earlier, more anecdotal commentators such as Cratis Williams, Crozier explicitly identifies the references he uses, lays out his methodology, and uses more systematic methods than any previous scholars. Using four published dictionaries and glossaries on Ulster English and one on Scottish English, several comprehensive British and American dictionaries, and ref-

Table 11.1 Scottish Contributions to Appalachian English

Key: G = Grammar; P = Pronunciation; V = Vocabulary

V backset—n., setback (in health)

V blinked (milk)—adj., sour

V clever—adj., neighborly, accommodating

G done—v., have, as in "I *done* finished my lessons."

G don't care to—phrase, would like to

P fixin—n., she-fox (i.e., *vixen*)

G fornenst—prep., next to

V haet—n., the smallest thing that can be conceived

G hoove—v., heaved (past participle of *heave*)

G how soon—conj., that, as in "I hope *how soon* we get some rain"

V ill—adj., bad-tempered

P ingern—n., onion

V pooch—v., protrude

V redd up—phrase, set in order, clean up

G -s suffix on verbs with plural subjects, as in "Moonshiners needs to be treated right"

G several—adj., many

V skift—n., light covering, as of snow

17 Items (2 Pronunciation; 7 Grammar; 8 Vocabulary)

Source: Wylene Dial, "The Dialect of the Appalachian People," *West Virginia History* 30 (1969): 463–71.

erence works from various British and American dialect atlas projects, he searches for items similar in meaning and form in the speech of both Ulster and Pennsylvania, the colony that in the eighteenth century attracted most Scotch-Irish immigrants. Crozier's careful approach, governed by prudent caveats against leaping to the conclusion that a term found both there and in the United States must have originated in Ulster, is as follows: "To make a case for Scotch-Irish influence one must demonstrate that features common to Ulster and America are recorded in those areas of the United States where the Scotch-Irish are known

Table 11.2   Ulster Contributions to American English

Key: G = Grammar; P = Pronunciation; V = Vocabulary

G   agin, again—conj., by the time that

G   all the (one)—noun phrase, the only (one)

G   anymore—adv., nowadays (in positive sentences)

P   becaise—conj., (pronunciation of "because")

G, P   boilt—v., past tense of "boiled"

V   bonny-clabber—n., curdled sour milk

V   bottom(s)—n., low-lying land

V   bucket—n., pail

V   cabin—n., rude log house of the American frontier

V   cruddled milk—n., curdled sour milk

V   diamond—n., town square

V   dornick—n., roundish stone

G   driv, druv—v., past tense forms of "drive"

P   drooth—n., (pronunciation of "drouth, drought")

V   evening—n., (includes afternoon)

V   fireboard—n., mantelpiece

V   flannel cake—n., type of cornbread

V   granny—n., midwife

V   hap—n., quilt

V   hull—v., shell

V   muley—n., hornless cow

V   nicker—n., whinny

P   nothing—(pronounced with low central vowel, as *nah-thing*)

V   piece—n., short distance

V   poke—n., bag

V   singletree—n., pivoted crossbar to which traces are fastened to yoke a horse to a plow

V   slut—n., light made from a grease-soaked rag in a dish or bottle

Table 11.2 continued on next page

Table 11.2 (continued)

Key:	G = Grammar; P = Pronunciation; V = Vocabulary
V	sook—interj. (a call to livestock)
V	spouting—n., gutter
G	till—prep., to
G	want out—v., same as "want to get out"
V	wattle—n., stout stick with a lash used for driving oxen
G	you-all—second-person-plural pronoun
G	you'ns—second-person-plural pronoun
G	yous—second-person-plural pronoun

36 Items (4 Pronunciation, 10 Grammar, 23 Vocabulary [*boilt* considered both a pronunciation and a grammatical form])

SOURCE: Alan Crozier, "The Scotch-Irish Influence on American English," *American Speech* 59 (1984): 310–31.

to have settled in large numbers, and preferably only in those areas. Even then, the case may not be conclusive."[14] His findings, based on published sources, are considerably more informative and convincing than previous studies.

Crozier concludes that, with various degrees of certainty, four pronunciations, ten grammatical forms, and twenty-three vocabulary items used in Pennsylvania probably derive from Ulster. For example, he cautiously includes *agin* and *again* (conjunctions meaning by the time that); the present study, as seen in Table 11.3, classifies these as having a General British source. Some items—like *diamond* (a type of town square)—are found today only in Pennsylvania, whereas others have much wider currency—like the "positive" *anymore* (as in the affirmative sentence, "When I go to New York, I always stay in a hotel *anymore*"). His general conclusion suggests that further research would be fruitful: "It is clear therefore that a few characteristics—mainly lexical—of Ulster English survived the assimilation of the Scotch-Irish into the American people, and it is very possible that more traces of Ulster speech remain to be discovered in the dialects of the Midland region."[15] (The Midland region, according to cultural and linguistic geographers, is an area spreading westward and opening in a fanlike shape from the eastern Pennsyl-

vania–Delaware Valley cultural hearth from which it developed. It includes all of Appalachia, as well as the Lower Midwest and the Upper
South. Linguistically it is marked by a folk vocabulary setting it off from
the North and the South.)

In an extended critique of historian Fischer's work, Michael Ellis has
most recently compared aspects of Appalachian speech, particularly vocabulary, with that of five regions in the British Isles.[16] Ellis takes twenty
traditional terms collected in East Tennessee and seeks their distribution according to English and Scottish dictionaries and linguistic at-
lases. Only four of these—*galluses* (suspenders), *palings* (of a fence), *sook*
(a call to cattle), and *stake* (fence post)—are classified as Scotch-Irish
or northern British English. On the other hand, sixteen terms were
found in the English West Midlands, suggesting that "a more extensive
comparison of Appalachian and British regional vocabulary might result
in a better understanding of the ancestry of Appalachian vocabulary."[17]

As interesting as the findings of Dial, Crozier, and Ellis are, these
studies are quite limited in scope. They take for comparison between
Scotch-Irish and Appalachian-American English a small, mixed group
of terms. Although the results may tell us about individual forms, it is
difficult to calculate with precision or state with generality the extent of
influence from Scotch-Irish English. Can they provide any relative assessment of the Scotch-Irish contribution to Appalachian English as opposed to some other contribution, such as that from speakers originating
from southern England? Can they answer the questions in the title of
this chapter about the breadth and depth of the Scotch-Irish influence?
The answer to both questions, except to some extent for Ellis's study, is
no. A methodology that involves identifying individual, highly selective
correspondences, whether done by romanticizers pointing out "Elizabe-
thanisms" and "Chaucerianisms" or by more recent writers like Dial and
Crozier who tally common vocabulary items, pronunciations, and grammatical usages, can ultimately reveal little. No matter how striking, or
actually how numerous, the resemblances may be, they constitute little
more than curiosities without a valid perspective. An approach that
searches for and tallies only resemblances cannot tell us what part of the
whole they represent. In short, these studies cannot grant us a larger
view or permit us to address important, general questions because they
are based on unsystematic comparisons of Appalachian English with varieties of British English.

This chapter, which argues that a thorough comparison of Scotch-

Irish versus Appalachian English can overcome the stubborn realities cited earlier and tell us much more than previous studies, provides surprising answers about the breadth and depth of the Scotch-Irish influence. Perhaps the most important keys to this effort are found in local and unpublished sources available only in the British Isles. Equally important is adherence to a systematic, objective methodology consisting of three steps: First, a wide range of forty grammatical features, all noted in the literature as typical of Appalachian speech, were systematically isolated.[18] In other words, it began by characterizing the variety in its own terms. This avoided the problem of haphazardly and impressionistically choosing items to compare and established a principled approach for drawing comparative conclusions. Second, the most likely British source (Scotch-Irish, Southern British, or General British) was determined, where possible, for each of the forty features.[19] Third, to assess their relative contributions to Appalachian English, those features attributable to different regions of the British Isles were counted and interpreted. Taken together, these steps have enabled the ancestry of each feature to be plotted more reliably, achieving the most general comparative view possible.

The Scope of the Challenge

Why is it that research has, until the present study, made no truly general assessment of the Scotch-Irish and English elements in Appalachian speech, especially given the keen, century-long interest in tracing the ancestry of Appalachian people? Beyond the lack of an appropriate methodology, there is the problem of knowledge and sources. American researchers tend to know little about the earlier stages of English spoken in Scotland and Ireland. A general familiarity with the writings of Shakespeare and his contemporaries no doubt has led many to "recognize" older elements in Appalachian English and thus to believe that it is more "Elizabethan" than is actually the case. Few, if any, of those writing on Appalachian speech have apparently known that there is not one, but two multivolume historical dictionaries of Scottish English: the *Scottish National Dictionary* and the *Dictionary of the Old Scottish Tongue*.[20] Questions about Scotch-Irish influence cannot be addressed by using solely the *Oxford English Dictionary*, the best-known and most comprehensive historical dictionary of the language, because its coverage of nonliterary and regional varieties of English, particularly from Ireland, is limited. All historical dictionaries are only as good and complete as their citation files, and being heavily biased toward literary language, these files offer little direct evidence of the speech patterns of common people. These volumes also suffer from the problem of negative evidence; that is, though the entry of a word in a dictionary indicates something about when, where, and how that word has been used, we cannot necessarily conclude from the absence of a word that it did not exist, or from the absence of a citation that a word was not used at a certain time and place. Even the best dictionaries fall considerably short of being based on a complete documentary record.

Thus it is necessary to go beyond dictionaries and consult other types of material—local glossaries, linguistic studies, and original sources themselves. An extensive literature on Scottish English does exist, though it is largely tucked away in major British libraries, and there is as yet no good bibliography for it. The literature on the English language of Ulster is also largely inaccessible to Americans,[21] and some of the larger studies and sources of data are unpublished.[22]

This chapter, which is part of an extensive effort to detail the roots of Appalachian English, draws on reference works for British, Irish, and American English[23] and on three other types of sources: (1) primary, archival material, such as letters from seventeenth- and eighteenth-century Scots in Ulster and early Ulster emigrants to America; (2) secondary sources, such as local glossaries and studies of Scottish and Ulster English consulted in Scotland and Ireland; and (3) the author's consultations with authorities in both Ireland and Scotland and first-hand observations of contemporary speech. Focusing on grammatical features rather than vocabulary or pronunciation, I have relied on a variety of sources not used heretofore by American linguists.

The focus of this study, grammar, has been shown by linguists to be deeper in a language and to be more resistant to change, at least rapid change, than either vocabulary or pronunciation. Grammatical features and forms usually exist in relation to one another (for example, singularity to plurality for nouns) and participate in certain systems, like the expression of verb tense or noun plurality, or they are certain classes of words, like conjunctions or prepositions, that connect words to one another. For these reasons and others that will be discussed later, grammatical features are more likely to preserve traceable elements. By comparison, vocabulary is more easily and quickly borrowed across languages and dialects; for example, English has borrowed thousands of nouns from French but almost no grammar. Pronunciation is also less stable; even in isolated communities it continually evolves according to the social dynamics of the speakers, much more so than grammar. Grammatical features have two further advantages for the language historian wishing to compare them across dialects. They can be unambiguously identified from earlier written documents (whereas spelling can easily disguise pronunciation), and they can be counted and sometimes quantified by a percentage (percentages are especially useful for comparative purposes).

Calculating the Scotch-Irish Contribution

We turn now to the first step of the methodology outlined—that of identifying a comprehensive list of forty grammatical features that are characteristic of Appalachian English and that comprise the basis for our comparison to varieties of British and Irish English. These are listed by part of speech in Table 11.3. A grammatical feature considered characteristic of Appalachian English is a structure or category whose occurrence, so far as can be determined, is more or less limited to Appalachia or to the Midland region or that occurs to a significantly higher degree in these regions than elsewhere in the United States. Not every feature in Table 11.3 is unique to the region. In fact, some are still found in scattered distribution in older-fashioned American English (such as *blowed* and *growed* as past-tense forms), and others were prevalent in rural areas outside Appalachia until a generation or two ago. Nor can it be argued that all forty are used by all Appalachian speakers or are found throughout Appalachia. Some of them are quite rare, others are definitely recessive, but all have been identified in the literature by several sources as occurring in the southern mountain region. Although these assessments reflect the fullest information available from reference works, original documents, and other sources, they are only as reliable as the sources on which they are based and so cannot be claimed to be absolutely definitive. As stated earlier, reference works never give us the negative information of whether a certain form did *not* occur at a particular time and place. Though the number and range of sources from which information is drawn enhances the reliability of the assignment of features to categories according to origin, for some forms (such as *get to* and *go to*, both meaning "begin to") no information has been found on the regional demarcations either in the British Isles or in the United States.

Such forms are included in this assessment because they are quite common in Appalachian speech, are discussed in studies of Appalachian speech, and are apparently not widely found in rural and old-fashioned speech elsewhere in the country. In some cases the classification of grammatical features is subjective to a degree, but grammatical forms widely used throughout the United States—including *ain't*, combinations of objective pronouns (*me and him*) used as a subject, *was* with plural subjects (*they was*), and a number of others—are excluded, even if common in Appalachia.

Relying on as many sources as could be found, the researcher took the second step—that of determining, when sources permitted, whether the historical currency of each of the forty features was general in the British Isles or was limited to a particular region. The result of this investigation into the origin and history of each feature is shown in Table 11.3's left-hand column. Thus, a feature like the *-s* suffix on third-person-plural present-tense verbs is classified as Scotch-Irish because its distribution in the British Isles has historically been and continues to be in Scotland, northern England, and in Ireland, its distribution in the United States is strongest in Appalachia, and the suffix has the same meaning and use in all these regions.

The forty Appalachian features can be divided into the following groups based on the British ancestry assigned to them.

(1) Eighteen (45 percent) are Scotch-Irish: A1, A4, A7, A9, A10, B1–B4, B8, D3–5, E2, E4, F1, F2, F5.
(2) Four (10 percent) are Southern British: A2, A6, B5, C2.
(3) Thirteen (32.5 percent) are General British: A5, B6, B7, B9–B11, C1, D2, D6, E1, E5, F3, F4.
(4) Five (12.5 percent) are of uncertain origin (dictionaries and other reference works provide no information): A3, A8, B12, D1, E3.

This comparison, also depicted in Table 11.4, provides the most direct and broadest view to date, suggesting two things: (1) the exclusively Scotch-Irish contributions to the grammar of Appalachian English significantly outnumber exclusively Southern British ones and appear to be largely responsible for the distinctive grammar of Appalachian English today; and (2) a third of the forty grammatical features, the thirteen classified as General British, were shared by more than one immigrant group whose descendants settled in Appalachia.

Table 11.3 Appalachian Grammatical Features

Key: SI = Scotch-Irish; SB = Southern British; GB = General British; Un = Unclear

A. Verbs

1. SI Suffix -*s* (and Linking Verb *is*) in the present tense with plural noun subjects but not with plural pronoun subjects: "people *knows*" vs. "they *know*"; "people *is*" vs. "*they are.*"

2. SB Regular Past Tense Suffix -*ed* in *blowed, throwed*, etc.: "Who *blowed* up the church house?"

3. Un *get to* / *go to* (= begin to): "Just after he left, the roof *went to* leaking again"; "We *got to* laughing and giggling."

4. SI Multiple Modal Verbs: "We *might should* break the bad news to him."

5. GB *liked to* (= almost): "I got lost and *liked to* never found my way out."

6. SB *a-* Prefix: "All of a sudden that bear come *a-runnin'* at me."

7. SI Completive or Emphatic *done:* "They have *done* landed in jail again."

8. Un Preposed *used to:* "*Used to* Pa wouldn't have done a thing like that."

9. SI *used to* + *would, could:* "I can't do it now but I *used to could.*"

10. SI *need* + Past Participle of Verb: "That boy *needs taught* a lesson."

B. Pronouns

1. SI *y'all* / *you all:* "Can *y'all* / *you all* give me a hand with this load?"

2. SI *you'uns* / *we'uns*, etc.: "*You'uns* come down with me."

3. SI *ye* (= you): "I told *ye* to keep away from there."

4. SI Combinations with *all* (*we-all, us-all, they-all, you-all, who-all, what-all, where-all, why-all*, etc.): "*Who-all* is going?"

5. SB -*n* (Suffix on *hisn, hern, theirn, ourn, yourn*): "I didn't like that look of *hern*"; "Is this a book of *yourn?*"

6. GB *hisself* / *theirselves:* "You can meet Mister Jones *hisself.*"

7. GB Personal or Ethical Dative (as *me* = "myself"): "I bought *me* a dog."

8. SI *they* Existential (= "there"): "*They's* about five people in that house."

Table 11.3 continued on next page

Table 11.3 *(continued)*

9. GB *it* Existential (= "there"): "*It*'s many people that think so."

10. GB Deletion of Subject Relative Pronoun: "They's about five people who could have done it."

11. GB *hit* (= it): "*Hit*'s a long time since I tasted it."

12. Un *everwhat, everwhich, everwho* (= whatever, etc.): "*Everwho* was here sure left in a hurry."

C. Nouns

1. GB No Suffix *-s* on Noun after Quantifier Adjective: "Five *bushel*"; "Many *mile*."

2. SB *-es* Plural Suffix after *-sp, -st, -sk: waspes, postes, deskes.*

D. Prepositions

1. Un Compounding of Prepositions: "Come *out from up under* the table"; "Cal, ain't you a-going *across down over* to Rose's?"

2. GB *anent* (= opposite, nearby): "He was layin' on the road *anent* the spring-house."

3. SI *fornent / fernenst* (= against, next to): "It's over *fernenst* the wall."

4. SI *till* (= to): "It's quarter *till* five."

5. SI *wait on* (= wait for): "Would you mind *waiting on* me?"

6. GB *again / against* (= before, by the time that): "She'll be back *again* five o'clock."

E. Conjunctions

1. GB *again / against* (= before, by the time that): "I'll be ready *again* you are."

2. SI *whenever* (= at the time that, as soon as): "*Whenever* I was young, people didn't do that"; "*Whenever* I heard about them, I bought one right away."

3. Un *till* (= so that): "They . . . got 'em in a good jail there *till* the mob can't get 'em." (Jesse Stuart)

Table 11.3 continued on next page

Table 11.3 (continued)

Key: SI = Scotch-Irish; SB = Southern British; GB = General British; Un = Unclear

4. SI *and* in Absolute Phrases: "They all wore mother hubbard dresses, *and* them loose."

5. GB *nor* (= than): "He's better *nor* you."

F. Adverbs

1. SI Positive / Affirmative *anymore*: "It's a pretty skilled job *anymore*."

2. SI *all the far* (= as far as): "That's *all the far* I want to go."

3. GB *right* (= very, quite): "It's *right* airish this morning."

4. GB *yonder*: "That's my field down *yonder*."

5. SI *yan* (= yon): "Snakes was everywhere going here and *yan*."

Table 11.4 Types of Grammatical Features by Source

Feature Type	Source			
	Scotch-Irish	Southern British	General British	Uncertain
Suffix	1	3	1	0
Word Order Pattern	7	0	1	2
Categorical Difference	3	1	2	1
Difference in Form of Pronoun	2	0	2	1
Function Word	5	0	7	1
Total	18	4	13	5

The preceding list views each of the forty grammatical features as equivalent in significance and level of structure; another way to classify them is according to their type of grammatical structure, described as follows and also shown in Table 11.4:

(1) Five are suffixes added to verbs, pronouns, or nouns: A1, A2, B5, C1, C2. Of these, one is Scotch-Irish, three Southern British, and one General British in origin.

(2) Ten involve word-order patterns (the combination of two or

more words in a distinct way): A4, A8, A9, A10, B4, B10, D1, E4, F1, F2. Of these, seven are Scotch-Irish, none Southern British, one General British, and two uncertain in origin.

(3) Seven involve categorical differences involving a grammatical category not found in other dialects (often a familiar form such as *done* is employed in a way unfamiliar to other dialects): A3, A5, A6, A7, B1, B2, B7. Of these, three are Scotch-Irish, one Southern British, two General British, and one uncertain in origin.

(4) Five are pronouns that vary from other dialects: B3, B6, B8, B11, B12. Of these, two are Scotch-Irish, none Southern British, two General British, and one uncertain in origin.

(5) Thirteen are function words (prepositions, adverbs, and conjunctions) that relate other words or elements in a clause to one another: B9, D2, D3, D4, D5, D6, E1, E2, E3, E5, F3, F4, F5. Of these, five are Scotch-Irish, none Southern British, seven General British, and one uncertain in origin.

Scotch-Irish English has contributed all five types of grammatical features to Appalachian English. This is particularly true for word-order patterns—like A4 ("We *might should* go on") and A10 ("That boy *needs taught* a lesson")—and function words—like D4 (*till*) and D5 (*wait on*). Only four items can be traced back specifically to southern Britain: the *a-* prefix (A6), and three suffixes—the long plural of an additional syllable in nouns like *postes* and *waspes* (C2); possessive pronouns ending in *-n*, like *hern* and *yourn* (B5); and regularized past-tense forms with *-ed*, like *blowed* (A2). These have not been current, so far as sources indicate, in Ireland, Scotland, or northern Britain over the past five centuries. Although this suggests a minimal Southern British contribution, we must remember that the English of southern Britain and Scotland shared thirteen grammatical features that are now identified as Appalachian, including the auxiliary verb *liked to* (A5) and the ethical dative use of pronouns (B7). Moreover, there are hundreds of grammatical features not in our tables that are shared as the common core of English everywhere.

Explaining the Scotch-Irish Contribution

The preceding comparison strongly suggests that the Scotch-Irish influence on Appalachian English, at least on its grammar, was broad in terms of the variety and deep in terms of the number of patterns. This work also shows that many features contributed by Ulster emigrants continue to thrive in modern-day Appalachia, that they were not leveled away.[24] Why might this be so? Explanations that rely on demographic factors alone, citing the numerical dominance of the Scotch-Irish and their descendants in southern Appalachia, are much too simple, for they ignore the fact that settlers from various areas of England predominated in some parts of the region. Isolation cannot account for this prevalence of Ulster speech patterns either. Appalachian residents have had continuing contact with speakers of more mainstream, more prestigious varieties of American English since the settlement period. Nor does the use of Scotch-Irish features as markers of identity with an ethnic group provide a plausible explanation, given the statement of James Leyburn cited earlier and the lack of popular awareness of Irish or Scotch-Irish ancestry in the mountains today; that is, unless Scotch-Irish features have come to symbolize Appalachian cultural identity.

Why did descendants of the Scotch-Irish in Appalachia not abandon more of their distinctive usages and shift to a more general variety of English, or at least one with fewer distinctive usages, as did the speakers of so many other dialect and language groups? This is how the North American melting pot is supposed to have worked, at least for immigrants from the British Isles. Were grammatical features brought from Ulster simply retained in the speech of immigrants and their descendants, in which case they would probably contrast most directly with Southern British forms? Or did they evolve, undergoing changes in meaning or form that can explain their preservation? Further insight into these questions, and work toward a reasonable linguistic explanation (not a social one, which is still a long way from formulation), of how and why the Scotch-Irish influence has been preserved comes by approaching the eighteen Appalachian grammatical features traceable to the Scotch-Irish in a third way. This involves formulating a typology for connections between Scotch-Irish and Appalachian English in terms of the evolutionary processes that account for their present-day patterning.

In studying these connections, we draw on concepts from the study of creole languages that carefully distinguish between the form of a grammatical feature and its meaning or function. Linguists have shown that in a creole language, for example, Gullah (the English creole spoken on the Sea Islands of South Carolina and Georgia), a form that sounds and looks like a form in the dominant language (American English) may continue to be used, but its meaning and function may differ, often subtly so. The effect is to camouflage some parts of the language, making speakers of both the dominant language and the creole believe that they use the same words in the same way, when they do not. For instance, the English verb form *been* has been adapted in Gullah to refer to an action that took place long ago (*He been go* thus means "He left a long time ago"). This same process applies to newly formed varieties like Appalachian English and may well account for the retention of a number of grammatical features. Although it is not yet clear how all eighteen features determined earlier to be of Scotch-Irish origin can be classified, three types of processes characterizing transatlantic linguistic connections can be proposed: straight retentions, disguised retentions, and reinterpretations. Table 11.5 lists seventeen grammatical features grouped under these three processes.

The first type of process, straight retentions, involves items whose form, meaning, and function are either the same or very similar in Appalachia and Ulster. However, though their form in Appalachian English is different from American English generally, their meaning and function are equivalent to other forms in American English. This is represented in Table 11.6. One example is the preposition *fornent*. Although quite distinct in form, it means the same as "against" or "next to." It is such Scotch-Irish forms that we would expect to have competed most directly with those from British English (like *against*), and in fact these straight retentions tend to be recessive in modern-day Appalachia, probably because of their salience, and are more common among older speakers than younger ones. These straight retentions include the following: the pronoun *you'uns* (B2), equivalent to *y'all*, *you*, or other plural pronouns; the pronoun *ye* (B3), equivalent to *you*;[25] and the adverb *yan* (F5), equivalent to *yon*, *yonder*, or *over there*.

The second type is disguised retentions, items whose form, meaning, and function, like straight retentions, are the same or very similar in Appalachia and Ulster. But whereas their form in Appalachian English is identical to that in American English generally, their meaning or function is at least partially different. This is represented in Table 11.7. These retentions are camouflaged in Appalachian English because the form of an item is usually more salient than its meaning or function. An example that has the same form and might at first appear to have the same meaning in Appalachian English as elsewhere is the conjunction *whenever*. In American English generally, it has several meanings. In re-

Table 11.5 Types of Grammatical Features[a] by Process

I. Straight Retentions (5)

A9. *used to + would, could*

B2. *you'uns / we'uns*, etc.

B3. *ye* (you)

D3. *fornent / fernenst* (against, next to)

F5. *yan* (yon)

II. Disguised Retentions (8)

A1. 3rd plural-present-tense *-s* (and *is*) with noun subjects but not pronoun subjects

A10. *need* + past participle of verb

B4. combinations with *all* (*what-all, where-all*, etc.)

B8. *they* Existential (there)

D4. *till* (to)

D5. *wait on* (wait for)

E2. *whenever* (at the time that, as soon as)

E4. *and* in absolute phrases

III. Reinterpretations (4)

A4. multiple modal verbs

A7. completive / emphatic *done*

B1. *y'all / you all*

F1. positive *anymore*

[a]As described in Table 11.3.

Table 11.6 Straight Retention Relationships

Appalachian English		American English Generally
Form	≠	Form
Meaning/Function	=	Meaning/Function

Table 11.7 Disguised Retention Relationships

Appalachian English		American English Generally
Form	=	Form
Meaning/Function	≠	Meaning/Function

ferring to an intermittent event, it is equivalent to "as often as" (as in "*Whenever* I work late, I order a pizza"); in referring to a hypothetical event it is equivalent to "at whatever time" or "at the moment that" ("I will be there *whenever* he arrives"). But in Appalachian and Ulster English it can be used in the past tense to mean "at the moment that" or in both the present and past tense to mean "as soon as." As a result, speakers of other varieties of American English interpret the following sentences, collected in Tennessee and South Carolina, as referring to intermittent occurrences, which of course in each case does not actually make sense.

(1) *Whenever* we were going out, I said to him . . .
(2) *Whenever* his Daddy died, he took over the farm.
(3) I was home on Wednesday and *whenever* I got on the interstate on Thursday my car broke down and I was stuck three four or five hours.
(4) As my school years continued, I inevitably expanded my knowledge of vocabulary. However, there seemed to be a change [in] my language *whenever* I reached my senior year in high school.
(5) *Whenever* I heard about the course, I signed up for it right away.

Thus, an Appalachian speaker stating "I'll come *whenever* I can" may be using the word to mean "as soon as," expressing urgency, but may be understood as saying "I'll come *at whatever time* I can" by outsiders. A friend of the author who moved to South Carolina from Michigan recently had to call a plumber about a desperate situation. When the plumber said that he would be over "*whenever* he could," she angrily told him not to come, thinking that he was going to take his time. He was actually going to come at his very next free moment.

Other Ulster grammatical features retained in Appalachian English also disguise their distinctiveness in their function; though identical with forms found elsewhere in American English, in Appalachian speech they are used in different grammatical contexts. Examples are third-person-plural -s (A1), as in "the men knows," which is camouflaged by its likeness to third-person-singular -s, as in "the man knows"; need + past participle (A10), as in needs taught, disguised by its similarity to need + infinitive + past participle (needs to be taught); and till (D4), which many speakers of American English mistakenly believe is a clipped form of until. The preposition-conjunction till originally came from Norse; it has long been a variant of the preposition to in Scottish English and still is in some places in North America, especially in phrases to tell time (quarter till ten).

Sometimes these disguised retentions have both different meanings and different contextual distributions, as with the form they (B8) when used to introduce a sentence that states the existence of something, and wait on (D5) as equivalent to wait for. Because they are disguised and Appalachian speakers are often unaware of how these grammatical features differ from other kinds of American English, they continue to flourish in mountain speech.

A third process, reinterpretation, has affected some Appalachian features that come from Scotch-Irish English. Their meaning and function has been thoroughly or completely expanded or shifted since arriving from Ulster in the eighteenth century. Although originally brought to the Midland region by the Scotch-Irish, today they are prevalent not only in Appalachian English but beyond as well. Three are common in the Lower South—multiple modal verbs (A4), the perfective done (A7), and y'all, you all (B1)—whereas the positive use of anymore (F1) has spread through much of the Midwest. The reinterpreted Scotch-Irish features that spread to the Lower South are now used by both whites and blacks throughout the region.

Reinterpretations contrast with other varieties of American English not only in form, as straight retentions do, but also in meaning and function. This is represented in Table 11.8. These grammatical features have survived and expanded because they developed specific functions in Appalachian and Midland English as well as derivative varieties that have given them a niche in the face of their lack of equivalence. The two best examples of these reinterpretations are combinations of modal verbs like might could and might should (A4) and the pronouns y'all and you all (B1). Though modal combinations are attested in Scotland, Ulster, and northern England, and though the most common combinations on both sides of the Atlantic are largely the same, the range of

Table 11.8 Reinterpretation Relationships

Appalachian English		American English Generally
Form	≠	Form
Meaning/Function	≠	Meaning/Function

combinations found in Appalachian and southern American English appears to be open ended and apparently much broader than the range of permissible combinations in the British Isles.[26] *Y'all*, still used to a very limited extent in Scotland today, is equivalent only to the phrase "all of you." Apparently after migrating to North America, it developed its semantic qualities (for example, as an associative plural, used in addressing one person but referring to others associated with the addressee). For many speakers, *y'all* represents a contraction of "you all," which it probably was not originally.[27]

In recent years linguistic scholars elsewhere have examined the elements of colonial varieties of European languages—sometimes called "extraterritorial" or "exported" varieties—pointing out that the competition of dialects in colonial territories often led to the formation of new dialects—not just a new inventory of forms selected from the dialects of the mother country, but sometimes entirely new patterns.[28] The reinterpretations discussed here are further evidence of the dynamic nature of such varieties, in this case Appalachian English. This typology outlines ways to explore the evolution of grammatical patterns of Old World English into New World English. The three processes sketched herein bring us much closer to an account of how distinctive Old World patterns, in this case from Scotch-Irish English, have been preserved in New World English. This typology, in addition to helping us understand how individual forms have or have not evolved over the past three hundred years, provides, particularly for disguised forms, an explanation of why the Scotch-Irish impact on Appalachian English has been underestimated in the past.

In attempting to assess this impact, this chapter has offered the broader dimensions of a case that still requires much to be filled in; more data, particularly from original documents, needs to be gathered. Each of the disguised and reinterpreted grammatical forms deserves a full-length description of its history to enable us to develop specific hypotheses that account for its development. Little more than their classification can be presented here. The same type of analysis should be undertaken for vocabulary and pronunciation.[29]

This chapter has focused on tracing connections in grammatical patterns between Appalachian English and varieties of British English. Such an effort, even at a relatively shallow time-depth of less than three hundred years, faces analytical and documentary challenges that the current investigation has sought to meet by consulting an unprecedented range of published and unpublished sources. By comparison, previous attempts to make the connection were small-scale, unsystematic, and tentative. If we assume some degree of homogeneity in the varieties that we have been calling Scotch-Irish English and Appalachian English, and if we assume the correct identification and comparison of grammatical forms from our work with dictionaries and grammars, local linguistic literature, original documents, and consultation with local observers, we can posit a strong link in the grammatical systems of Scotch-Irish English and Appalachian English. This link is both broad and deep, extending across different types of grammatical features. As a result, we are much closer to saying just how "Scotch-Irish" Appalachian English is.

12 Scotch-Irish Frontier Society in Southwestern North Carolina, 1780–1840

H. Tyler Blethen
Curtis W. Wood, Jr.

At the close of the American Revolution, the territory west of the Blue Ridge and Allegheny Mountains quickly opened to the first legal white settlement. Southwestern North Carolina was one of many regions that received a flood of new people. Between 1780 and 1840, this western-most part of North Carolina was occupied by new settlers of diverse ethnic backgrounds: primarily English, German, and Scotch-Irish. The census of 1840 records a population of approximately 34,000 from Buncombe County westward, including Henderson, Haywood, Macon, and Cherokee Counties. In the half century that the Old West frontier moved through southwestern North Carolina, a new society rapidly evolved. Never static or isolated, it was in fact a constantly growing, changing region.[1] This chapter will attempt to gauge the status and role of the Scotch-Irish in this process by examining the dimensions of the Scotch-Irish community in the region; the history of Presbyterianism, the most visible institution of that community; and an essential characteristic of any rural people, the ways in which they settled and used the land.

Some years ago the eminent Ulster geographer and folklorist E. Estyn Evans wrote that the story of the Scotch-Irish on the American Old West frontier in the eighteenth and nineteenth centuries would require the cooperation of historian, geographer, social anthropologist, and folklorist,[2] for the sources are scattered, fragmentary, and diverse and require painstaking research, a variety of approaches, and imaginative insight. In pursuing a case study of Scotch-Irish frontier history, the first step is to assess the dimensions of the early Scotch-Irish community in the southwestern mountains of North Carolina. What proportion of the new settlers could trace their origins to the north of Ireland? It is impossible on the basis of surname examination alone to arrive at accurate information on the numbers of Scotch-Irish within a community of peoples who emigrated from Europe, Ireland, and Great Britain. Yet a careful approximation with acknowledged limitations is useful as a basis to consider cultural impact, comparisons with other areas, and changes in the proportion of Scotch-Irish in the region. We have attempted to tabulate ethnic statistics with the assumption that Scottish names common in Appalachia are likely to have arrived from Ulster rather than Scotland, given the minimal Scottish migration into southern Appalachia in the first decades of settlement. The larger problem is determining the origin of certain English names common in Ulster and found in the southern mountains, names such as Brown, Wilson, Rogers, Thompson, Smith, and Thomas. Passenger lists of ships from Ulster arriving in colonial ports indicate a high frequency of such names in the eighteenth century.

Our estimates are based primarily on the surname handbooks of Sir Robert Matheson and Edward MacLysaght, as well as on data from genealogies and family histories and traditions.[3] We have consistently eliminated names of settlers known to be Scottish or Welsh. More important, we have excluded English names common in Ulster, unless we had information about specific families that allowed us to include them. It is our opinion that the estimates that follow are low and represent minima. But since the criteria have been applied consistently, the relationship between Scotch-Irish and non-Scotch-Irish names should remain constant. We have applied the resulting surname information to a number of population lists from the region. The resulting estimates suggest the Scotch-Irish role in white settlement as it advanced across southwestern North Carolina between 1790 and 1840.

The 1790 census of that part of Burke County, which was located west of the Blue Ridge and which at that time encompassed all non–Native American settlements in southwestern North Carolina, yields a figure of 40 percent Scotch-Irish, or 35 out of 88 heads of families.[4] The census of 1800 for Buncombe County, recently created out of Burke County and then the only North Carolina county open for settlement west of the Blue Ridge, yields a figure of 43 percent, or 385 out of 888 heads of families.[5] The 1810 census for the newly created county of Haywood, to the west of Buncombe, reveals 120 out of 384 heads of families, or 31.3 percent.[6] In the sale of Cherokee lands in 1819, in what would in 1828 become Macon County, 38 percent of the 144 land purchasers bore Ulster names.[7] An analysis of the 1830 census for Macon County indicates that 30.5 percent, 248 of 813 heads of families, were of Scotch-Irish origin. Among the purchasers of Cherokee lands in 1838 in what would become Cherokee County, 28 percent of the 355 purchasers bore Scotch-Irish names.[8] Finally, the 1840 census for Cherokee County yields 25 percent, or 125 of 501 families, as distinctly Scotch-Irish[9] (see Figure 12.1).

Several observations arise from these estimates. The most obvious is the perceptible decline in the size of the Scotch-Irish element in the newly settled lands as the frontier moved west between 1790 and 1840, an approximate decline from 40 percent to 20 percent. A reasonable hypothesis is that the earliest settlers were drawn from large concentrations of Scotch-Irish immigrants who had traveled down the Great Wagon Road from Pennsylvania into the Carolina piedmont and the Watauga settlement of East Tennessee in the thirty years before the Revolution. After 1783, these two areas served as population reservoirs from which southwestern North Carolina drew many of its settlers, among them men who had hunted and fought in the mountains and knew the land well. The high percentage of Scotch-Irish in those two areas must have declined as many of those early settlers dispersed—some moving into southwestern North Carolina, others moving further south or west—and were replaced by newcomers of varied origins. Consequently, by about 1810 new settlers in the mountain region were being drawn from a wider and more varied population.

A second observation seems to support the first—our estimates for southwestern North Carolina are considerably higher than those that have been compiled for the state as a whole. Howard F. Barker and Marcus L. Hansen, in an early and widely used report that calculated the ethnic makeup of the American population in 1790, concluded that 11.1 percent of all settlers in North Carolina were from Ireland. Forrest McDonald and Ellen Shapiro McDonald have argued that 13.3 percent of the population of North Carolina in 1790 bore Irish and 27.6 percent bore Scottish names, a combined total of 40.9 percent. Because neither study makes an effort to estimate what proportion of this number was Scotch-Irish, except to suggest that a majority of these Scottish and Irish names must have come from Ulster, it is difficult to use their estimates. Thomas L. Purvis has recently critiqued and refined their figures and concluded that 15.8 percent of North Carolina's 1790 population was Scotch-Irish.[10] Our figures for southwestern North Carolina in 1790

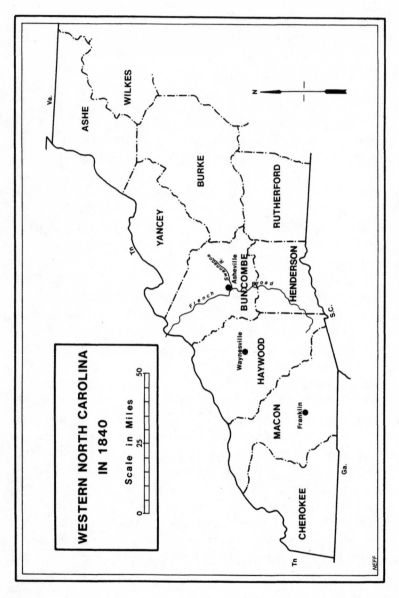

Figure 12.1 Western North Carolina in 1840.

and 1800 are remarkably higher than all of these estimates for the state as a whole. If the commonly accepted notion that the Scotch-Irish were highly mobile settlers and inclined to follow the frontier westward in search of more and better land is true, then it would follow that they would dominate the first phase of frontier settlement but that they would be among the first to move on. There is certainly evidence to support this thesis in contemporary accounts and in family histories, and there is tentative evidence for it in various demographic sources.

Scotch-Irish dominance in the early frontier period also appears when name analysis is used to investigate their sociopolitical role in the region. We have applied the same name analysis technique to several samples to develop an understanding of the Scotch-Irish role in community leadership. Of the sixteen landowners in the new town of Asheville in 1800, ten, or 63 percent, had names and family histories that indicate Scotch-Irish origins, as did five of the ten justices of the peace for Buncombe County in 1792 and five of seven county office holders.[11] A compilation of those individuals who claimed over 1,000 acres in land grants in Buncombe and Haywood Counties from 1788 to 1810 and who were also resident there, as opposed to absentee speculators, indicates that nineteen of thirty, or 63.3 percent, were Scotch-Irish.[12] It appears from these figures that in the first generation of settlement, Scotch-Irish individuals and families played a larger part in western North Carolina society than even their numbers might suggest. By the 1840s and 1850s in Cherokee County, an examination of the names of ninety-four men who served as justices of the peace[13] indicates that 35 percent bore Scotch-Irish names at a time when 25 percent of the population can be identified by the same method as members of that group. It is apparent that during the half century of settlement the Scotch-Irish element in southwestern North Carolina was in flux. But though it formed only a substantial minority of a mixed and still inchoate society, its social prominence probably outweighed its size.

Perhaps the most visible manifestation of Scotch-Irish culture on the new Carolina frontier was the Presbyterian church. Throughout the eighteenth century there was a distinct relationship between Presbyterianism, the Scotch-Irish, and the advance of the American frontier south and west.[14] The Presbyterian church appeared in the history of the mountain settlements almost as early as the Scotch-Irish themselves, and the early organization and administration of churches in these settlements were haphazard and uncertain. Initially the westernmost area of North Carolina was under the supervision of the Abingdon Presbytery, which, organized in 1786, also covered southwestern Virginia and the Watauga settlement; meanwhile Burke and Rutherford Counties were administered by the Concord Presbytery of the Carolina Synod. But just as most of the Scotch-Irish immigrants entered the Blue Ridge Mountains from the Carolina piedmont, so too did the Church. The birthing and nurturing of the earliest congregations within the mountain settlements were largely the work of piedmont Carolinians.[15]

The central figure in this early missionary work was James Hall, one of the most distinguished ministers of his time. His father, also James, left Ireland in 1730 and apparently came to Philadelphia, where he married Prudence Roddy. James, Jr., was born in Carlisle, Pennsylvania, in 1744 and moved with his family to the North Carolina piedmont in 1751. He graduated in 1774 from Nassau Hall, the Presbyterian seminary that later became known as Princeton University, served as captain of cavalry and army chaplain during the Revolutionary War, and became a pastor in what would soon be the Concord Presbytery. In 1790 he began his ministry as one of the great frontier missionaries,[16] preaching in the mountains of North Carolina.

According to the 1797 minutes of the General Assembly of the Presbyterian Church, three churches had existed since 1794 in the Asheville area of Buncombe County: Reems Creek, Swannanoa, and Head of the French Broad River.[17] But James Hall's report to the Synod of the Carolinas in October 1793, describing his recent visit there, indicates that these congregations were established at least as early as 1790, although they were not provided with resident clergymen.[18] In 1797 Reverend George Newton, born in York County, Pennsylvania,[19] left piedmont North Carolina to accept a call from the united congregations of Swannanoa and Reems Creek.[20] Subsequently these congregations and the Reverend Mr. Newton were instrumental in the formation of other churches further west: Armageddon Church in the Turkey Creek–Sandy Mush–New Foord areas and Bethsalem Church in the Pigeon River–Richland Creek area. Both were founded in 1800 in what would soon be Haywood County, three years earlier than the first Baptist churches. Newton was engaged to supply these new Presbyterian congregations as well.[21]

In the same period, an academy was established by the Scotch-Irish Presbyterians of Buncombe County near the mouth of the Swannanoa River on land owned by William Forster, an immigrant born in Ireland in 1748.[22] Robert Henry, of Scotch-Irish descent and a veteran of the Battle of King's Mountain, taught in this first North Carolina school west of the Blue Ridge,[23] and in 1797 George Newton assumed direction of this academy, later named for him. With a curriculum that offered Greek and Latin as well as "fundamental learning," the academy produced among its early students two governors of North Carolina (David Lowry Swain and Zebulon Baird Vance) and a governor of South Carolina. The trustees of the academy comprised a roster of the regional elite, with many Scotch-Irish among them. In 1810 a group of prominent citizens interested in "literary advancement" undertook on behalf of the academy to organize a lottery with a $7,000 prize to raise money to establish a female academy in Asheville. The lottery failed, "owing to the extreme scarcity of cash," and the money was refunded.[24]

But it was not only the Scotch-Irish ideal of learning that encountered trouble on the Carolina frontier. The Presbyterian Church also experienced difficulty in maintaining its traditional position in Scotch-Irish society. In 1809, following a tour of the churches in the region, the Reverend James Hall reported that "respecting the State of religion it is not as in years past." Deploring the disastrous impact of the emotional revivalism of the second Great Awakening that had swept the Carolinas early in the nineteenth century, for its "most wild and delusive fanaticism" and its "horrid and extravagant conduct," he also complained about the lack of qualified ministers, a consequence of Presbyterians' insistence on an educated ministry. This problem must have been common among Presbyterian congregations throughout the frontier: "Our vacant churches in those counties," Hall observed, "still look up to us, for public instructions and the administrations of the sealing ordinances of the Gospel; but lament that they have from us too few supplies. On this account in sundry places, from principles of necessity, they employ preachers of other denominations to impart to them, some of their ministerial labours. For this and other causes, our members are dropping off, and our societies annually melting away; so that unless some remedy be afforded they will ere long cease to exist."[25]

The shortage of qualified ministers was complicated by the remoteness of the mountain counties, both from the center of the Presbytery in the piedmont and from its national center in Pennsylvania, and by the stress on connectionalism, the insistence that ministers and churches be directly connected to and under the authority of a presbytery and through it joined to the hierarchy of synod and general assembly.[26] The church west of the Blue Ridge did not flourish under these requirements. The congregations of Armageddon and Bethsalem seem to have had a short life—they were heard from no more after their founding. Between 1805 and 1813 Newton attended only one meeting of the Presbytery, and when he left Buncombe County for greener pastures in Tennessee in 1813 he was not replaced for four years. But the original congregation in Buncombe County and the academy there did survive, and Presbyterianism did maintain a presence across the western counties and an identification with the Scotch-Irish community throughout the period.

In the 1820s there was a renewal of Presbyterian activity, associated with the work of Reverend Christopher Bradshaw. He first served in the southern part of Buncombe County, where in 1828 he organized the Davidson River Church, along with three elders and twenty-seven members. Sixty-five new members had been added by 1834, and by 1836 an academy was associated with the church.[27] In 1833 Bradshaw was involved in organizing the Franklin Presbyterian Church in Macon County, which recorded 101 members in 1836 but was inactive by the 1840s.[28] In 1834 the Reverend William Hall reported that he had organized a church in Haywood County, to be known as the Ebenezer Church.[29] Finally, in 1841, Bradshaw organized a church in the newly created county of Cherokee called the Hiwassee Church, and he moved west to serve it. Hiwassee was small and grew slowly, but it survived. The session books of the Davidson River and Hiwassee churches have also survived[30] and provide us with a list of elders and members. There is no mistaking the Scotch-Irish identity of these congregations and their role as the core of a small continuing Presbyterian tradition within the region. But the great majority of their fellows had found new religious loyalties. The Presbyterian Church was completely overshadowed after about 1810 by the rapid growth of the Baptist and Methodist churches, and there can be no doubt but that many old Presbyterian families rapidly joined one of those denominations. By the early 1840s there were only six Presbyterian churches serving fewer than three hundred members across southwestern North Carolina.[31] In comparison, there were thirty-seven Baptist and thirty-two Methodist congregations in the region, according to the census of 1850.[32]

A final issue is the role of the Scotch-Irish in the creation and development of rural mountain society after 1790. How significant were ethnic heritage and historical experiences, both in Ulster and in migration, on the development of regional land-use and settlement patterns?

Numerous scholars have addressed these questions in studies of other regions. The historical geographer James Lemon, in his pioneering work on the settlement of southeastern Pennsylvania, dismissed ethnicity as a convincing explanation of the extensive farming practices and dispersed settlement patterns that the Scotch-Irish practiced there. He argued that dispersed settlement patterns did not develop in Ulster until the nineteenth century, and that other ethnic groups settled in dispersed patterns and farmed extensively in Pennsylvania both before the Scotch-Irish arrived (e.g., the Quakers) and after their presence was established (e.g., the Germans). Instead he insisted that there was a general trend in the Western world in the eighteenth century toward dispersed settlement, as peasant values were abandoned in favor of a trend toward individualism.[33]

E. Estyn Evans rejected Lemon's findings, arguing that folkways are not fully revealed by statistical analyses such as those Lemon applied to tax lists and estate inventories and that Lemon had not examined the Scotch-Irish outside of Pennsylvania.[34] Although Evans acknowledged the role of the frontier in shaping Scotch-Irish (and other groups') agricultural practices and settlement patterns, he insisted that "their experience in Ulster and their cultural inheritance" also played an important part and that their influence on "the patterns of land-use, economy and society" were among their most significant contributions to American life.[35]

More recently Forrest McDonald, Ellen Shapiro McDonald, and Grady McWhiney have attempted to explain just about all of southern history in terms of ethnicity. In various works they argue that by 1850, three-quarters or more of the South was Celtic (they lump Scots, Irish, Welsh, and Scotch-Irish together in this category) and that this ethnic dominance explains the "fundamental differences between northern and southern Americans." Celts were culturally preadapted by their British and Irish experiences to practice livestock-raising and dispersed settlement in the New World, and this distinguished them from other ethnic groups such as the English or Germans, who reproduced a settled village life based on their customs and experiences in the Old World.[36] In essence, they assert that the Scotch-Irish "practiced an open-range pastoralism and disdained mere tillage of the soil. They were 'indolent to a high degree, unless roused to war, or to any animating amusement.' They preferred personal arbitration to law; they had little respect for property rights in land. Politically, they were disputatious and often adroit, but they were inept at governing and nearly impossible to govern. In an orderly English or Anglo-American society, in other words, they were misfits; and when they appeared in sufficient numbers they composed a disruptive element indeed."[37] In light of this controversy, the following comments offer a regional study of Scotch-Irish land-use practices and settlement patterns based on information about Ulster and colonial agriculture and an initial investigation of practices in southwestern North Carolina.

Settlers on the Old West frontier practiced extensive mixed farming, a combination of tillage and livestock that was favored in circumstances where land was plentiful, labor scarce, and markets remote or nonexistent. Corn was grown on plots of land cultivated by hoe, and cattle and hogs were raised on unfenced common pasture land. The land which the early pioneers entered was not completely forested, as the Cherokee who had lived there for centuries had engaged in tillage and cleared much of the valley land for cultivation.[38] More often than has been recognized the early white settlers were confronted with a choice: whether to take over cultivation of existing fields or to clear their own. Though cleared land was preferred and brought higher prices in land sales, the choice was not always an obvious one. Uncleared land was not always undesirable, for taking over cleared land implied a commitment to plowing and manuring, a more intensive agriculture best suited to areas with a larger labor supply and market-oriented efficiency. Farming on uncleared land meant girdling and burning trees, utilizing the soil's natural fertility, and cultivating among the trees or stumps by hoe, altogether a more rational use of scarce labor. Eventually, though, the soil wore out, and at that point "new ground" was cultivated and the process begun again.[39]

As for livestock raising, the preferred method was open-range grazing, whereby animals were turned loose on any land not fenced for tillage, primarily woods and upland pastures. Animals were branded or otherwise marked and then allowed to fend for themselves. The great attraction of this method of stock raising was that it utilized uncleared land to produce a commercial commodity that transported itself to distant markets.[40]

As James Lemon has pointed out, it cannot be argued that the Scotch-Irish alone practiced this kind of agriculture, with its emphasis on extravagant use of land, simple tools, and livestock, for it was characteristic of the frontier South and particularly North Carolina. The anonymous author of *American Husbandry*, originally published in 1775, observed of North Carolina, "Such herds of cattle and swine are to be found in no other colonies, and when this is better settled, they will not be so common here; for at present the woods are all in common." He continued, "In this system of crops they change the land as fast as it wears out, clearing fresh pieces of wood land, exhausting them in succession, after which they leave them to spontaneous growth. . . . It presently becomes such wood as the rest of the country is; and woods here are the pasture of the cattle."[41]

The piedmont area he was describing was heavily settled by Scotch-Irish, but observers also recorded such practices among the Highland Scots in the Cape Fear region and German farmers in the piedmont.[42] This use of the land was appropriate to the environment and the labor resources of the first settlers, and it was highly flexible and adaptable. There was no sharply defined line between extensive subsistence-oriented farming and more intensive farming for market. This frontier agriculture was suited to progressive modification as land became less plentiful and markets and labor more available.[43]

It can, however, be argued that the Scotch-Irish who settled in southwestern North Carolina were predisposed to adopt the extensive pattern—which they found familiar and congenial—because of their historical experiences. In Ulster, although there existed a wide variety of farming practices and although agriculture was in flux in the late seventeenth and eighteenth centuries, extensive farming methods did play a major role. The system of agriculture known as infield-outfield was common in both Scotland and Ireland. Crops were grown intensively on some plots of land known as the infield and were supplemented by other land cultivated as outfield. The latter was an extensive form of tillage in which the land was seldom fertilized and was allowed for long periods to lie fallow, returning to grass or bush. Tillage was supplemented by livestock grazing on the outfield and common pasture land, often upland pastures. This system provided many of the elements for the agriculture that the Scotch-Irish evolved in their American migration.[44] The slash-and-burn practices of Native American agriculturists were well suited to the vast resources of land available, and the Scotch-Irish were not slow to borrow them. The underpopulation of America, particularly in the South and West, invited extensive use of the land by both the Native Americans and by the early white settlers.

By the time that the Scotch-Irish arrived in southwestern North

Carolina, they had accumulated a wide variety of agricultural experiences involving the practice of extensive agriculture. In addition they had entered into an environment characterized in the extreme by abundant land and a scarcity of labor and markets. Consequently the early generations of pioneers chose extensive methods of land use, and they settled on single-family homesites surrounded by their lands. Unlike the English in New England and the Germans in Pennsylvania, the Scotch-Irish did not settle in tightly knit, highly organized villages. They spread out across the land, surrounding themselves with the many acres that their style of farming required, ready to move should their soil become exhausted and their pastures restricted, but also willing to adapt.

The controversy over the ethnic origins of dispersed settlement patterns continues. Evans argues for Ulster origins, as do the McDonalds and McWhiney. But Ruth Sutter in her history of communities in North America sees the phenomenon in a broader perspective: "Around the Atlantic fringes of Europe, from Finland to parts of the Iberian peninsula, the traditional settlement pattern was one of single family and more or less self-sufficient farms. Homesteads were dispersed, and a sense of neighborhood was probably maintained through kinship, trading associations, crossroads fairs, religious gatherings, and rural courts. . . . [T]hese were scattered elsewhere in Europe too, but through much of England and trans-alpine Europe the community took the form of a compact village, a cluster of households separate from fields."[45] Whatever the source, dispersed settlements characterized the Old West frontier and southwestern North Carolina from the start.

Four particular categories of evidence suggest much about agricultural practices in the highland region of southwestern North Carolina: (1) the 1839 *Letter of James Patton, One of the First Residents of Asheville, North Carolina, to his Children;* (2) a census of economic activity appended to the 1810 census for Haywood County; (3) the surviving wills and inventories for Haywood County in the period 1825–36; and (4) the first agricultural census of the United States (1850).

Patton—born in Tamlacht, County Londonderry, in 1756 and trained as a weaver—emigrated to America in 1783. In the Philadelphia area he found various employment as a casual laborer until, in 1789, having accumulated enough money to purchase a supply of goods, he set out for western North Carolina. This marked the beginning of his career as a traveling merchant, taking trade goods south to the North Carolina mountains and driving livestock north to the cities of Washington, Baltimore, and Philadelphia.

Patton's experiences give a good idea of what it took to prosper as a merchant working the Great Wagon Road, and his observations on conditions in western North Carolina provide information about the first decades of settlement. During his life, he saw economic activity grow from the late 1780s, when there was little money available in the mountains, to the 1830s, when his inventories of trade goods reveal a significant expansion of commerce. The primary "cash crop" that mountaineers raised was livestock—which according to Patton was driven out of the mountains in large numbers—supplemented by furs, feathers, beeswax, and medicinal roots such as ginseng and snake root. He observed, "I settled in the upper part of North Carolina at that time the poorest part of the country I ever saw to make property; but I do not entertain the same opinion now. Changes and improvements have convinced me that there are few sections of country superior to the western part of North Carolina."[46]

Allowing for regional pride, Patton's narrative records the steady if not rapid development of the southwestern counties since the 1790s and the emergence of a relatively populous region of small farms engaged in increasingly commercialized mixed farming. Patton's descriptions are of course impressionistic, but they can be supplemented by statistical data, especially for Haywood County. The picture that emerges from the 1810 census data and from county wills and inventories supports Patton's impressions.

The wills and inventories (only nineteen such documents survive in county records)[47] portray a population engaged in mixed farming. Much livestock is listed, along with tools and implements for tillage. Grains were the dominant crops, with Indian corn far and away the leader, followed by oats, wheat, and barley. Plows are listed in sixteen of the inventories, indicating that in addition to hoe cultivation, as agriculture moved out of the pioneer phase, many fields were being cleared and plowed. Other crops such as flax and cotton were also grown, though in small amounts for local use.

As for the reliance on livestock, the wills do not support the picture of large herds that the McDonalds and McWhiney draw. Hogs, cattle, horses, and sheep were listed, but not in great numbers.[48] In his study of colonial North Carolina, Harry Roy Merrens points out that during the 1780s, when piedmont settlers were driving large numbers of cattle to northern markets, the average size of herds was six to sixteen head.[49] In southwestern North Carolina, hogs were the most common type of stock raised, the average holding being twenty-two hogs, with seven estates listing over thirty. Cattle were held in smaller numbers, with an average holding of eight and with three estates listing over twenty. Sheep, listed in only half of the wills and inventories, averaged six per estate.[50] Finally, according to the agricultural census of 1850, in Cherokee County, where the land had been open to white settlement only since 1838, the average holdings were twenty-seven hogs, fourteen cattle, and eleven sheep, numbers quite comparable to those found in Haywood wills and inventories.[51]

Having examined the changing dimensions of the Scotch-Irish element in southwestern North Carolina, the decline of Presbyterianism, and the regional land-use and settlement patterns, the impression that remains is of a numerous and still identifiable people who were rapidly and quite willingly absorbing the colors of their surroundings. The McDonalds and McWhiney's contention that three-quarters of the settlers in the antebellum South were of Celtic origins is not borne out by the evidence, at least not for southwestern North Carolina, nor is their description of the Scotch-Irish as factious herders who scorned mere tillage. Mountain herds, though unquestionably important to the regional economy, were smaller—and tillage much more important—than the McDonalds and McWhiney would have it. It is our conclusion that the Scotch-Irish played a major role in formulating the kind of agriculture we do find, that they were highly proficient at it, and that they found it and the local social order of scattered family homesteads congenial to their experiences and expectations. If, as Evans argues, their land-use and settlement patterns are their most important contributions to American life, it was a way of life the Scotch-Irish shared with those around them. By 1840 ethnic identities must have been largely submerged in rural mountain culture by the appearance of new generations and new people. Yet a few still lived who had personal memories of a home across the ocean. James Patton, for one, lived until September 1845, and the census of 1850, the first to record place of birth, suggests another: 78-year-old Fannie Ferguson, widow of Robin Ferguson and one of the first settlers in the Crabtree community of Haywood County. By her name is the note: born "Tirone County, Ireland."

Notes

Abbreviations

AWM	*American Weekly Mercury*
Bos. N.L.	*Boston News Letter*
DB	Deed Book
HLA	Handley Library Archives, Winchester, Virginia
IESH	*Irish Economic and Social History*
JSH	*Journal of Southern History*
NNLGB	Northern Neck Land Grant Book, Virginia State Library and Archives, Richmond, Virginia
PRO	Public Records Office, Kew, London
Ormonde MSS	*Calendar of the Manuscripts of the Marquess of Ormonde*, n.s., 7 (London: Historical Manuscripts Commission, 1912)
OSM	Ordnance Survey Memoirs, Royal Irish Academy, Dublin
PGM	*Pennsylvania Genealogical Magazine*
PRONI	Public Record Office of Northern Ireland
TCD	Trinity College, Dublin
VSL&A	Virginia State Library and Archives, Richmond, Virginia
WB	Will Book
WMQ	*William and Mary Quarterly*

Foreword

I am grateful to Frank Lelievre, H. Tyler Blethen, and Curtis W. Wood, Jr., for their recollections of the symposium's origins.

1. Nathan Glazer and Daniel Patrick Moynihan, *Beyond the Melting Pot* (Cambridge, MA: M.I.T. Press, 1970), lxxvii.
2. *The Scotch-Irish in America, Proceedings of the Scotch-Irish Congress at Columbia, Tennessee, May 8–11, 1889* (Cincinnati: R. Clarke, 1889).
3. "Scotch-Irish," Grady McWhiney and Forrest McDonald, in *Encyclopedia of Southern Culture*, ed. Charles Reagan Wilson and William Ferris

(Chapel Hill: University of North Carolina Press, 1989). It is curious to note, though, that the entry for the Scotch-Irish occupies less space than those for Greeks, Gypsies, and Italians.

4.   Richard Blaustein, introduction to *A Portrait of Appalachia*, by Kenneth Murray (Boone, NC: Appalachian Consortium Press, 1985).

5.   *The Scotch-Irish in America*, 1889.

1. Introduction

1.   Kenneth W. Keller, "What is Distinctive about the Scotch-Irish?" in *Appalachian Frontiers: Settlement, Society and Development in the Preindustrial Era*, ed. Robert D. Mitchell (Lexington: University Press of Kentucky, 1990), 70; Maldwyn A. Jones, "The Scotch-Irish in British America," in *Strangers Within the Realm: Cultural Margins of the First British Empire*, ed. Bernard Bailyn and Philip D. Morgan (Chapel Hill: University of North Carolina Press, 1991), 284–85.

2.   M. Perceval-Maxwell, *The Scottish Migration to Ulster in the Reign of James I* (London: Routledge & Kegan Paul, 1973); *The Outbreak of the Irish Rebellion of 1641* (Montreal: McGill-Queen's University Press, 1994).

3.   R. J. Dickson, *Ulster Emigration to Colonial America*, 2d ed. (Belfast: Ulster Historical Foundation, 1988); Louis Cullen, *The Emergence of Modern Ireland, 1600–1900* (London: Batsford Press, 1972).

4.   E. Estyn Evans, "The Scotch-Irish: Their Cultural Adaptation and Heritage in the American Old West," in *Essays in Scotch-Irish History*, ed. E. R. R. Green (London: Routledge and Kegan Paul, 1969), 86.

5.   James Leyburn, *The Scotch-Irish: A Social History* (Chapel Hill: University of North Carolina Press, 1962); David Hackett Fischer, *Albion's Seed: Four British Folkways in America* (New York: Oxford University Press, 1989); Rodger Cunningham, *Apples on the Flood: Minority Discourse and Appalachia* (Knoxville: University of Tennessee Press, 1987); and the following works by Forrest McDonald and Grady McWhiney: "The Antebellum Herdsman: A Reinterpretation," *JSH* 41 (1975): 147–66; "The South from Self-Sufficiency to Peonage: An Interpretation," *American Historical Review* 85 (1980): 1095–1118; "Celtic Origins of Southern Herding Practices," *JSH* 51 (1985): 165–82.

6.   See Paul Salstrom, *Appalachia's Path to Dependency: Rethinking a Region's Economic History, 1730–1940* (Lexington: University Press of Kentucky, 1994), xix.

7.   Karl Nicholas and Hal Farwell, *Smoky Mountain Voices: A Lexicon of Southern Appalachian Speech Based on the Research of Horace Kephart* (Lexington: University Press of Kentucky, 1993).

8.   For critical discussions of *Albion's Seed*, see "Albion's Seed: Four British Folkways in America—A Symposium," *WMQ* 48 (1991): 223–308; and

"Culture Wars: David Hackett Fischer's *Albion's Seed*," *Appalachian Journal* 19 (1992): 161–200.

9. David N. Doyle, *Ireland, Irishmen and Revolutionary America, 1760–1820* (Dublin and Cork: Mercier Press, 1981).

2. Prophecy and Prophylaxis: A Paradigm for the Scotch-Irish?

I am indebted to Athol Gow, with whom I am working on a study of Scottish prophecy.

1. James G. Leyburn, *The Scotch-Irish: A Social History* (Chapel Hill: University of North Carolina Press, 1962).
2. David Hackett Fischer, *Albion's Seed: Four British Folkways in America* (Oxford: Oxford University Press, 1989). See also Edward J. Cowan, "Back-home and the Back-country: David Fischer's *Borderlands* Revisited," *Appalachian Journal* 19 (1991): 166–73; and "The MacRoots Phenomenon or, the Myth of Scottish America," *Now and Then* 9 (1992): 24–25.
3. Edward J. Cowan, "Myth and Identity in Early Medieval Scotland," *Scottish Historical Review* (1984): 111–24.
4. Kenneth Jackson, *The Gododdin* (Edinburgh: Edinburgh University Press, 1969).
5. Geoffrey of Monmouth, *The History of Kings of Britain*, trans. Lewis Thorpe (Harmondsworth: Penguin Books, 1966), 170–85.
6. Robin Frame, *The Political Development of the British Isles 1100–1400* (Oxford: Oxford University Press, 1990), 140.
7. James A. M. L. Murray, ed., *The Romance and Prophecies of Thomas of Erceldoune* (London: Early English Text Society, 1875), xxx.
8. Francis James Child, *English and Scottish Popular Ballads*, ed. H. C. Sargent and G. L. Kittredge (Boston and New York: Houghton Mifflin, 1904), 63–66.
9. Murray, *The Romance and Prophecies of Thomas of Erceldoune*, xlii–xliii, lxxxv.
10. Arthur H. Williamson, *Scottish National Consciousness in the Age of James VI* (Edinburgh: John Donald Publishers, 1979), 21–24, 102–3.
11. *Collection of Ancient Scottish Prophecies in Alliterative Verse: Reprinted from Waldegrave's Edition MDCIII* (Edinburgh: Bannatyne Club, 1833), 16–17.
12. I am indebted to Tim Sauer of the University of Guelph library for compiling a bibliography of the editions of *The Whole Prophecies of Scotland*.
13. Alexander Mackenzie, *The Prophecies of the Brahan Seer* (Stirling: Eneas Mackay, 1899 and subsequent editions).
14. Hilda Davidson, ed., *The Seer in Celtic and Other Traditions* (Edinburgh: John Donald Publishers, 1989), 22.

15.   Ibid., 11.
16.   Gillian Bennett, *Tradition of Belief: Women and the Supernatural* (London: Penguin, 1987), 15, following David J. Hufford, *The Terror That Comes in the Night: An Experience-Centred Study of Supernatural Assault Traditions* (Philadelphia: University of Pennsylvania Press, 1982).
17.   Murray, *The Romance and Prophecies of Thomas of Erceldoune*, lxii.
18.   James King Hewison, *The Covenanters: A History of the Church in Scotland from the Reformation to the Revolution*, 2 vols. (Glasgow: John Smith and Sons, 1913), 2:11, 434ff. See also Ian B. Cowan, *The Scottish Covenanters 1660–88* (London: Victor Gollancz, 1976).
19.   On the legends that grew up around covenanting persecution, see the classic by Robert Wodrow, *Analecta: or Materials for a History of Remarkable Providences* (Edinburgh: Maitland Club, 1842); and James Aikman, *Annals of the Persecution in Scotland from the Restoration to the Revolution* (Edinburgh: Hugh Paton, 1842).
20.   For example, Cowan, *The Scottish Covenanters*.
21.   Leyburn, *The Scotch-Irish*, 61.
22.   See Marilyn Jeanne Westerkamp, *Triumph of the Laity: Scots-Irish Piety and the Great Awakening 1625–1760* (New York: Oxford University Press, 1988), 15–73. A parallel study that underplays the Irish dimension is Leigh Eric Schmidt, *Holy Fairs: Scottish Communions and American Revivals in the Early Modern Period* (Princeton, NJ: Princeton University Press, 1989).
23.   Andrew Hook, *Scotland and America: A Study of Cultural Relations, 1750–1835* (Glasgow: Blackie, 1975), especially chap. 5.
24.   Gregory G. Smith, *Scottish Literature: Character and Influence* (London: MacMillan & Co., 1919), 19.
25.   Hugh MacDiarmid, *Scottish Eccentrics* (London: George Routledge & Sons, 1963), 284.

3. Ulster Presbyterians: Religion, Culture, and Politics, 1660–1850

1.   William Macafee, "The Population of Ulster, 1630–1841" (D.Phil. thesis, University of Ulster, 1987), 74–75.
2.   Raymond Gillespie, "The Presbyterian Revolution in Ulster, 1660–1690," in *The Churches, Ireland and the Irish*, ed. W. J. Sheils and Diana Wood (Oxford: Oxford University Press, 1989), 159–70; M. J. Westerkamp, *Triumph of the Laity: Scots-Irish Piety and the Great Awakening, 1625–1760* (Oxford: Oxford University Press, 1988), chap. 1.
3.   David Stevenson, *Scottish Covenanters and Irish Confederates* (Belfast: Ulster Historical Foundation, 1981); T. C. Barnard, *Cromwellian Ireland, 1649–1660* (Oxford: Oxford University Press, 1975), 122–26.
4.   J. I. McGuire, "The Dublin Convention, the Protestant Community and the Emergence of an Ecclesiastical Settlement in 1660," in *Parliament*

and *Community*, ed. Art Cosgrove and J. I. McGuire (Belfast: Appletree Press, 1983), 121–46.

5. John Neville, "Irish Presbyterians under the Restored Stuart Monarchy," *Eire-Ireland* 16 (1981): 2.

6. J. C. Beckett, "Irish-Scottish Relations in the Seventeenth Century," in *Confrontations: Studies in Irish History* (London: Faber, 1972); *Calendar of the Manuscripts of the Marquess of Ormonde* (London: Historical Manuscripts Commission, 1912), 7:96, 102, 108, 181.

7. Macafee, "The Population of Ulster, 1630–1841," 94–103.

8. J. C. Beckett, *Protestant Dissent in Ireland, 1687–1780* (London: Faber & Faber, 1948), 40–63; David W. Hayton, *Ireland after the Glorious Revolution* (Belfast: PRONI, 1976), 6–10, 23.

9. Beckett, *Protestant Dissent in Ireland, 1687–1780*, 71–96.

10. K. Theodore Hoppen, *Elections, Politics and Society in Ireland 1832–1885* (Oxford: Clarendon Press, 1984), 265.

11. Brian M. Walker, *Ulster Politics: The Formative Years, 1868–86* (Belfast: Ulster Historical Foundation, 1989), 32. See also Richard McMinn, "Presbyterians and Politics in Ulster, 1871–1900," *Studia Hibernica* 21 (1981): 127–32.

12. John Stevenson, *Two Centuries of Life in Down, 1600–1800* (Belfast: McCaw, Stevenson and Orr, 1920), 169–87; J. M. Barkley, "The Presbyterian Minister in Eighteenth-Century Ireland," in *Challenge and Conflict: Essays in Irish Presbyterian History and Doctrine*, ed. J. L. M. Haire et al. (Antrim: W. & G. Baird, 1981), 52–53.

13. King to William Wake, archbishop of Canterbury, March 24, 1716, TCD, Ms 2533, p. 165; King to St. George Ashe, February 8, 1716, TCD, p. 135.

14. L. M. Cullen, *The Emergence of Modern Ireland, 1600–1900* (London: Batsford Academic and Educational, 1981), 55–56.

15. A. C. Hepburn, "Work, Class and Religion in Belfast 1871–1911," *IESH* 10 (1983): 33–50.

16. William Shaw Mason, *A Statistical Account or Parochial Survey of Ireland* (Dublin: Gainsberry and Campbell, 1814–19), 1:314.

17. Angelique Day and Patrick McWilliams, eds., *Ordnance Survey Memoirs of Ireland*, vol. 2, *Parishes of County Antrim (i) 1838–9* (Belfast: Institute of Irish Studies, 1990), 2:113, 11.

18. *Calendar of State Papers Relating to Ireland 1660–62* (London: Her Majesty's Stationery Office, 1860–1912 [24 vols.]), 164–65.

19. Samuel M'Skimmin, *Narrative of Some Strange Events that Took Place in Island Magee and Neighbourhood in 1711* (Belfast: J. Smyth, 1822), 12.

20. OSM, 12/III/2; John Dubourdieu, *Statistical Survey of the County of Antrim* (Dublin: Dublin Society, 1812), 497–98.

21. For example, Day and McWilliams, eds., *Ordnance Survey Memoirs of Ireland*, 2:12, 24, 63.

22. OSM 47/III/1, Termoneeny, County Londonderry (1836); Mason, *A Statistical Account*, 1:124 and 3:207.

23. Mason, 1:594.

24. Historical Manuscripts Commission, *Ormond Manuscripts* 8 (1920): 78, 86, 112, 132.

25. A. T. Q. Stewart, " 'The Harp New Strung': Nationalism, Culture and the United Irishmen," in *Ireland and Irish Australia*, ed. Oliver MacDonough and W. F. Mandle (London: Croom Helm, 1986), 261–62.

26. PRONI, Dio 4/5/3/84, examinations against James Henderson and others.

27. Caroline Robbins, *The Eighteenth-Century Commonwealthman* (Cambridge, MA: Harvard University Press, 1959), 168–85; A. T. Q. Stewart, *A Deeper Silence: The Hidden Origins of the United Irish Movement* (London: Faber and Faber, 1993).

28. Sean Murphy, "The Dublin Anti-Union Riot of 3 December 1759," in *Parliament, Politics and People*, ed. Gerard O'Brien (Dublin: Irish Academic Press, 1989), 59.

29. For a discussion of the unusual independence of the County Antrim electorate, as well as of the limitations of the challenge offered even there to landlord control, see Edith M. Johnston, *Great Britain and Ireland, 1760–1800: A Study in Public Administration* (Edinburgh: Oliver & Boyd, 1963), 179–87.

30. Stewart, " 'The Harp New Strung,' "; Marianne Elliott, *Partners in Revolution: The United Irishmen and France* (New Haven: Yale University Press, 1982), 21–23, 46–48, 67–68, 95–96; Nancy J. Curtin, "The Transformation of the Society of United Irishmen into a Mass-Based Revolutionary Organisation, 1794–6," *Irish Historical Studies* 24 (1986): 468–73, 486–88; "Paine and Ireland," in *The United Irishmen*, ed. David Dickson, Daire Keogh, and Kevin Whelan (Dublin, 1993), 138.

31. J. R. R. Adams, *The Printed Word and the Common Man: Popular Culture in Ulster, 1700–1900* (Belfast: Institute of Irish Studies, 1987), 38–40; R. B. McDowell, *Ireland in the Age of Imperialism and Revolution, 1760–1801* (Oxford: Clarendon Press, 1979), 473.

32. David W. Miller, "Presbyterianism and 'Modernisation' in Ulster," *Past & Present* 80 (1978): 77–84.

33. A. T. Q. Stewart, "The Transformation of Presbyterian Radicalism in the North of Ireland, 1792–1825," master's thesis, Queen's University, Belfast (1956), 111–39, 152.

34. National Archives, Dublin, State of the Country Papers 1091/6, Major General A. Campbell, Belfast, December 2, 1806; G. F. Hill to Peel, March 9, 1806, State of the Country Papers, 1567/10; Edward Wakefield, *An Account of Ireland, Statistical and Political* (London: Printed for Longman, Hurst, Rees, Orme, and Brown, 1812), 2:547.

35. OSM 8/II/1, p. 22.

36. W. J. O'Neill Daunt, *Personal Recollections of the Late Daniel O'Connell M.P.* (London: Chapman and Hall, 1848), 2:7.

37. Information signed "S.C.," June 3, 1798, Rebellion Papers 620/38/36, National Archives, Dublin; enclosure in Earl of Carysfort to Grenville, November 13, 1803 (Historical Manuscripts Commission, *Calendar of*

the *Manuscripts of J. B. Fortescue Esq.*, *Preserved at Dropmore*, 10 vols. [London: 1892–1927], 7:196).

38. Stewart, "The Transformation of Presbyterian Radicalism in the North of Ireland, 1792–1825," 194–95.

39. R. Finlay Holmes, *Henry Cooke* (Belfast: Christian Journals, 1981), 109–20, 176–83, 205–8.

40. Hoppen, *Elections, Politics and Society in Ireland, 1832–1885*, 265–73.

41. Day and McWilliams, eds., *Ordnance Survey Memoirs of Ireland*, 2:23; OSM, 9/III/3, p. 56.

42. Walker, *Ulster Politics*, 143.

43. R. F. G. Holmes, "Controversy and Schism in the Synod of Ulster in the 1820's," in *Challenge and Conflict*, Haire et al. 26–28.

44. For a fuller discussion of this theme, see Peter Brooke, *Ulster Presbyterianism: The Historical Perspective 1610–1970* (Dublin: Gill and Macmillan, 1987), 190–91; Miller, "Presbyterianism and 'Modernisation,' " 85–90.

45. Brooke, *Ulster Presbyterianism*, 228, n. 151.

4. The Demographic History of Ulster, 1750–1841

1. K. H. Connell, *The Population of Ireland, 1750–1845* (Oxford: Oxford University Press, 1950).

2. The first critique of Connell's work was by Michael Drake, "Marriage and Population Growth in Ireland, 1750–1845," *Economic History Review*, 2d ser., 16 (1963): 301–13. However, Joseph Lee, "Marriage and Population in Pre-Famine Ireland," *Economic History Review*, 2d ser., 21 (1968): 283–95, was not convinced that Drake had succeeded in excluding falling age at marriage as a possible factor in pre-Famine demographic change and concluded that if the conflicting hypotheses were to be tested, more use would have to be made of parish registers. This led to a series of papers by Valerie Morgan: "The Church of Ireland Registers of St. Patrick's, Coleraine, as a Source for the Study of a Local Pre-Famine Population," *Ulster Folklife* 19 (1973): 56–67; "Mortality in Magherafelt, County Derry, in the Early Eighteenth Century," *Irish Historical Studies* 19 (1974): 125–35; "A Case Study of Population Change over Two Centuries: Blaris, Lisburn, 1661–1848," *IESH* 3 (1976): 5–16. The findings related to Magherafelt were revised in William Macafee and Valerie Morgan, "Historical Revision XXI: Mortality in Magherafelt, County Derry, in the Early Eighteenth Century," *Irish Historical Studies* 23 (1982): 50–60. More recently, work by the present author and Morgan has looked more closely at age at marriage: Valerie Morgan and William Macafee, "Irish Population in the Pre-Famine Period: Evidence from County Antrim," *Economic History Review*, 2d ser., 37 (1984): 182–96, as well as William Macafee, "Pre-Famine Population in Ulster: Evidence from the Parish Register of Killyman," in *Rural Ireland: Modernisation and Change, 1600–1900*, ed. Patrick O'Flanagan, Paul Ferguson, and

Kevin Whelan (Cork: Cork University Press, 1987). This latter work was extended in William Macafee, "The Population Of Ulster, 1630–1841: Evidence from Mid-Ulster" (unpublished D.Phil. thesis, University of Ulster, Coleraine, 1987). Other sources, particularly the Census and Hearth Returns, have been reassessed in Joseph Lee, "On the Accuracy of the pre-Famine Irish Censuses," in *Irish Population, Economy, and Society: Essays in Honour of the Late K. H. Connell*, ed. J. M. Goldstrom and L. A. Clarkson (Oxford: Oxford University Press, 1981), 37–56; and David Dickson, Cormac O'Grada, and Stuart Daultrey, "Hearth Tax, Household Size, and Irish Population Change, 1672–1821," *Proceedings of the Royal Irish Academy* 82 (1982): 125–81. In addition to these more detailed studies, there have been a number of general critiques and attempts at reinterpreting the pre-Famine demographic history of Ireland. The most important of these are L. A. Clarkson, "Irish Population Revisited, 1687–1821," in *Irish Population, Economy, and Society: Essays in Honour of the Late K. H. Connell*, ed. J. M. Goldstrom and L. A. Clarkson (Oxford: Clarendon Press, 1981), 13–35; and Joel Mokyr and Cormac O'Grada, "New Developments in Irish Population History, 1700–1850," *Economic History Review*, 2d ser., 37 (1984): 473–88. Contemporaneous with these revisions of Irish demographic history there has been a reinterpretation of economic history. Most prominent in this field has been the work of L. M. Cullen: "Problems in the Interpretation and Revision of Eighteenth Century Irish Economic History," *Transactions of the Royal Historical Society*, 1st ser., 17 (1966): 1–22; *Anglo-Irish Trade, 1660–1800* (Manchester: Manchester University Press, 1968); *An Economic History of Ireland since 1660* (London: Batsford Press, 1972); *The Emergence of Modern Ireland, 1600–1900* (London: Batsford Press, 1981); "Population Growth and Diet, 1600–1850," in *Irish Population, Economy, and Society*, ed. Goldstrom and Clarkson, 89–112. Within Ulster the work of W. H. Crawford has been the most prominent: "The Origins of the Linen Industry in North Armagh and the Lagan Valley," *Ulster Folklife* 17 (1971): 42–51; "Ulster Landowners and the Linen Industry," in *Land and Industry*, ed. J. T. Ward and R. T. Wilson (Newton Abbot: David and Charles, 1971); *Domestic Industry in Ireland: The Experience of the Linen Industry* (Dublin: Gill and Macmillan, 1972); "Landlord-Tenant Relations in Ulster, 1609–1820," *IESH* 2 (1975): 5–21; "Economy and Society in South Ulster in the Eighteenth Century," *Clogher Record* (1975), 241–58; "Change in Ulster in the Late Eighteenth Century," in *Penal Era and Golden Age*, ed. Thomas Bartlett and D. W. Hayton (Belfast: Ulster Historical Foundation, 1979), 186–203.

3. Connell, *The Population of Ireland, 1750–1845*, 10.
4. Ibid., 13, 25.
5. Ibid., 24–25.
6. Dickson et al., "Hearth Tax, Household Size, and Irish Population Change, 1672–1821."
7. G. A. T. O'Brien, *The Economic History of Ireland in the Eighteenth Century* (Dublin: Maunsel, 1918).

8. Cullen, *The Emergence of Modern Ireland, 1600–1900*, 25.
9. Ibid., 26.
10. Cullen, "Problems in the Interpretation and Revision of Eighteenth Century Irish Economic History," 11–13.
11. Ibid., 13.
12. W. H. Crawford, *Eighteenth Century Emigration: Thomas Davis Lecture* (Dublin: Radio Telefis Eireann, 1972), 3.
13. Cullen, *Anglo-Irish Trade, 1660–1800*, 214–15.
14. Clarkson, "Irish Population Revisited, 1687–1821," 17.
15. Dickson et al., "Hearth Tax, Household Size, and Irish Population Change, 1672–1821," 134–43.
16. Clarkson, "Irish Population Revisited, 1687–1821," 26.
17. Dickson et al., "Hearth Tax, Household Size, and Irish Population Change, 1672–1821," 144–45.
18. Clarkson, "Irish Population Revisited, 1687–1821," 24.
19. Dickson et al., "Hearth Tax, Household Size, and Irish Population Change, 1672–1821," 153.
20. Macafee, "The Population of Ulster, 1630–1841," 148–58, 205–9.
21. These figures are taken from Gearoid O'Tuathaigh, *Ireland before the Famine* (Dublin: Gill and Macmillan, 1972), 129.
22. These growth rates have been taken from M. W. Flinn, *The European Demographic System* (Brighton: Harvester Press, 1981), 124–27.
23. Drake, "Marriage and Population Growth in Ireland, 1750–1845," 312.
24. Morgan, "A Case Study of Population Change over Two Centuries," 12, and "Mortality in Magherafelt, County Derry, in the Early Eighteenth Century," 130–31.
25. Macafee, "The Population of Ulster, 1630–1841," 107–8.
26. Ibid., 114–19.
27. Ibid., 160–64.
28. Cullen, "Population Growth and Diet, 1600–1850," 95.
29. Cullen, *The Emergence of Modern Ireland, 1600–1900*, 93–94.
30. Ibid., 93.
31. Clarkson, "Irish Population Revisited, 1687–1821," 33.
32. John Walter and Roger Schofield, eds., *Famine, Disease and the Social Order in Early Modern Society* (Cambridge: Cambridge University Press, 1991).
33. E. A. Wrigley and R. S. Schofield, *The Population History of England, 1541–1871: A Reconstruction* (London: Edward Arnold, 1981).
34. Connell, *The Population of Ireland, 1750–1845*, 50–52.
35. Mokyr and O'Grada, "New Developments in Irish Population History, 1700–1850," 477.
36. Morgan and Macafee, "Irish Population in the Pre-Famine Period," 186–87.
37. Kevin O'Neill, *Family and Farm in Pre-Famine Ireland: The Parish of Killashandra* (Madison: University of Wisconsin Press, 1984).
38. Morgan, "The Church of Ireland Registers of St. Patrick's, Coleraine," 62.
39. William Macafee and Valerie Morgan, "Population in Ulster, 1660–

1760," in *Plantation to Partition: Essays in Honour of J. L. McCracken,* ed. Peter Roebuck (Belfast: Blackstaff Press, 1981), 56.

40.   D. Dickson, "A Note on the Cromwellian Transplantation Certificates" (unpublished paper, Trinity College, Dublin, 1982).

41.   D. E. C. Eversley, "The Demography of the Irish Quakers, 1650–1850," in *Irish Population, Economy, and Society,* ed. Goldstrom and Clarkson, 57–88.

42.   Macafee, "Pre-Famine Population in Ulster," and "The Population of Ulster, 1630–1841."

43.   Church of Ireland register of baptisms, marriages, and burials for the parish of Killyman, PRONI, T.679/383, 384, 386, 387, and 393.

44.   For a fuller discussion of the method used, see Macafee, "The Population of Ulster, 1630–1841," 173–74.

45.   Mokyr and O'Grada,. "New Developments in Irish Population History, 1700–1850," 479.

46.   Flinn, *The European Demographic System,* 124–27.

47.   Clarkson, "Irish Population Revisited, 1687–1821," 35.

48.   Cullen, "Population Growth and Diet, 1600–1850," 94.

49.   For a fuller discussion of the method used, see Macafee, "The Population of Ulster, 1630–1841," 170–71.

50.   Conrad Gill, *The Rise of the Irish Linen Industry* (Oxford: Clarendon Press, 1925), 221–26.

51.   Church of Ireland register of baptisms, marriages, and burials for the parish of Donaghmore, PRONI, T.679/17, T.786.

52.   Church of Ireland register of baptisms, marriages, and burials for the parish of Magheralin, PRONI, T.679/376.

53.   Connell, *The Population of Ireland, 1750–1845,* 29.

54.   Mokyr and O'Grada, "New Developments in Irish Population History, 1700–1845," 473.

55.   Macafee, "The Population of Ulster, 1630–1841," 31–32.

56.   Dickson et al., "Hearth Tax, Household Size, and Irish Population Change, 1672–1821," 170.

57.   K. F. Helleiner, "The Vital Revolution Reconsidered," in *Population in History: Essays in Historical Demography,* ed. D. V. Glass and D. E. C. Eversley (Chicago: Aldine, 1965), 79–86.

5. The Household Economy in Early Rural America and Ulster: The Question of Self-Sufficiency

1.   Benjamin Franklin, 1772, quoted in Gary B. Nash, "Urban Wealth and Poverty in Pre-Revolutionary America," *Journal of Interdisciplinary History* 6 (1976): 545.

2.   D. Forde and M. Douglas, "Primitive Economics," in *Tribal and Peasant Economies,* ed. George Dalton (Austin, TX: University of Texas Press, 1978), 48.

3.   J. Bell, "Relations of Mutual Help between Ulster Farmers," *Ulster Folk-life* 24 (1978): 48.
4.   See, for example, Duane E. Ball, "Dynamics of Population and Wealth in Eighteenth-Century Chester County, Pennsylvania," *Journal of Interdisciplinary History* 6 (1976); J. P. Greene and J. R. Pole, *Colonial British America: Essays in the New History of the Early Modern Era* (Baltimore: Johns Hopkins University Press, 1984); J. A. Henretta, *The Evolution of American Society, 1700–1815: An Interdisciplinary Analysis* (Lexington, MA: Heath Publishing, 1973); J. A. Henretta, "Families and Farms: Mentalité in Pre-Industrial America," *WMQ*, 3d ser., 35 (1978); J. T. Lemon, *The Best Poor Man's Country: A Geographical Study of Early Southeastern Pennsylvania* (Baltimore: Johns Hopkins University Press, 1972); J. T. Lemon, "Early American Economy and Society," *Agricultural History Review* 35 (1987); John J. McCusker and R. R. Menard, *The Economy of British America, 1667–1789* (Chapel Hill: Published for the Institute of Early American History and Culture by the University of North Carolina Press, 1985); J. T. Main, *Society and Economy in Colonial Connecticut* (Princeton, NJ: Princeton University Press, 1985); Michael Merril, " 'Cash is Good to Eat': Self-Sufficiency and Exchange in the Rural Economy of the United States," *Radical History Review* 4 (1977); R. D. Mitchell, *Commercialism and Frontier: Perspectives on the Early Shenandoah Valley* (Charlottesville: University of Virginia Press, 1972); G. H. Nobles, "Breaking into the Back Country: New Approaches to the American Frontier," *WMQ*, 3d ser., 46 (1989); Carole Shammas, "How Self-Sufficient Was Early America?" *Journal of Interdisciplinary History* 13 (1982); J. B. Pruitt, "Self-Sufficiency and the Agricultural Economy of Eighteenth-Century Massachusetts," *WMQ*, 3d ser., 41 (1984); Daniel Vickers, "Competency and Culture in Early America," *WMQ*, 3d ser., 47 (1990).
5.   Shammas, "How Self-Sufficient Was Early America?" 252.
6.   Pruitt, "Self-Sufficiency and the Agricultural Economy of Eighteenth-Century Massachusetts," 333.
7.   Mitchell, *Commercialism and Frontier*, 133–60.
8.   Lemon, *Best Poor Man's Country*, 180.
9.   Nobles, "Breaking into the Back Country," 656.
10. Pruitt, "Self-Sufficiency and the Agricultural Economy of Eighteenth-Century Massachusetts," 349.
11. See especially the following by W. H. Crawford: "The Significance of Landed Estates in Ulster, 1600–1820," *IESH* 17, no. 18 (1990): 44–61; "The Political Economy of Linen: Ulster in the Eighteenth Century," in *Ulster: An Illustrated History*, ed. Ciarah Brady, Mary O'Dowd, and Brian Walker (London: Batsford Press, 1989); "Economy and Society in South Ulster in the Eighteenth Century," *Clogher Record* 8 (1975): 241–58; *Domestic Industry in Ireland: The Emergence of the Linen Industry* (Belfast: PRONI, 1972). See also L. M. Cullen, *The Emergence of Modern Ireland, 1600–1900* (London: Batsford Press, 1981), and the following by

Raymond Gillespie: *Settlement and Survival on an Ulster Estate: The Brownlow Leasebook, 1667–1711* (Belfast: PRONI, 1988); *Colonial Ulster: The Settlement of East Ulster, 1600–1641* (Cork: Cork University Press, 1985); "The Small Towns of Ulster, 1600–1700," *Ulster Folklife* 36 (1990): 23–31. Also see G. E. Kirkham, " 'To Pay the Rent and Lay up Riches': Economic Opportunity in Eighteenth-Century North West Ulster," in *Economy and Society in Scotland and Ireland, 1500–1939*, ed. R. Mitchison and P. Roebuck (Edinburgh: John Donald Press, 1988), 95–104; Phillip Robinson, *The Plantation of Ulster: British Settlement in an Irish Landscape, 1600–1670* (Dublin: Gill and Macmillan, 1984).

12.   Quoted in L. M. Cullen, "Economic Development, 1691–1750," in *A New History of Ireland*, ed. T. W. Moody (Oxford: Oxford University Press, 1986), 4:135.

13.   Ibid., 123.

14.   J. H. Andrews, "Land and People, c. 1685," in *A New History of Ireland*, ed. T. W. Moody, F. X. Martin, and F. J. Byrne (Oxford: Oxford University Press, 1976), 3:459.

15.   See, for example, V. Morgan and W. Macafee, "Population in Ulster, 1660–1760," in *Plantation to Partition: Essays in Honour of J. L. McCracken*, ed. P. Roebuck (Belfast: Blackstaff Press, 1981), 46–63.

16.   L. M. Cullen, "Economic Development, 1691–1750," 140–43; see also D. Dickson, *New Foundations: Ireland, 1660–1800* (Dublin: Gill and Macmillan, 1987), 95–103.

17.   Rev. W. Henry, "A Natural History of the Parish of Killesher," MS vol. G.I. 14, Armagh Public Library, Armagh.

18.   Ibid., 10.

19.   Ibid., 12–13.

20.   Ibid., 6.

21.   Charles O'Hara, "Survey of the Economic Development of Co. Sligo," PRONI, T2812/19/1, year 1700.

22.   Ibid., years 1717 and 1718.

23.   Ibid., October 6 and 18, 1764.

24.   Ibid.

25.   Ibid., January 12, 1766.

26.   Arthur Young, *A Tour in Ireland, 1776–1779* (Dublin: Irish University Press Reprint, 1970), 1:120.

27.   Alan Gailey, "The Ballyhagan Inventories, 1716–1740," *Ulster Folklife* 15 (1977): 36.

28.   These related to the contents of Springhill House, Moneymore, County Tyrone, in 1787, and Ballynesport House, Lecale, County Down, in 1731.

29.   Farm Accounts, Orr Family, Glassdrummond, PRONI, T3301.

30.   Farm Accounts, Holmes Family, Moyar, County Tyrone, PRONI, D1782/3.

31.   Mick Reed, " 'Gnawing it Out': A New Look at Economic Relations in Nineteenth-Century Rural England," *Rural History* 1 (1990): 83.

32.   Ibid.

33. Ibid., 84.
34. Ibid., 83.
35. Ibid., 92.
36. C. Clarke, "Economics and Culture: Change in Rural Massachusetts, 1780–1860" (unpublished paper presented to the "Peasants" seminar, Institute of Commonwealth Studies, University of London, March 1987), as quoted in Reed, "Gnawing it Out," 91.
37. Reed, "Gnawing it Out," 91.
38. Ibid., 92.

6. Ulster Emigration to North America, 1680–1720

1. The research on which this paper is based was partly conducted under the auspices of the Garfield Weston Research Project, "Emigration from Ulster to North America," at the University of Ulster at Coleraine, 1982–85. Acknowledgments are due to the following individuals and institutions for permission to cite and quote from documents: the late Lord Carew; the late Sir John Heygate; the late Mrs. Lenox Conyngham; the late H. K. Worsley; Dermot O'Hara, Esq.; the Irish Georgian Society; the Merchant Taylors' Company, London; the Public Record Office, London (Crown copyright); the Deputy Keeper of the Records, Public Record Office of Northern Ireland; Essex Record Office; the Board of Trinity College Dublin; Dublin Corporation—Gilbert Library; Library Company of Philadelphia; Scottish Record Office; the executors of the late Mrs. Murray Usher; Baker Library, Graduate School of Business Administration, Harvard University.

2. TCD, MS 750/5, pp. 79–80, King to Rev. Henry Maule, November 29, 1718. I am indebted to Dr. Sean Connolly for providing me with this and other references from Archbishop King's correspondence.

3. A. C. Myers, *Immigration of the Irish Quakers into Pennsylvania, 1682–1750* (Swarthmore, PA: 1902; reprint, Baltimore, MD: Genealogical Publishing Co., 1969), 53, 61, table between 82–83. See also Marion Balderston, "William Penn's Twenty-three Ships," PGM 23 (1963): 27–67; Balderston, "Pennsylvania's 1683 Ships and Some of Their Passengers," PGM 24 (1965): 76–77, 92–93, 98.

4. N. C. Landsman, *Scotland And Its First American Colony, 1683–1765* (Princeton, NJ: Princeton University Press, 1985), 113–14, 144n. R. J. Dickson notes one of the promoters' volumes as having been published in Belfast in the early 1680s in *Ulster Emigration to Colonial America, 1718–1775* (London: Routledge and Kegan Paul, 1966; reprint, Belfast: Ulster Historical Foundation, 1988), 86n., 303.

5. H. J. Ford, *The Scotch-Irish in America* (Princeton, NJ: Princeton University Press, 1915), 215; Landsman, *Scotland And Its First American Colony, 1683–1765*, 103–4.

6. *Ormonde MSS*, 59–60, Viscount Mountjoy, Newtownstewart, County

Tyrone, to Duke of Ormonde, July 2, 1683; *Ormonde MSS*, 107, same to same, August 17, 1683. I am indebted to Dr. Raymond Gillespie for drawing my attention to these references.

7.   Wait Winthrop, Boston, to Fitz-John Winthrop, Connecticut, December 29, 1684, quoted in C. K. Bolton, *Scotch Irish Pioneers in Ulster and America* (Boston: Bacon and Brown, 1910), 12–13.

8.   William Macafee, "The Population of Ulster, 1630–1841: Evidence from Mid Ulster" (unpublished D.Phil. thesis, University of Ulster, 1987), 107–8; *Ormonde MSS*, 175–76, Capt. William Hamilton, Caledon, County Armagh, to William Ellis, January 2, 1683/4; J. S. Curl, *The Londonderry Plantation, 1609–1914* (Chichester, Sussex: Phillimore, 1986), 98; J. H. Andrews, "Land and People, c. 1685," in *A New History of Ireland: III, Early Modern Ireland, 1534–1691*, ed. T. W. Moody, F. X. Martin, and F. J. Byrne (Oxford: Clarendon Press, 1976), 462.

9.   *Ormonde MSS*, 181, Viscount Mountjoy, Newtownstewart, to Duke of Ormonde, January 13, 1683/4.

10. A. G. Lecky, *The Laggan and its Presbyterianism* (Belfast: Davidson and McCormack, 1905); reprinted as *Roots of Presbyterianism in Donegal* (Omagh, County Tyrone: Graham and Sons, 1978), 17.

11. *Analecta Hibernica* 27 (1972): 157, [Capt.] Paul Rycaut, Dublin, to John Cooke, Whitehall, July 16, 1686. See also J. C. Beckett, *Protestant Dissent in Ireland, 1687–1780* (London: Faber and Faber, 1948), 21; *Ormonde MSS*, 423–24, Archbishop Boyle, Dublin, to Duke of Ormonde, June 5, 1686.

12. W. Macafee and V. Morgan, "Population in Ulster, 1660–1760," in *Plantation to Partition: Essays in Ulster History in Honour of J. L. McCracken*, ed. Peter Roebuck (Belfast: Blackstaff Press, 1981), 57; J. C. Beckett, "William King's Administration of the Diocese of Derry, 1691–1703," *Irish Historical Studies* 4 (1944): 171; Tom Bartlett, "The O'Haras of Annaghmore c. 1600–c. 1800: Survival and Revival," *IESH*, 40–41; TCD, MS 1995-2008/391, Bishop King [of Derry] to Archbishop of Canterbury, November 2, 1694; TCD, MUN/P/24/273, "Account of how the College Lands held by Capt. Hamilton are now set, and how before the Wars," n.d.

13. T. M. Truxes, *Irish-American Trade, 1600–1783* (Cambridge: Cambridge University Press, 1988), 20–22, 79.

14. PRONI, HAR 1F/1, Belfast harbour records 1683–87 (nineteenth century copy); PRO, CO 5/749(i), CO 5/1441, CO 5/848, f. 29, 21, Naval Office Shipping Lists for Maryland, Virginia, and Massachusetts.

15. Truxes, *Irish-American Trade, 1600–1783*, 22. Ralph Davis, in *Rise of the English Shipping Industry*, (Newton Abbot, Devon: David and Charles, 1972), 287, has suggested that most vessels involved in the tobacco trade carried passengers to offset uncertain trading conditions.

16. PRO, CO 5/1441, Naval Office Shipping List, Virginia.

17. Ford, *The Scotch-Irish in America*, 172–75, 178; Bolton, *Scotch Irish Pioneers in Ulster and America*, 21–23, 27–28; C. A. Hanna, *The Scotch-*

Irish (New York: G. P. Putnam and Sons, 1902; reprint, Baltimore, MD: Genealogical Publishing Co., 1968), 2:7, 107.

18. Quoted in Ford, *The Scotch-Irish in America*, 177. The work was probably George Scott, *A Brief Advertisement Concerning East New Jersey in America* (Edinburgh: John Reid, 1685). I am indebted to Dr. Sean Connolly for making this identification.

19. Edward Randolph, James City, to Commissioners of Customs, June 27, 1692, quoted in Bolton, *Scotch Irish Pioneers in Ulster and America*, 25. At least six Ulster vessels arrived in the Pocamoke naval district of Somerset County in the period 1689–92 (PRO, CO 5/749(i), Naval Office Shipping List, Maryland).

20. Sir Thomas Lawrence, Secretary of Maryland, June 25, 1695, quoted in Ford, *The Scotch-Irish in America*, 180.

21. *Calendar of State Papers, Colonial Series: America and the West Indies. Dec. 1, 1702–1703* (London: His Majesty's Stationery Office, 1913), 263, 269–70.

22. Dickson, *Ulster Emigration to Colonial America, 1718–1775*, 20.

23. PRO, CUST 15, Ledgers of Imports and Exports of Ireland. This source does not show individual voyages and does not distinguish between trade to North American destinations and the Caribbean.

24. Myers, *Immigration of the Irish Quakers into Pennsylvania, 1682–1750*, table between 82–83; Scotland General Assembly Papers, vol. 28, quoted in Sean Beattie, "Emigration from North Donegal," *Donegal Annual* 44 (1992): 14; *Boston News Letter* (hereafter cited as *Bos. N.L.*), June 3–10, 1717; E. S. Bolton, *Immigrants to New England, 1700–1775* (Salem, MA: 1931; reprint, Baltimore, MD: Genealogical Publishing Co., 1966), 149.

25. PRONI, D. 501, Macartney Letter Book, 1704–7; Ralph Davis, *The Rise of the Atlantic Economies* (London: Weidenfeld and Nicolson, 1973), 134–35; R. D. Mitchell, "American Origins and Regional Institutions: The Seventeenth Century Chesapeake," *Annals of the Association of American Geographers* 73 (1983): 409, 413–15.

26. PRONI, HAR 1F/1, unidentified press cuttings of antiquarian notes on Belfast trade, included in the diary of the Secretary of Belfast Harbour Commisioners for the early 1850s. This source also reports three sailings for Barbados. It is not clear whether the data relate to 1714–15 or 1715–16; PRO, CUST 15 shows exports from Belfast to the "Plantations" in both years.

27. See Appendix to chapter 6; *Dublin Courant*, August 19, 1721; *AWM*, August 17–24, 1721, and November 30–December 7, 1721; PRO, CO 5/1442, Naval Office Shipping Lists, Virginia, f. 13, 23; see D. N. Doyle, *Ireland, Irishmen and Revolutionary America, 1760–1820* (Cork: Mercier Press, 1981), 63; R. K. MacMaster, "Captain James Patton Comes to America, 1737–1740," *Augusta Historical Bulletin* 16 (1980): 5. See also Truxes, *Irish-American Trade, 1600–1783*, 143.

28. TCD, MS 2535, p. 80, King, Dublin, to Archbishop [of Canterbury]

Wake, February 6, 1717/18; TCD, MS 750/5, p. 23, King to Samuel Moly-neux, August 25, 1718.

29. Library Company of Philadelphia (on deposit at the Historical Society of Pennsylvania), Letter Book of Jonathan Dickinson, Dickinson to John Askew, October 24, 1717. I am extremely grateful to Mary Anne Hines of the Library Company of Philadelphia for supplying me with tran-scripts of this and other Dickinson letters.

30. Dickinson Letter Book, Dickinson to [Joshua Crosby], November 17, 1719; see also Dickinson Letter Book, Dickinson to John Harriot, No-vember 12, 1719.

31. W. T. Latimer, "Ulster Emigration to America," *Journal of the Royal So-ciety of Antiquaries of Ireland* 32 (1903): 387.

32. *Dublin Courant*, February 10, 1719. A Cavan family emigrated via Dub-lin in 1725; see George Francis Donovan, *The Pre-Revolutionary Irish in Massachusetts, 1620–1775* (Menosha, WI: Geo Banta, 1931; reprint, Ann Arbor, MI: University Microfilms, 1981), 84.

33. Bolton, *Scotch Irish Pioneers in Ulster and America*, 1.

34. Scottish Record Office, Broughton and Cally Muniments, GD, 10/1421/Vol. 1, 46, Alexander McCulloch, Ballycopeland, to [Alexan-der?] Murray, Scotland, September 1718.

35. PRONI, MIC 170/2, Edmond Kaine, Clones, County Monaghan, to Hon. Dacres Barrett, Essex, December 18, 1718. The original letters cited here and subsequently under this reference are held by the Essex Record Office, D/DL C24-40a.

36. PRONI, MIC 170/2, Kaine to Barrett, March 17, 1718/19. Fifty tates of land was probably equivalent to the same number of townlands and sug-gests the departure of a substantial number of households. Alexander Hamilton, one of the principal Ulster settlers on the Kennebec River in Maine, was from Enniskillen, County Fermanagh (PRONI, T. 580/1, Tran-scripts of the State Papers, Ireland, Humble Petition of Alexander Hamil-ton, May 1724).

37. PRONI, T. 2812/6/55, Patrick Brett, Cloonamanagh, to Kean O'Hara, Dublin, November 14, 1718. I am indebted to Dr. Sean Conolly for this reference.

38. Dickson, *Ulster Emigration to Colonial America, 1718–1775*, 25–31. K. A. Miller, however, has recently reasserted the primacy of Presbyte-rian "oppressions" in prompting the exodus of the late 1710s; see *Emi-grants and Exiles: Ireland and the Irish Exodus to North America* (Oxford: Oxford University Press, 1985), 158–59.

39. Dickson, *Ulster Emigration to Colonial America, 1718–1775*, 25.

40. *Records of the General Synod of Ulster from 1691–1820* (Belfast: Synod of the Presbyterian Church, 1890), 1:274, 275, 296, 322, 329, 336, 350, 455, 456, 486; James Seaton Reid, *History of the Presbyterian Church in Ireland*, ed. W. D. Killen, 3 vols. (Belfast: W. Mullan, 1867), 3:47; Dick-son, *Ulster Emigration to Colonial America, 1718–1775*, 27–28.

41. Introduction by Rev. Increase Mather to a sermon of Boyd's, printed in

Boston in 1719, quoted in Bolton, *Scotch Irish Pioneers in Ulster and America*, 92; Dickson, *Ulster Emigration to Colonial America, 1718–1775*, 21.

42. Reid, *History of the Presbyterian Church in Ireland*, 3:58–59, 67–80, 88–89; Beckett, *Protestant Dissent in Ireland*, 111–12; Dickson, *Ulster Emigration to Colonial America, 1718–1775*, 26–27.

43. Ibid., 31.

44. Reid, *History of the Presbyterian Church in Ireland*, 2:472, 2:522–23, 3:85n.; TCD, MS 1489/2, p. 187, Bishop King, Derry, to [?], Annesley, April 6, 1703; Beckett, *Protestant Dissent in Ireland, 1687–1780*, 85–86, 142–43.

45. Beckett, *Protestant Dissent in Ireland, 1687–1780*, 139–41. See, for example, TCD, MS 2533, p. 134, King to Bishop of Clogher, February 8, 1715/16.

46. Rev. R. Choppin, Derry, to Rev. Thos. Steward, Dublin, July 8, 1712, quoted in Thomas Witherow, *Historical and Literary Memorials of Presbyterianism in Ireland* (London and Belfast: W. Mullan, 1879), 1:326.

47. Rev. Lang, Loughbrickland, to Rev. Wodrow, [Edinburgh?], January 23, 1712, quoted in Reid, *History of the Presbyterian Church in Ireland*, 3:20 n.

48. TCD, MS 2533, p. 165, King to Wm. Wake, Archbishop of Canterbury, March 24, 1715/16.

49. TCD, MS 750/5, p. 192, King to Archbishop of Canterbury, August 1, 1719.

50. Reid, *History of the Presbyterian Church in Ireland*, 3:22–23.

51. Scottish Record Office, Broughton and Cally Muniments, GD, 10/1421/12/511, Samuel Delap, Donegal, to Alexander Murray, Cally [Gatehouse of Fleet, Scotland], June 7, 1744; Edmond Kaine to Dacres Barrett, May 11, 1715, noted in W. H. Crawford, "Economy and Society in South Ulster in the Eighteenth Century," *Clogher Record* 8 (1975): 242.

52. *Records of the General Synod of Ulster from 1691–1820*, 1:252, 443, 468, 476.

53. TCD, MS 750/5, pp. 79–80, King to Rev. Henry Maule, November 29, 1718; see also TCD, MS 750/5, p. 32, King to Bishop of Down, September 2, 1718.

54. TCD, MS 750/5, p. 166, King to Archbishop of Canterbury, June 2, 1719.

55. Jos. Marriott, August 12, 1718, quoted in Dickson, *Ulster Emigration to Colonial America, 1718–1775*, 29. The original is held, with other documentary material, in the archive of the Merchant Tailors Company in London. Requests to the company for access to this and other material have been refused.

56. Bolton, *Scotch Irish Pioneers in Ulster and America*, 240.

57. Calculated from data in Lorcán Ó Mearáin, "The Bath Estate, 1700–1777," *Clogher Record* 6 (1967): 339–45.

58. PRONI, T. 656/44, T. 656/45, Rent rolls for the Clothworkers Proportion, c. 1717.

59. W. H. Crawford, "Landlord-Tenant Relations in Ulster, 1609–1820," *IESH* 2 (1975): 13.

60. Calculated from PRONI, D. 2860/4/25, 1719 rent roll, and D. 2860/36, new leases, 1720.

61. PRONI, MIC 170/2, Edmond Kaine, Clones, to Hon. Dacres Barrett, Essex, September 20 and December 18, 1718.

62. On the Brownlow estate the area let in the years 1710–19 was more than the total for the previous three decades (Crawford, "Landlord-Tenant Relations in Ulster, 1609–1820," 13). Occasional press advertisements reveal substantial areas to be leased; for two Antrim examples, see *Dublin Courant,* January 10, 1719, and June 22, 1720.

63. PRONI, D. 2094/21, Copy of the Rent Roll of the Vintners' Proportion sent to them by Amos Strettele, October 18, 1718.

64. Crawford, "Landlord-Tenant Relations in Ulster, 1609–1820," 10.

65. PRONI, D. 2094/21, Rent Roll of the Vintners' Proportion, October 18, 1718.

66. T. H. Mullin, *Aghadowey: A Parish and Its Linen Industry* (Belfast: Century Services, 1972), 45.

67. PRONI, MIC 170/2, Edmond Kaine, Clones, to Hon. Dacres Barrett, Essex, December 2, 1717, March 17, 1719. See also same to same, June 9, 1718.

68. L. M. Cullen, *Anglo-Irish Trade 1660–1800* (Manchester: Manchester University Press, 1968), 157, 178, 195; TCD, MS 2535, p. 88, Archbishop King to Lady Dun, February 24, 1717/18; TCD, MS 2535, pp. 111–12, King to Thomas Knox, March 14, 1717/18.

69. TCD, MS 2535, p. 84, King to Bishop [Nicolson] of Carlisle, February 21, 1717/18.

70. All export figures are calculated from PRO, CUST 15. These data are for fiscal years ending March 25; 1717/18, for example, refers to the period between March 1717 and March 1718.

71. PRONI, T. 2825/C/27/2, Robert McCausland, [Limavady, County Derry], to Ld. Justice [William] Conolly, November 13, 1718.

72. G. E. Kirkham, " 'To Pay The Rent and Lay Up Riches': Economic Opportunity in Eighteenth-Century North-West Ulster," in *Economy and Society in Scotland and Ireland, 1500–1939,* ed. Rosalind Mitchison and Peter Roebuck (Edinburgh: John Donald Publishers, 1988), 99–100.

73. F. E. Dixon, "An Irish Weather Diary of 1711–1725," *Quarterly Journal of the Royal Meteorological Society* 85 (1959): 378–80, 382; Dublin Municipal Library, Gilbert MS 27, pp. 185–89, Bishop Nicolson, Derry, to Archbishop Wake, August 1, 1718.

74. Gilbert MS 27, pp. 178–80, Bishop Nicolson, Derry, to Archbishop Wake, June 24, 1718. TCD, MS 750/4/2, Archbishop King to Earl of Sunderland, December 31, 1714; TCD, MS 2535, p. 211, King to Lord Fitzwilliam, July 13, 1718; Sean Conolly, "Violence and Order in the Eighteenth Century," in Rural Ireland: *Modernisation and Change,* ed.

P. O'Flanagan, P. Ferguson, and K. Whelan (Cork: Cork University Press, 1987), 45.

75. Macafee, "The Population of Ulster, 1630–1841," 119.

76. PRONI, T. 2529/1/310, Edmond Kaine, Clones, County Monaghan, to Hon. Dacres Barrett, Essex, April 20, 1720 (photocopy of an original letter held by Essex Record Office, D/DL C24-40a). TCD, MS 750/6, p. 76, King to Bishop of Clogher, May 12, 1720.

77. Gilbert MS 27, pp. 297–300, Bishop Nicolson, Derry, to Archbishop Wake, October 21, 1720; Gilbert MS 27, pp. 286–87, Nicholson to Wake, June 2, 1721; Appendix to chapter 6; *New England Courant*, October 16–23, 1721; *AWM*, November 2–9, 1721 (two vessels); *Bos. N.L.*, July 23–30, 1722; *AWM*, September 26–October 4, 1723, November 7–14, 1723.

78. R. L. Meriwether, *The Expansion of South Carolina, 1729–1765* (Kingsport, TN: Southern Publishers, 1940; reprint, Philadelphia: Porcupine Press, 1974), 17.

79. R. H. Akagi, *The Town Proprietors of the New England Colonies* (Philadelphia: University of Pennsylvania Press, 1924; reprint, Gloucester, MA: Peter Smith, 1963), 256–62.

80. "A Petition of Archibald Boyd, James MacGregory [sic] and sundry others," quoted in Bolton, *Scotch Irish Pioneers in Ulster and America*, 240.

81. Thomas Lechmere, Boston, to [Governor] Winthrop, [Connecticut], August 11, 1718, quoted in Bolton, *Scotch Irish Pioneers in Ulster and America*, 139.

82. Doyle, *Ireland, Irishmen and Revolutionary America, 1760–1820*, 53; Logan's comment is quoted in Ford, *The Scotch-Irish in America*, 264.

83. Meriwether, *The Expansion of South Carolina, 1729–1765*, 17; Truxes, *Irish American Trade, 1600–1783*, 22.

84. TCD, MS 2535, pp. 111–12, Archbishop King, Dublin, to Thomas Knox, March 14, 1717/18.

85. *Records of the General Synod of Ulster from 1691–1820*, 1:336–37.

86. PRONI, D354/363, Charter party for the *Hanover* of Belfast, August 17, 1717; PRONI, D. 354/369, Charter party for the *Friendship* of Belfast, August 19, 1718; PRO, CO 5/508, f. 71, Naval Office Shipping List, South Carolina. The *Friendship* had already made one voyage to Charleston, arriving in mid-March 1718; the venture to which the charter party refers arrived in April 1719 (Appendix to chapter 6).

87. William G. Saltonstall, *Ports of Piscataqua* (Cambridge, MA: Harvard University Press, 1941), 26, quoted in Truxes, *Irish-American Trade, 1600–1783*, 23. I am extremely grateful to Richard E. Winston III of New Hampshire's Portsmouth Public Library for supplying copies of the relevant portions of this work. A vessel from Cork arrived at Piscataqua in May 1718, and vessels from Waterford came in 1716 and 1719 (*Bos. N.L.*, May 12–19, 1718, July 19, 1716, May 11–18, 1719).

88. *Bos. N.L.*, September 23–30, 1717.

89. Ibid., June 23–30, 1718.
90. Baker Library, Harvard Business School, MSS 766, F-7-168, papers of A. MacPheadris and Jonathan Warner 1716–1813, Archibald MacPheadris, Portsmouth, [NH], to Messrs. Robert Wilson & Co., Belfast, August 28, 1718. I am indebted to staff at the Baker Library for supplying me with a transcript of this document.
91. Ibid. Truxes (*Irish-American Trade, 1600–1783*, 23) has misread this passage, interpreting the comments on the potential success of iron production to refer to the profitability of importing servants. It is clear from the full text that this is not the case.
92. *Bos. N.L.*, July 23–30, 1722; *AWM*, July 26–August 2, 1722.
93. Truxes, *Irish-American Trade, 1690–1783*, 23.
94. Appendix to chapter 6.
95. TCD, MS 750/5, pp. 131–32, King to Lord Chancellor Middleton, March 4, 1718/19; *Dublin Intelligence*, January 6, 1719; *Dublin Courant*, February 10, 1719.
96. *Dublin Courant*, November 16, 1719.
97. Donovan, *Pre-Revolutionary Irish in Massachusetts, 1620–1775*, 79.
98. *Bos. N.L.*, August 1–8, 1720; *AWM*, September 8, 1720.
99. Graeme Kirkham, "The Origins of Mass Emigration from Ireland," in *Migrations: The Irish At Home and Abroad*, ed. Richard Kearney (Dublin: Wolfhound Press, 1990), 86. For the background to changes in domestic prosperity, see Kirkham, " 'To Pay The Rent and Lay Up Riches.' "
100. PRONI, T. 2812/6/55, Patrick Brett, Cloonamanagh, to Kean O'Hara, Dublin, November 14, 1718.
101. PRONI, MIC 170/2, Edmond Kaine, Clones, to Hon. Dacres Barrett, Essex, September 20, 1718; same to same, December 18, 1718. For a discussion of lease interest, see Crawford, "Landlord-Tenant Relations in Ulster 1609–1820," 10–12.
102. PRONI, D. 673/4a, Magilligan Rent Book, 1718–63; Bolton, *Scotch Irish Pioneers in Ulster and America*, 131.
103. PRONI, D. 673/4a, Magilligan Rent Book.
104. Thomas Lechmere, Boston, to [Governor] Winthrop, Connecticut, July 28, 1718, quoted in Bolton, *Scotch Irish Pioneers in Ulster and America*, 133.
105. Same to same, August 11, 1718, quoted in ibid., 139.
106. Quoted in Bolton, *Scotch Irish Pioneers in Ulster and America*, 157, 136.
107. R. J. Hunter, "Dublin-Boston, 1719," *Éire-Ireland* 6 (1971): 22.
108. Dickinson Letter Book, Dickinson to "Couzon" [Joshua Crosby], November 17, 1719; Dickinson to John Harriot, November 12, 1719.
109. PRONI, T. 2825/C/27/2, Ro[bert] McCausland, [Limavady], to Lord Justice [William] Conolly, November 13, 1718.
110. See, for example, Edmond Kaine's accounts from Clones in 1718 and 1719 (notes 35, 36). For reports of "families from the north of Ireland" settled in Sussex County, Delaware, and "two hundred families . . . from Ireland" settled around Head of Christiana Creek in southeastern Penn-

sylvania in the period before 1723, see J. G. Leyburn, *The Scotch-Irish: A Social History* (Chapel Hill: University of North Carolina Press, 1962), 330, and G. S. Klett, *Presbyterians in Colonial Pennsylvania* (Philadelphia: University of Pennsylvania Press, 1937), 31–32. See also the variety of references to the arrival and settlement of Ulster families in New England in Bolton, *Scotch Irish Pioneers in Ulster and America*, 133, 135, 142, 205, 225, 240, 250.

111. Appendix to chapter 6.
112. *Bos. N.L.*, June 18–25, 1716.
113. Ibid., August 4–11, 1718.
114. Runaways have been noted from a search of the *Boston News Letter* and *American Weekly Mercury* for these years. The advertisement for servants from the *Globe* in 1716 referred to them specifically as Protestant (*Bos. N.L.*, June 18–25, 1716).
115. Dickson, *Ulster Emigration to Colonial America, 1718–1775*, 22–23.
116. This is somewhat lower than the figure suggested by Dickinson's report of nearly 2,000 passengers to the Delaware on twelve or thirteen vessels in 1719 (note 30). Passenger numbers may be underestimated. Leonard Cotton traveled from Dublin to Boston in 1719 and noted "57 full passengers, which made about 80 souls in all" (Hunter, "Dublin-Boston, 1719," 22). It is not clear whether Cotton's total included crew members, but presumably children were being counted as less than full passengers.
117. For example, Edmond Kaine's experience of forty households leaving the Clones area during 1718 and one hundred families passing through on their way to embark in 1719 (notes 35, 36).
118. Mullin, *Aghadowey*, 50–51.

7. Philadelphia Here I Come: A Study of the Letters of Ulster Immigrants in Pennsylvania, 1750–1875

1. PRONI, T.1336/1/20, John Dunlap, Philadelphia, to Robert Rutherford, Strabane, County Tyrone, May 12, 1785. I am grateful to the Deputy Keeper of the Records, Dr. A. P. W. Malcomson, for permission to quote from this and other PRONI sources cited.
2. PRONI, T.3700/1, Job Johnston, Oxford, Pennsylvania, to his brothers John, Robert, and James, Slaghtabogy, parish of Maghera, County Londonderry, March 2, 1766.
3. Ibid.
4. Ibid.
5. *Belfast Newsletter*, November 20, 1771.
6. For example, *Belfast Newsletter*, November 20, 1771, September 7–10, 1773, June 14–17, 1774.
7. R. J. Dickson, *Ulster Emigration to Colonial America, 1718–1775*, 2d ed. (Belfast: Ulster Historical Foundation, 1988), 230.

8. *Belfast Newsletter,* September 7–10, 1773, "To Capt. Robert Ewing, Commander of the Brigantine *Agnes,* now lying in the Delaware River, off Newcastle. . . . Sir, we the passengers who sailed on board your vessel from Belfast, in Ireland, to Philadelphia in North America . . . "

9. PRONI, T.1592/2, James Horner, Philadelphia, to his father, Thomas, and mother, Boveagh, near Newtownlimavady, County Londonderry, August 18, 1801.

10. PRONI, D.1828/7, Robert Smith, Philadelphia, to his father, James, Moycraig, parish of Billy, County Antrim, August 7, 1837.

11. PRONI, T.1592/2, James Horner to Thomas and Boveagh Horner, August 18, 1801.

12. Ibid.

13. PRONI, T.2493/1, David Lindsey, County Tyrone, to his cousins Andrew and Thomas Fleming, Pennsylvania, March 19, 1758.

14. Ibid.

15. McNish Manuscripts, #2086, Cornell University Library, Ithaca, New York, letters from John Kerr, south Tyrone, March 22 and April 24, 1806, as quoted in Kerby A. Miller, *Emigrants and Exiles: Ireland and the Irish Exodus to North America* (Oxford: Oxford University Press, 1985), 178–79.

16. PRONI, D.1044/404, Joseph Wilson, New York, to Thomas Greer, merchant, Dungannon, County Tyrone, December 19, 1774.

17. PRONI, D.1044. This collection of almost one thousand items relates to the linen business carried on by a Quaker, Thomas Greer of Dungannon, County Tyrone. Of particular interest are the papers relating to importing flax seed from America and exporting linen cloth to America in the 1770s, particularly through Samuel and John Morton of Philadelphia.

18. PRONI, D.1044/400, Thomas Wright, Plumstead, Bucks County, Pennsylvania, to Thomas Greer, merchant, Dungannon, County Tyrone, June 14, 1774.

19. PRONI, T.3525, Samuel Brown, Philadelphia, to his brother David, Mill Street, Belfast, December 23, 1793.

20. Ibid.

21. E. R. R. Green, "Ulster Emigrants' Letters," in *Essays in Scotch-Irish History,* ed. E. R. R. Green (Belfast: Ulster Historical Foundation, 1992), 93.

22. Miller, *Emigrants and Exiles.*

23. PRONI, T.2294/1, John Dennison, Franklin, Pennsylvania, to his brother Samuel, c/o J. Waddel, Esq., of Springfield near Dromore, County Down, January 15, 1789.

24. PRONI, D.1859/17, H. Riddle, Pittsburgh, to William Anderson, Ballinrees, parish of Aghadowey, County Londonderry, February 23, 1857.

25. PRONI, T.1727/2, James Wray, Spruce Creek, Philadelphia, to his mother and his brother Thomas, Quilley Coleraine, parish of Dunboe, County Londonderry, October 1, 1818.

26. "Irish Educational Inquiry," *Second Report from the Commissioners,* House of Commons, 1826–27, xii.

27. PRONI, MIC144/1/3, John Kerr, c/o Rev. Alexander Wright, Pittsburgh, Allegheny County, Pennsylvania, to James Graham, Newpark, County Antrim, June 16, 1843.

28. Denis Clark, *The Irish in Philadelphia* (Philadelphia: Temple University Press, 1973), 34.

29. W. F. Adams, *Ireland and Irish Emigration to the New World* (Baltimore: Genealogical Publishing Co., 1980), 108.

30. Cormac Ó Gráda, "Across the Briny Ocean: Some Thoughts on Irish Emigration to America 1800–1850," in *Ireland and Scotland 1600–1850: Parallels and Contrasts on Economic and Social Development,* ed. T. M. Devine and David Dickson (Edinburgh: John Donald, 1983), 120.

31. Miller, *Emigrants and Exiles,* 216.

32. PRONI, T.2294/1, John Denison, Pennsylvania to Samuel Denison, c/o J. Waddell, Springfield, Dromore, County Down, January 15, 1789.

33. PRONI, D.1859/3, Joseph Anderson, West Salem, Mercer County, Pennsylvania, to his family, Ballinrees, parish of Aghadowey, County Londonderry, September 14, 1840.

34. PRONI, D.1828/3, William Smyth, Philadelphia, to Robert Smyth, Moycraig, parish of Billy, County Antrim, March 30, 1837.

35. PRONI, D.2892/1/4, passenger book, 1853–71, of J. & J. Cooke, shipping agents, Londonderry.

36. Herbert Gans, *The Urban Villagers: Group and Class in the Life of Italian-Americans,* (Glencoe: The Free Press, 1962).

37. PRONI, T.3525/1, Samuel Brown, Philadelphia, to David Brown, Mill Street, Belfast, December 23, 1793.

38. PRONI, D.1828/7, Robert Smyth, Philadelphia, to his father James, Moycraig, parish of Billy, County Antrim, August 7, 1837.

39. PRONI, D.1828/3, James Smyth, Moycraig, parish of Billy, County Antrim, to his brother William, Lombard Street and 12th Street, Philadelphia, December 4, 1836.

40. PRONI, T.3588/7, Henry Johnston, Loughbrickland, County Down, to his brother Moses, Northumberland County, Pennsylvania, May 11, 1800.

41. PRONI, T.3397, Henry Keenan, Ballyscullion East, parish of Ballyscullion, County Antrim, to his brother Daniel Keenan, corner of Bank and Charles Street, Baltimore, Maryland, July 15, 1849, as described in Trevor Parkhill, "At Home with the Emigrants: The Role of Emigrants' Letters in Locating Family Homes," in *Ulster Genealogical & Historical Guild Newsletter* 1 (1984). I am grateful to Professor Richard K. McMaster, Bluffton College, Ohio, for drawing this source to my attention.

42. PRONI, D.1140/2, Margaret Duncan, Philadelphia, to William Weir, Merchant, Stewartstown, County Tyrone, December 1774.

43. PRONI, T.2046/12, Andrew Greenlees, Dayton, Ohio, to his brother

John, Magheramorne, County Antrim, September 7, 1863. I am grateful to Professor Ronald A. Wells, Calvin College, Grand Rapids, Michigan, for drawing this source to my attention.

44.   Brian Friel, *Philadelphia Here I Come* (London: Faber & Faber, 1965).

8. The Scotch-Irish and Immigrant Culture on Amherst Island, Ontario

1.   I thank the Social Science and Humanities Research Council of Canada and the Institute of Irish Studies (Belfast) for their funding and support of this project.

2.   T. W. Moody, "The Ulster Scots in Colonial and Revolutionary America, Part I," *Studies* (1945): 86.

3.   Ibid., 87–90; William Forbes Adams, *Ireland and Irish Emigration to the New World from 1815 to the Famine* (New Haven: Yale University Press, 1932), 65; E. Evans, "The Scotch-Irish," in *Essays in Scotch-Irish History*, ed. E. R. R. Green (London: Routledge & Kegan Paul, 1969).

4.   Kerby Miller, *Emigrants and Exiles: Ireland and the Irish Exodus to North America* (New York: Oxford University Press, 1985); Rory Fitzpatrick, *God's Frontiersmen: The Scots-Irish Epic* (London: Weidenfeld and Nicolson, 1989).

5.   R. Cole Harris, Pauline Roulston, and Chris de Freitas, "The Settlement of Mono Township," *The Canadian Geographer* 19 (1975): 7–15; John T. Mannion, *Irish Settlement in Eastern Canada: A Study of Cultural Transfer and Adaptation* (Toronto: University of Toronto Press, 1974), 173.

6.   Today the United Parish of St. Andrews no longer exists and has been replaced by the individual parishes of Ballywalter, Inishargy, and Ballyhalbert.

7.   John P. Maxwell, *The Scottish Migration to Ulster in the Reign of James I* (London: Routledge & Kegan Paul, 1973), 59, 288; Raymond Gillespie, *Colonial Ulster: The Settlement of East Ulster 1600–1641* (Cork: Cork University Press, 1985), 5, 32; Phillip Robinson, *Plantation of Ulster* (Dublin: St. Martin Press, 1984).

8.   Gillespie, *Colonial Ulster*, 5; Maxwell, *The Scottish Migration to Ulster in the Reign of James I*, 59, 69, 248–49, 288.

9.   Maldwyn A. Jones, "Scotch-Irish," in *Harvard Encyclopedia of American Ethnic Groups*, ed. Stephan Thernstrom (Cambridge, MA: Harvard University Press, 1980), 895, 904–5.

10.   *Account of the Population of Ireland*, vol. 2, House of Commons, 1824, xxii, 276–86.

11.   *First Report from the Commissioners for Inquiry into the Condition of the Poorer Classes in Ireland*, Supplement to Appendix F, House of Commons [38], 1836, xxxiii, pp. 323–24, 419 (hereafter *Poor Law Inquiry*); First Valuation of the Parish of Inishargy, 1838, PRONI, VAL 1B/311A and B.

12.   *Poor Law Inquiry*, Supplement to Appendix E, pp. 323–24; Ordnance

Survey Memoir of the Parish of Inishargy, 1836, PRONI, MIC 6C/8, p. 4; *Down Recorder*, December 21, 1839, p. 2.

13. *First Report of the Commissioners of Inquiry into the State of the Irish Fisheries & Appendix to First Report*, House of Commons, 1837, xxii, pp. 25–29.

14. *Poor Law Inquiry, Supplement to Appendix F*, pp. 319, 323–24; Greyabbey, Ballywalter, and Kircubbin Tenant Farmers Association, *Letters etc., Republished from Newspapers on the Land Question* (Belfast, 1881), p. 5, Dufferin and Ava Papers, PRONI, D. 1071 H/T/63; *Evidence Taken Before the Commissioners Appointed in Inquiry into the Occupation of Land in Ireland Part I*, House of Commons [606], 1845, xix, pp. 575–77.

15. Graeme Kirkham gives an excellent summary of important revisions to the subject in his introduction to the most recent edition of R. J. Dickson, *Ulster Emigration to Colonial America, 1718–1775* (Belfast: Ulster Historical Foundation, 1988), vii–xviii.

16. I began the process of linking the two communities by doing genealogical research on island families using local parish registers, gravestone inscriptions, and obituaries, and then doing the same kind of research at the Public Record Office of Northern Ireland to establish the Irish link. Unless otherwise noted, information on individual families derives from this process. Sources are too numerous to list here but are available on request.

17. Kircubbin Presbyterian Church Marriage Register, PRONI, D.1758/1D/12; 1851 Manuscript Census for Amherst Island, Document Center, Queen's University, Kingston, Ontario; Hitchins Rental Book, 1826, Burleigh Papers, 3d ser., Queen's University Archives, Kingston, Ontario.

18. Cloughy Presbyterian Church Marriage Register, PRONI, MIC 1P/314; 1851 Manuscript Census for Amherst Island.

19. Glastry Presbyterian Church Marriage Records, PRONI, MIC 1P/111/2; 1861 Manuscript Census for Amherst Island.

20. Adams, *Ireland and Irish Emigration*, 96–97; Jim Blaney, "Portaferry Shipping in Two Centuries," *Upper Ards Historical Society Journal* 11 (1987): 10–15.

21. *Poor Law Inquiry, Supplement to Appendix F*, pp. 323–24; *Belfast Newsletter*, April 22, 1831, p. 4.

22. Alexander Pentland to John Henderson, September 13, 1846; and J. & J. Pentland to Mrs. Polly, August 17, 1857; both letters are courtesy of Mrs. D. P. Holmes. Also correspondence with genealogists Mrs. Margaret Pentland Pritchard, May 1987; Mary Charles, September 15, 1987; and Mrs. A. J. Peppin, April 27, 1987. Mrs. Donald Lobb, "Goderich Township Families," 1985.

23. For wages, see *Poor Law Inquiry, Supplement to Appendix D*, pp. 323–24; Robert Stanton, *Upper Canada Assembly Journal 1833–34: Appendix* (Toronto, 1834); and Robert Stanton, *Upper Canada Assembly Journal 1836–37: Appendix* (Toronto, 1837). For rents, see the following: 1835 Rental, Moore Hill Papers, PRONI, D.3817; *Inquiry in the Occupation of*

Land in Ireland, pp. 575–76; *Poor Law Inquiry, Supplement to Appendix F*, pp. 323–24.

24. Letter from Mary Charles (genealogist), Woodstock, Ontario, September 15, 1987.

25. Copybooks for Lennox and Addington County, Queen's University Archives, Kingston, Ontario.

26. William Moutray's Ledger, Queen's University Archives, Kingston, p. 14; J. Neilson's Ledgers and his Pay Book for 1880, Lennox and Addington County Museum, Napanee, Ontario.

27. Moutray's Ledger, p. 8.

28. Burleigh Papers, Box 16, F24, Queen's University Archives, Kingston, Ontario.

29. Interview with Bruce Caughey, August 21, 1986.

30. For historians who have shown that tenancy acted as an agricultural ladder, see Sung Bok Kim, *Landlord and Tenant in Colonial New York* (Chapel Hill: University of North Carolina Press, 1978); Donald L. Winter, "The Agricultural Ladder in Southern Agriculture: Tennessee, 1850–1870," *Agricultural History* 61 (1987): 36–52; Jeremy Atack, "The Agricultural Ladder Revisited: A New Look at an Old Question with Some Data for 1860," *Agricultural History* 63 (1989): 1–25.

31. *The Canada Farmer*, ser. 2, vol. 2 (May 15, 1870): 2.

32. *Censuses of Canada 1665–1871: Statistics of Canada*, vol. 4 (Ottawa: I. B. Taylor, 1876), 168.

33. Currency can be a problem in making comparisons of this sort. Ards money values are in British sterling, and Amherst Island money values are in Halifax currency. The exchange rate was 5 shillings Halifax currency = 4 shillings British sterling. Even when Ards values are translated into currency, the difference is impressive. For the purpose of comparison, Irish rents in cunningham acres have been converted into statute acres. For rents in St. Andrews, see Clanmorris Papers, PRONI, D.3735/3; Wallace Documents, PRONI, T.1009/67 and T.1009/61; Misc. Estate Papers from Martin and Henderson Solicitors, PRONI, D.2223/15/43; Tenant Farmers Association, *Letters on the Land Question* (Belfast, 1881), pp. 3–5, Dufferin and Ava Papers, PRONI, D.1071 H/T/63; and *Poor Law Inquiry, Supplement to Appendix F*, pp. 319, 323–24.

34. 1835 Rental, Moore Hill Papers, PRONI.

35. Ibid.; Thomas Rolph, *Emigration and Colonization* (London: John Mortimer, 1844), 354.

36. Land Registry Abstract for Amherst Island, Lennox and Addington County Registry Office, Napanee, Ontario. For tenant right in east Ulster, see Liam Kennedy and Philip Ollerenshaw, eds., *An Economic History of Ulster, 1820–1940* (Manchester: Manchester University Press, 1985), 9; and for specific examples from the Ards, see Deed, William Little of Ballymullen to James Little of Killivolgan, November 1, 1814, Registry of Deeds, Dublin, 681-32-468570; and Deed of Conveyance, James Moreland of Ballyhalbert to James Gowan of Ballyesborough, March 24, 1836, Registry of Deeds, Dublin, 1836-7-202.

37. 1855 Rental List, Moore Hill Papers, PRONI, D.387/3/3; Land Registry
     Abstract for Amherst Island.

38. The most thorough discussion of tenant right is found in W. E.
     Vaughan, *Landlords and Tenants in Ireland* (Dublin: Economic and Social
     History Society of Ireland, 1984), 17–25.

39. Only three recorded cases of tenant right have survived for Amherst Is-
     land: Frances K. Smith, *Daniel Fowler of Amherst Island 1810–1894*
     (Kingston: Agnes Etherington Art Center, 1979), 129; William Perceval
     to Robert Perceval Maxwell, July 13, 1858, PRONI, Moore Hill Papers;
     and "Account of Captain Hugh Glenn," in the private possession of
     Ruth Glenn, Amherst Island.

40. Rolph, *Emigration and Colonization,* 346; Spencer Perceval to Robert Per-
     ceval Maxwell, November 6, 1857, Moore Hill Papers.

41. These figures are deduced from the rental lists for these years and do not
     include families where the household head died or retired; 1835 Rental
     List and 1855 Rental List for Amherst Island, Moore Hill Papers, PRONI,
     D.3817/1/1 and D.3817/3/3; "Corrected Valuation for Amherst Island,
     June 10, 1871," Moore Hill Papers.

42. Ibid.; Land Registry Abstract for Amherst Island.

43. Eva M. Glenn, "The Glenn Family of Amherst Island," 1968; Land Reg-
     istry Abstract for Amherst Island; 1871 Rental List, Moore Hill Papers,
     PRONI; interview with Fred Brown, Ballywalter, Ards Peninsula, Septem-
     ber 9, 1987.

44. Robert Perceval Maxwell to William Perceval, October 30, 1865, Per-
     ceval Maxwell Papers, PRONI, D.1556/2/2/304–305; "Statement showing
     amount of property sold by William H. Moutray on Amherst Island Es-
     tate, May 6, 1879," Moore Hill Papers.

45. William Perceval to Robert Perceval Maxwell, July 13, 1858, Moore Hill
     Papers; *Kingston Chronicle & Gazette,* August 25, 1841, p. 3; and two il-
     luminated addresses in the private possession of Mr. Syl Apps, Amherst
     Island. (An illuminated address was a formal letter embellished with or-
     namental borders and color.)

46. Kircubbin Presbyterian Church Records, April 17, 1837, PRONI.

47. Glastry Presbyterian Church Records, June 21, 1835, PRONI.

48. Interview with Kenneth Miller, August 1982, Amherst Island Oral His-
     tory Project, Interview No. 32, Lennox and Addington County Museum,
     Napanee, Ontario.

49. Poetry in the private possession of Mrs. Edwin Landry. Alexander
     McGrattan was a Roman Catholic but was married to Mary Wilson, a
     Presbyterian, and was the son of a Presbyterian mother. As with the
     Scotch-Irish migration in the 1700s, the emigrants were not entirely
     Presbyterian or of Scottish ancestry but included some native Irish
     Catholics and members of the established church who were of English
     descent.

50. Correspondence with genealogists Randi Kennedy and Mrs. Edwin Lan-
     dry. David McGrattan was Presbyterian.

51. Walter D. Kamphoefner, *The Westfalians: From Germany to Missouri*

(Princeton, NJ: Princeton University Press, 1987), 9, 38, 178–79; John Bodnar, *The Transplanted: A History of Immigrants in Urban America* (Bloomington: Indiana University Press, 1985), 54–56.

52. Kamphoefner, *The Westfalians*; Bodnar, *The Transplanted*; Bruce S. Elliott, *Irish Migrants in the Canadas: A New Approach* (Kingston: McGill-Queen's University Press, 1988); Cecil J. Houston and William M. Smyth, *Irish Emigration and Canadian Settlement* (Toronto: University of Toronto Press, 1990); and Jon Gjerde, *From Peasants to Farmers: The Migration from Balestrande, Norway to the Upper Middle West* (New York: Cambridge University Press, 1985); Robert C. Ostergren, *A Community Transplanted* (Madison: University of Wisconsin Press, 1988).

53. Kamphoefner, *The Westfalians*, chap. 6, and p. 167.

9. Scotch-Irish Landscapes in the Ozarks

1. Colonel A. K. McClure, "Scotch-Irish Achievement," in *The Scotch-Irish in America, Proceedings of the Scotch-Irish Congress at Columbia, Tennessee, May 8–11, 1889* (Cincinnati: R. Clarke, 1889), 178.

2. F. McDonald and E. S. McDonald, "The Ethnic Origins of the American People, 1790," *WMQ*, 3d ser. 37 (1980): 199.

3. Robert D. Mitchell, "The Shenandoah Valley Frontier," *Annals of the Association of American Geographers* 62 (1972): 471.

4. Robert L. Kincaid, *The Wilderness Road* (Middlesboro, KY: Robert L. Kincaid, 1973), 64.

5. Madison Grant, *The Conquest of a Continent* (New York: C. Scribner's Sons, 1933), 146.

6. E. Estyn Evans, "Cultural Relics in the Old West of North America," *Ulster Folklife* 11 (1965): 33.

7. Kerby Miller, *Emigrants and Exiles: Ireland and the Irish Exodus to North America* (New York: Oxford University Press, 1985), 161.

8. Floyd C. Shoemaker, "Missouri's Tennessee Heritage," *Missouri Historical Review* 49 (1955): 130.

9. Carl O. Sauer, *The Geography of the Ozark Highland of Missouri*, bulletin no. 7 (Chicago: Geographical Society of Chicago, 1920): 159.

10. U.S. Census Office, *Eighth Census of the United States: 1860*, 386.

11. U.S. Census Office, *Eighth Census of the United States: 1860,* Population Schedules, Missouri.

12. Harbert L. Clendenen, "Settlement Morphology of the Southern Courtois Hills, Missouri, 1820–1860" (unpublished Ph.D. diss., Louisiana State University, Baton Rouge, 1973), 18–21.

13. Ibid., 25.

14. U.S. Bureau of the Census, *Census of Population and Housing: 1980*, Summary Tape File 4, *Technical Documentation*, appendix C3, 109–13.

15. A select seventeen groups claiming three ancestries were separated out. For a listing of these groups, see U.S. Bureau of the Census, *Ancestry of the Population by State: 1980*, 6.

16. Patrick J. Blessing, "Irish," in *The Harvard Encyclopedia of American Ethnic Groups*, ed. Stephan Thernstrom (Cambridge, MA: Belknap Press of Harvard University, 1980), 530.

17. U.S. Census Office, *Preliminary Report of the Eighth Census: 1860*, 268–71.

18. U.S. Census Office, *Compendium of the Eleventh Census: 1890*, 646–747.

19. U.S. Census Office, *The Seventh Census of the United States: 1850*, 689–90.

20. Russel L. Gerlach, *Immigrants in the Ozarks* (Columbia: University of Missouri Press, 1976), 38.

21. Charles O. Paullin, *Atlas of the Historical Geography of the United States* (Washington, DC: Carnegie Institution of Washington, 1932), 87.

22. Gerlach, *Immigrants in the Ozarks*, 38, 49.

23. Bernard Quinn, Herman Anderson, Martin Bradley, Paul Goetting, and Peggy Shriver, *Churches and Church Membership in the United States: 1980* (Atlanta: Glenmary Research Center, 1982), 164–73.

24. Robert Flanders, "Caledonia: An Ozark Village: History, Geography, Architecture," (Springfield, MO: unpublished MS, 1984), 1–2; Flanders, "Caledonia: Ozark Legacy of the High Scotch-Irish," *Gateway Heritage* 6 (1986): 34–52.

25. Sauer, *The Geography of the Ozark Highland of Missouri*, 102–3.

26. Ibid., 148–49.

27. John W. Blake, "The Ulster-American Connection—Synopsis and Epilog," in *The Ulster-American Connection*, ed. J. W. Blake (Coleraine, Northern Ireland: New University of Ulster, 1981), 34–35.

28. James A. Banks and Geneva Gay, "Ethnicity in Contemporary American Society: Toward the Development of a Typology," *Ethnicity* 5 (1978): 248.

29. Carl O. Sauer, "The Morphology of Landscape," in *Land and Life: A Selection from the Writing of Carl Ortwin Sauer*, ed. John Leighly (Berkeley: University of California Press, 1969), 342–43.

30. James T. Lemon, "The Agricultural Practices of National Groups in Eighteenth Century Southeastern Pennsylvania," *Geographical Review* 56 (1966): 467–96.

31. Arthur Young, *A Tour in Ireland*, 2d ed., 2 vols. (London: Printed for T. Cadell, 1780); *Letters by a Farmer: originally published in the Belfast Evening Post with several alterations and additions* (Belfast: Printed by James Magee, 1787); John Mogey, *Rural Life in Northern Ireland* (London: Oxford University Press, 1947); J. G. Williams, "An Economic Survey of Small Holdings in Northern Ireland," *Journal of the Ministry of Agriculture for Northern Ireland* 3 (1931): 62–82; T. Jones Hughes, "Society and Settlement in Nineteenth Century Ireland," *Irish Geography* 5 (1964–1968): 79–96.

32. Richard H. Shryock, "British and German Farmers," *American-German Review* 4 (1938): 36–38; James G. Leyburn, *The Scotch-Irish: A Social History* (Chapel Hill: University of North Carolina Press, 1962); John C. Campbell, *The Southern Highlander and His Homeland* (Lex-

ington: University Press of Kentucky, 1921); Harry M. Caudill, *Night Comes to the Cumberlands* (Boston: Little, Brown, 1962); Maldwyn Jones, "Scotch-Irish," *Harvard Encyclopedia*, 895–908.

33. Young, *A Tour of Ireland*, 2:101.

34. *Letters by a Farmer*, 115; R. J. Dickson, *Ulster Emigration to Colonial America, 1718–1785* (London: Routledge & Kegan Paul, 1966), 13; Jones, "Scotch-Irish," in *The Harvard Encyclopedia of American Ethnic Groups*, 898.

35. Mitchell, "The Shenandoah Valley Frontier," 147.

36. David N. Doyle, *Ireland, Irishmen and Revolutionary America, 1760–1820* (Dublin: Mercier Press, 1981), 72.

37. Gerlach, *Immigrants in the Ozarks*, 107.

38. Milton D. Rafferty, *The Ozarks: Land and Life* (Norman: University of Oklahoma Press, 1980), 186–87.

39. Jones, "Scotch-Irish," in *The Harvard Encyclopedia of American Ethnic Groups*, 900.

40. E. Estyn Evans, "The Scotch-Irish: Their Cultural Adaptation and Heritage in the American Old West," in *Essays in Scotch-Irish History*, ed. E. R. R. Green (London: Routledge & Kegan Paul, 1969), 84.

41. Evans, "Cultural Relics of the Ulster-Scots in the Old West of North America," 35; John S. Otto and Augustus M. Burns III, "Traditional Agricultural Practices in the Arkansas Highlands," *Journal of American Folklore* 94 (1981): 168.

42. Mogey, *Rural Life in Northern Ireland*, 23–25.

43. Forest McDonald and Grady McWhiney, "The Celtic South," *History Today* 30 (1980): 13.

44. U.S. Census Office, *Seventh Census of the United States: 1850*, 555, 676–77.

45. Ozark moonshining has been so steeped in legend and lore that it can be difficult to distinguish fact from fiction. The operation of illegal stills has long been associated with the Scotch-Irish, both in Ulster and in America. According to data from the Bureau of Alcohol, Tobacco and Firearms, U.S. Department of the Treasury, from 1935 to the present nearly 6,000 stills have been raided by federal agents alone in the states of Arkansas and Missouri. Most of this activity was in the pre-1970 period, and today only a few stills are found in these two states annually. For the Ulster antecedents of this practice, see John McGuffin, *In Praise of Poteen* (Belfast: Appletree Press, 1978); for moonshining in the United States, see James Earl Dabney, *Mountain Spirits: A Chronicle of Corn Whiskey* (New York: Scribner, 1974); and for Ozark moonshining, see Russel L. Gerlach, "Moonshining in the Ozarks: Past and Present," *Ozarks Mountaineer* 24 (1976): 20, 30.

46. U.S. Census Office, *Seventh Census of the United States: 1850*, 554, 675–76. The average value per acre was obtained by dividing the combined acreage in farms for each county by the cash value of all farms in each county.

47. T. C. Porter and Frank Miller, "Missouri Fencing Laws," *Missouri Agricultural Experiment Station Bulletin* 711 (Columbia: University of Missouri, 1958), 3.

48. Allen Brohn and Thomas S. Baskett, "Free Livestock Range in Missouri," *Missouri Agricultural Experiment Station Bulletin* 761 (Columbia: University of Missouri, 1961), 1.

49. E. Estyn Evans, *The Personality of Ireland: Habitat, Heritage and History* (Belfast: Blackstaff Press, 1981), 83–84.

50. Mogey, *Rural Life in Northern Ireland*, 96.

51. John Solomon Otto and Nain Estelle Anderson, "The Diffusion of Upland South Folk Culture, 1790–1840," *Southeastern Geographer* 22 (1982): 93.

52. Evans, "Cultural Relics of the Ulster-Scots in the Old West of North America," 37.

53. Milton Newton, "Cultural Preadaptation and the Upland South," in *Man and Cultural Heritage, Geoscience and Man*, ed. H. J. Walker and W. G. Haag (Baton Rouge: Louisiana State University, 1974), 152.

54. Otto and Burns, "Traditional Agricultural Practices in the Arkansas Highlands," 166–86.

55. Evans, "The Scotch-Irish," 80–81.

56. John Fraser Hart, "Land Rotation in Appalachia," *Geographical Review* 67 (1977): 166.

57. Gerlach, *Immigrants in the Ozarks*, 60–65.

58. E. Estyn Evans, "The Prehistoric and Historical Background," in *Land Use in Northern Ireland*, ed. Leslie Symons (London: University of London Press, 1963), 36.

59. E. R. R. Green, "Scotch-Irish Emigration, An Imperial Problem," *Western Pennsylvania Historical Magazine* 35 (1952): 209

60. Government of Northern Ireland, *Report of the Agricultural Inquiry Committee*, Command Paper 249 (Babbington Report) (Belfast,1945), 259.

61. Williams, "An Economic Survey of Small Holdings in Northern Ireland," 82.

10. Land, Ethnicity, and Community at the Opequon Settlement, Virginia, 1730–1800

I thank Robert D. Cross, Richard K. MacMaster, Robert D. Mitchell, and D. Alan Williams for their guidance. Research was supported by a grant from the National Endowment for the Humanities. This essay is reprinted with minor changes from the July 1990 issue of the *Virginia Magazine of History and Biography*.

1. For discussion of community in general, see Darrett B. Rutman, "Community Study," *Historical Methods* 13 (1980): 29–41; and Darrett B. Rutman, "Assessing the Little Communities of Early America," *WMQ*, 3d ser., 43 (1986): 163–78.

2. William Henry Foote, *Sketches of Virginia, Historical and Biographical*, 2d ser., 2d ed. (Philadelphia: J. B. Lippincott, 1856), 19–20.

3. With the possible exception of William Hoge, who may have originated in Berwick, Scotland. See William D. Nichols, *The Hoge, Nichols and Related Families Biographical-Historical; A Sequential Arrangement of Genealogical Data* (Ann Arbor: University Microfilms, 1969), 14. For a general study of Scotch-Irish immigration, see R. J. Dickson, *The Ulster Emigration to Colonial America, 1718–1775* (London: Routledge and Kegan Paul, 1966).

4. Residential intermixing by diverse ethnic groups was perhaps greater at Opequon than elsewhere on the frontier during the first half of the eighteenth century. Ethnic group clustering within large areas already characterized Pennsylvania, with the possible exception of the Lancaster plain, where ethnic mixing was more common. Opequon was one of the earliest areas settled in the Shenandoah Valley; subsequent settlement tended to produce more exclusive concentrations of Scotch-Irish, notably in Augusta County, and Germans, in present-day Shenandoah and Rockingham Counties. Throughout the backcountry, from Pennsylvania to the Carolinas, residential intermixing increased during the late eighteenth century. See James T. Lemon, *The Best Poor Man's Country: A Geographical Study of Early Southeastern Pennsylvania* (Baltimore: Johns Hopkins Press, 1972), 42–70; James G. Leyburn, *The Scotch-Irish: A Social History* (Chapel Hill: University of North Carolina Press, 1962), 190; Robert D. Mitchell, *Commercialism and Frontier: Perspectives on the Early Shenandoah Valley* (Charlottesville: University of Virginia Press, 1977), 40–45; Thomas L. Purvis, "Patterns of Ethnic Settlement in Late Eighteenth-Century Pennsylvania," *Western Pennsylvania Historical Magazine* 70 (1987): 107–22.

5. Lemon, *Best Poor Man's Country*, 42–49; Allan Kulikoff, *Tobacco and Slaves: The Development of Southern Cultures in the Chesapeake, 1680–1800* (Chapel Hill: University of North Carolina Press, 1986), 92–99, 141–61; Frank W. Porter III, "From Backcountry to County: The Delayed Settlement of Western Maryland," *Maryland Historical Magazine* 70 (1975): 329–49.

6. The argument for Celtic influences on the culture of the eighteenth- and nineteenth-century South has been put most forcibly by Forrest McDonald and Grady McWhiney in a series of articles and books. The best summary can be found in Grady McWhiney, *Cracker Culture: Celtic Ways in the Old South* (Tuscaloosa: University of Alabama Press, 1988). For a critical analysis of the idea, see Rowland Berthoff, "Celtic Mist Over the South," *JSH* 52 (1986): 523–46.

7. Hite, a native of Bonfeld in Baden-Württemberg, joined the Palatine emigration to England in 1709 and in the next year to New York. He later acquired extensive landholdings along the Perkiomen Creek about twenty-five miles from Philadelphia. Hearing of opportunities in Vir-

ginia, Hite secured orders for Shenandoah Valley land in 1731 and arrived on the banks of the Opequon Creek early in 1732. See Klaus Wust, *The Virginia Germans* (Charlottesville: University of Virginia Press, 1969), 32–33; Henry Z. Jones, Ralph Conner, and Klaus Wust, *German Origins of Jost Hite: Virginia Pioneer, 1685–1761* (Edinburg, VA: Shenandoah History, 1979).

8. The subject of land policy and its effect on settlement west of the Blue Ridge is more fully explored in Warren R. Hofstra, "Land Policies and Their Consequences in the Northern Neck: Frederick County, Virginia, during the 18th Century," in *Appalachian Frontiers: Settlement, Society, & Development in the Preindustrial Era,* ed. Robert D. Mitchell (Lexington: University Press of Kentucky, 1990), 105–26. See also Manning C. Voorhis, "The Land Grant Policy of Colonial Virginia, 1607–1771" (Ph.D. diss., University of Virginia, 1940), 129–65.

9. In his study of western migration, Ray Allen Billington observed that "the best lands were occupied by Germans, forcing the Scotch-Irish into the hillier country" (Ray Allen Billington, *Westward Expansion: A History of the American Frontier,* 2d ed. [New York: Macmillan Co., 1949], 92). See also Carl Bridenbaugh, *Myths and Realities: Societies of the Colonial South* (Baton Rouge: Louisiana University Press, 1952), 123, 132–33.

10. According to Robert Mitchell, "commercial considerations were paramount in making decisions about where to settle," and there was "little correlation between the distribution of national groups and that of soil types" (Mitchell, *Commercialism and Frontier,* 40–41).

11. Lemon, *Best Poor Man's Country,* xv–xvi.

12. For the debate between Lemon and Henretta over the transition from subsistence-based, household economies to market-oriented, capitalist economies, see James A. Henretta, "Families and Farms: *Mentalité* in Pre-Industrial America," *WMQ,* 3d ser., 35 (1978): 3–32; for replies by both Lemon and Henretta, see *WMQ,* 3d ser., 37 (1980): 688–700. See also Allan Kulikoff, "The Transition to Capitalism in Rural America," *WMQ,* 3d ser., 46 (1989): 120–44.

13. On social instability and community organization in the seventeenth century, see Edmund S. Morgan, *American Slavery, American Freedom: The Ordeal of Colonial Virginia* (New York: Norton Co., 1975), and Allan Kulikoff, "The Colonial Chesapeake: Seedbed of Antebellum Southern Culture?" *JSH* 45 (1979): 513–40. The best review articles of the immense literature on the seventeenth-century Chesapeake are Thad W. Tate, "The Seventeenth-Century Chesapeake and Its Modern Historians," in *The Chesapeake in the Seventeenth Century: Essays on Anglo-American Society,* ed. Thad W. Tate and David L. Ammerman (Chapel Hill: University of North Carolina Press, 1979), 3–50; and Anita H. Rutman, "Still Planting the Seeds of Hope: The Recent Literature of the Early Chesapeake Region," *Virginia Magazine of History and Biography* 95 (1987): 3–24. For a provocative analysis of the Chesapeake

literature, see Jack P. Greene, *Pursuits of Happiness: The Social Development of Early Modern British Colonies and the Formation of American Culture* (Chapel Hill: University of North Carolina Press, 1988), 7–54, 81–100.

14.   In analyzing settlement at Opequon, I broke the population into three generations. The first generation consisted of those individuals who were the earliest mentioned members of their lineal family at Opequon and who can also be numbered among the initial settlers according to land records and family histories. Some confusion results from this method because in certain cases a man and his son-in-law, although of separate generations in family history, are of the same generation as I have reckoned generations because they represent separate family names. The first generation of husbands and wives as I have determined them at Opequon is Robert Allen and Sarah, John Beckett and Sarah Glass, Joseph Colvill and Elizabeth, Samuel Glass and Mary Gamble, William Hoge and Barbara Hume, William Marquis and Margaret Colvill, William Reid and Mary Allen, Andrew Vance and Elizabeth Colvill, John Wilson and Mary Marquis, Robert Wilson and Garrata Hoge, and Thomas Wilson and Mary. The children of these men and women constituted the second generation, and the second generation's children in turn made up the third generation. As a group the third generation was difficult to identify because of cross-generational marriages and outmigration. Estate inventories exist in Frederick County court records for seven members of the first generation. None of these inventories contains references either to tobacco crops or to any implements related to tobacco production. All Frederick County records are located in the Frederick County Courthouse, Winchester, Virginia, unless otherwise noted.

15.   *Hite et al. v. Fairfax* Papers, transcription by Hunter B. McKay, HLA, p. 1521; Mitchell, *Commercialism and Frontier*, 149–52.

16.   Whereas the eighteenth-century Piedmont was settled by a process of expansion from an already stabilized society to the east, and in fact by the children and grandchildren of those who helped build the first kinship communities and secure social hierarchies in the Tidewater, the backcountry to the west of the Blue Ridge was settled by immigrants who were often as unaccustomed to American conditions as were those first arrivals to the Chesapeake. Like their predecessors of the previous century, but unlike their counterparts in the Piedmont, the people of Opequon were cut off from kin, community, and familiar institutions. See Richard R. Beeman, *The Evolution of the Southern Backcountry: A Case Study of Lunenburg County, Virginia, 1746–1832* (Philadelphia: University of Pennsylvania Press, 1984), 3–119; Kulikoff, *Tobacco and Slaves*, 205–60; Darrett B. Rutman and Anita H. Rutman, *A Place in Time: Middlesex County, Virginia, 1650–1750* (New York: Norton Co., 1984), 94–127.

17.   Thomas and Mary Wilson may have had children, but they left no rec-

ord of them. Wills, deeds, inventories, and court orders provided the greatest and most reliable sources for genealogical information on the first three generations at Opequon. Gravestones at Opequon Presbyterian Church, Kernstown, Virginia, also furnished much helpful information on family origins and relations. Published and unpublished genealogical studies were less reliable because of poor documentation. See Margaret S. Beyer, "The Gilkeson Family," HLA; Marjorie L. Cherry, comp., "The Family of Andrew Vance" (typescript), HLA; William Henry Foote, "Genealogy of the Glass Family in Virginia" (typescript), comp. Mrs. Royal E. Burnham, Daughters of the American Revolution Library, Washington, DC; Marquis File, HLA; Nichols, *Hoge, Nichols and Related Families*; Vida Vance, "First Generation in America" (typescript), HLA.

18. James Vance, will, February 26, 1750, Frederick County WB 1, p. 495. References to county records refer only to the first page of the document because the county indexed them that way. For deeds of lease and release, references are generally to the deeds of release because they contain more information on grantors, grantees, and sale prices. Dates refer to the day the instrument was drafted, not recorded, unless otherwise specified.

19. Nichols, *Hoge, Nichols and Related Families*, 14; William Hoge, will, recorded November 15, 1749, Frederick County WB 1, p. 338.

20. Warren R. Hofstra, "These Fine Prospects: Frederick County, Virginia, 1738–1840" (Ph.D. diss., University of Virginia, 1985), 46; Chester R. Young, "The Effects of the French and Indian War on Civilian Life in the Frontier Counties of Virginia, 1754–1763" (Ph.D. diss., Vanderbilt University, 1969), p. 436, table 33; U.S. Census Office, *First Census of the United States, 1790, Return of the Whole Number of Persons within the Several Districts of the United States...*, 48.

21. These marriages include those made with families that were allied to the Opequon community after or at the time of settlement, namely Brown, Chipley, Fulton, Gilkeson, Rannells, Simrall, and White.

22. The children of John Wilson and Mary Marquis died in infancy.

23. Elizabeth Vance, will, November 12, 1781, Frederick County WB 5, p. 110. Samuel Vance married Jane Rannells; William Vance married three times, first to Nancy Gilkeson, next to Martha Colvill, and finally to Ann Glass; James David Vance married Mary Glass; Sarah Vance married John Gilkeson; and Mary Vance married Robert Wilson, Jr.

24. Robert Wilson to Peter Stephens, deed of gift, March 4, 1767, Frederick County DB 11, p. 330; Robert Wilson, will, November 1777, Frederick County WB 4, p. 444.

25. Jost Hite to James Vance, deed, November 26, 1742, Orange County DB 8, Orange County Courthouse, Orange, VA, p. 46; Thomas, Lord Fairfax, to James Vance, grant, January 10, 1752, NNLGB H, p. 100; Thomas, Lord Fairfax, to Elizabeth Vance, grant, August 7, 1752,

NNLGB H, p. 191. Mary Reid, wife of William Reed, also received a Fairfax grant after her husband died (Thomas, Lord Fairfax, to Mary Reid, grant, June 19, 1751, NNLGB H, p. 2).

26. For the pattern of inheritance in the Vance family, see Samuel Vance to John Gilkeson, deed, April 14, 1807, Frederick County DB 40, p. 530; William Vance, will, August 25, 1792, Frederick County WB 5, p. 392; Joseph Roberts to James David Vance, deed, May 2, 1775, Frederick County DB 17, p. 25; Joseph Wood to James David Vance, deed, April 1, 1798, Frederick County DB 24A, p. 458; James D. Vance's heirs to Robert Vance, deed, October 24, 1825, Frederick County DB 51, p. 73; Robert Beckett to John and Samuel Gilkeson, deed, November 7, 1780, Frederick County DB 19, p. 193; Isaac and Ebenezer Gilkeson to John Gilkeson, deed, August 28, 1792, Frederick County Superior Court DB 2, p. 32; John White to Sarah Gilkeson, deed, April 17, 1799, Frederick County Superior Court DB 3, p. 586; Samuel Rannells to Sarah Gilkeson, deed, February 28, 1801, Frederick County Superior Court DB 4, p. 264; Samuel Rannells to Sarah Gilkeson, deed, March 12, 1801, Frederick County Superior Court DB 4, p. 591; William F. Simrall to Sarah Gilkeson, deed, April 7, 1803, Frederick County Superior Court DB 4, p. 587; Robert Wilson to Mary Wilson, surrender, August 3, 1779, Frederick County DB 18, p. 224.

27. The argument that a father's conveying land by will and thereby delaying a son's inheritance and economic independence constituted a form of parental control is most fully developed by Philip J. Greven, Jr., in *Four Generations: Population, Land, and Family in Colonial Andover, Massachusetts* (Ithaca: Cornell University Press, 1970), 72–99, 125–72.

28. On November 12, 1735, William Hoge patented 411 acres on a tributary of the Opequon that came to be called Hoge's Run (Regal Government Land Book 16, VSL&A, p. 366).

29. "Life of Moses Hoge, 1752–1820," Moses Hoge Papers, Library of Congress, Washington, DC, p. 4.

30. William Hoge to David Vance et al., deed, February 19, 1745, Frederick County DB 1, p. 275. Grantees listed in the deed are David Vance, Joseph Colvill, Robert Wilson, Robert Allen, William Reid, John Wilson, William Chambers, Thomas Marquis, David Vance, "Gent.," James Vance, Robert Smith, James Hoge, Jr., Robert White, William McMachen, "Gent.," Samuel Glass, and David Glass. Unfortunately this deed is the only extant record indicating church membership at Opequon for the eighteenth century.

31. R. B. Woodworth, "Date of Organization of the Opequon Presbyterian Church," C. Langdon Gordon Collection, HLA, p. 6; Lennart Pearson, "Historic Opequon Church (typescript), C. Langdon Gordon Collection, pp. 1–15; John Craig, as quoted in Pearson, "Historic Opequon Church," p. 10.

32. Lemon, *Best Poor Man's Country*, 88–91, 151–69. For an analysis of interdependence and lack of self-sufficiency—even in food production for

domestic consumption—in eighteenth-century rural economies, see
Bettye Hobbs Pruitt, "Self-Sufficiency and the Agricultural Economy of
Eighteenth-Century Massachusetts," *WMQ*, 3d ser., 41 (1984): 333–64.

33. Inventory of James Vance, recorded February 12, 1752, Frederick
County WB 2, p. 17.

34. Account of James Vance's estate, recorded November 4, 1760, Frederick
County WB, p. 451.

35. Account of William Hoge's estate, recorded April 8, 1761, Frederick
County WB, p. 476.

36. Elizabeth Chapman Denny Vann and Margaret Collins Denny Dixon,
*Brumback-Hotsinpiller Genealogy; Some of the Descendants of Melchior
Brumback of the 1714 Germanna Colony in Virginia through his Daughter
Elizabeth Who Married Stephen Hotsinpiller and Allied Families of Afflick*
(Englewood, NJ: n.p., 1961), 21–26; Jost Hite to Stephen Hotsinpiller,
deed, March 24, 1736, Orange County DB 1, p. 431; account of
Stephen Hotsinpiller's estate, recorded October 2, 1787, Frederick
County WB 5, p. 176.

37. Inventory of Robert Allen, March 7, 1771, Frederick County WB 4,
p. 77.

38. Joseph Colvill, will, October 17, 1757, Frederick County WB 2, p. 294.

39. Thomas Bryan Martin to Philip Martin, June 28, 1790, Wykeham-Mar-
tin Papers, Colonial Williamsburg Foundation, Williamsburg, VA (on
microfilm); Luigi Castiglioni, as quoted in *Travels in Virginia in Revolutionary Times*, ed. A. J. Morrison (Lynchburg, VA: J. P. Bell Co.,
1922), 69.

40. Foote, *Sketches of Virginia, Historical and Biographical*, 22.

41. Selective migration for the third generation at Opequon conforms to a
pattern that Darrett Rutman has described for all of America's "little
communities" as "the orderly mobility of most of the young as they
moved out from a family of origin into a regional agricultural economy
(and occasionally beyond) in search of the means to establish themselves" (Rutman, "Little Communities," 173–74). For the land acquisi-
tions of Joseph, Robert, and David Glass, see Samuel Glass to Joseph
Glass, deed, May 22, 1752, Frederick County DB 2, p. 341; John
Beckett, Jr., to Joseph Glass, deed, February 28, 1772, Frederick County
DB 15, p. 305; Joseph Beckett to Joseph Glass, deed, March 18, 1778,
Frederick County DB 17, p. 518; Thomas, Lord Fairfax, to Robert Glass,
grant, November 2, 1754, NNLGB H, p. 529; Samuel Glass to David
Glass, deed, June 6, 1749, Frederick County DB 2, p. 12; Thomas, Lord
Fairfax, to David Glass, grant, June 30, 1761, NNLGB K, p. 294. For ge-
nealogical information on the Glass family, see Foote, "Genealogy of the
Glass Family," pp. 12, 23. For information on patterns of inheritance be-
tween the second and third generations of Glasses, see Joseph Glass,
will, January 23, 1792, Frederick County WB 6, p. 2; Robert Glass, will,
July 13, 1796, Frederick County WB 6, p. 250; David Glass, will, January 9, 1774, Frederick County WB 4, p. 298.

42.   Also serving as trustee was William Chipley, a member of an allied family at Opequon; serving as additional collectors of subscriptions were James Simrall, Hugh Brown, and Robert White, all members of allied families. For their activities, see *Bowen's Virginia Centinel & Gazette: or, the Winchester Political Repository*, March 16, 1791; and *Bartgis's Virginia Gazette, and the Winchester Advertiser*, August 20, 1791. When Adam Kern sold more land to the congregation in 1795, James Simrall, Joseph Lucky, and Alexander Feely were listed as elders of the church (Adam Kern to James Simrall, Joseph Lucky, and Alexander Feely, deed, December 1, 1795, Frederick County DB 24B, p. 330).
43.   Foote, *Sketches of Virginia, Historical and Biographical*, 22.
44.   W. A. Crawford, "Memorial Discourse of Opequon Presbyterian Church," June 23, 1876, Elizabeth Engle Collection, HLA, p. 12.
45.   Lemon, *Best Poor Man's Country*, xv; Henretta, "Families and Farms," 32.

11. The Scotch-Irish Element in Appalachian English: How Broad? How Deep?

1.   This was presumably contemplated by Lorimer in doing his translation, but abandoned. The devil speaks in Scots English in the version that reached publication, but one can hardly blame the PBS program for using the line. The research on which this chapter is based was supported in part by travel grants from the National Endowment for the Humanities and the Southern Regional Education Board and in part by a Research and Productive Scholarship grant from the University of South Carolina. The author especially thanks A. J. Aitken, John Kirk, Caroline Macafee, and Philip Robinson for their advice and observations on Scottish and Ulster English. Any errors of interpretation or any overstatements, however, are strictly mine.
2.   The first concerted effort in this regard was apparently undertaken by Calvin S. Brown in a series of four short studies: "Dialectal Survivals in Tennessee," *Modern Language Notes* 4 (1889): 205–9; "Other Dialectal Forms in Tennessee," *Publications of the Modern Language Association* 6 (1891): 171–75; "Dialectal Survivals from Spenser," *Dial* 16 (1894): 40; "Dialectal Survivals from Chaucer," *Dial* 22 (1897): 139–41.
3.   *A Dictionary of the Queen's English* (Raleigh, NC: Travel and Promotion Division, Department of Natural and Economic Resources, [1974?]).
4.   Cratis Williams, "Who are the Southern Mountaineers?" *Appalachian Journal* 1 (1972): 48–55; the earliest effort in this regard was apparently H. P. Burt, "The Dialects of Our Country," *Appleton's Journal* 5 (1878): 411–17.
5.   John C. Campbell, *The Southern Highlander and His Homeland* (New York: Russell Sage Foundation, 1921); Josiah Combs, *The Kentucky High-*

lands from a Native Mountaineer's Viewpoint (Lexington: J. L. Richardson & Co., 1913); Williams, "Who are the Southern Mountaineers?"

6. Helen Child Sargent and George Lyman Kittredge, Introduction to *English and Scottish Popular Ballads Edited from the Collection of Francis James Child*, ed. Sargent and Kittredge (Boston: Houghton Mifflin, 1904), xiii; Cecil J. Sharp, *English Folk Songs from the Southern Appalachians*, ed. Maud Karpeles, 2 vols. (London: Oxford University Press, 1932).

7. Henry Glassie, *Patterns in the Material Folk Culture of the Eastern United States* (Philadelphia: University of Pennsylvania Press, 1968).

8. For a discussion of the goals of the linguistic atlas, see Hans Kurath, "The Conference on a Linguistic Atlas of the United States and Canada," *Bulletin of the Linguistic Society of America* 4 (1929): 20–47. Three branches of the atlas project cover territory within Appalachia: the Linguistic Atlas of the Middle and South Atlantic States interviewed speakers in North Carolina, Virginia, and West Virginia in the 1930s; the Linguistic Atlas of the Gulf States surveyed Georgia, Tennessee, and Alabama in the late 1960s and 1970s; and the Linguistic Atlas of the North Central States covered Kentucky in the 1950s. For an overview of these projects, see Raven I. McDavid, Jr., "The Dialects of American English," in *The Structure of American English*, ed. W. Nelson Francis (New York: Ronald Press Co., 1958), 480–543.

9. One might compare Kurath's *Word Geography of the Eastern United States* (Ann Arbor: University of Michigan Press, 1949), whose first chapter, "The English of the Eastern States: A Perspective," focuses in detail on British and Continental European sources of American vocabulary, with Craig Carver's *American Regional Dialects: A Word Geography* (Ann Arbor: University of Michigan Press, 1987), a work comparable in scope, written a generation later. Carver says almost nothing about such sources.

10. James G. Leyburn, *The Scotch-Irish: A Social History* (Chapel Hill: University of North Carolina Press, 1962), vi.

11. In the present study, "Scotch-Irish English" refers to the general variety of English brought to North America in the eighteenth century by Ulster emigrants, the overwhelming majority of whom were of Scottish ancestry, according to Leyburn (*The Scotch-Irish*) and R. J. Dickson (*Ulster Emigration to Colonial America, 1718–1775*, 2d ed., with a new introduction by Graeme Kirkham [Belfast: Ulster Historical Foundation, 1988]). While seventeenth-century Lowland Scottish English and eighteenth-century Ulster English overlap considerably, Scotch-Irish English includes some features of Scottish English for which there is not yet evidence in Ulster (in part because of the scant earlier documentary record), and it contains some features that apparently derive from Ulster contact with Irish Gaelic—like positive *anymore* (F1)—but are unattested in Scotland.

12. Josiah Combs, "Language of the Southern Highlander," *Publications of*

the *Modern Language Association* 46 (1931): 1302–22; David Hackett Fischer, *Albion's Seed: Four British Folkways in North America* (New York: Oxford University Press, 1989); Wylene Dial, "The Dialect of the Appalachian People," *West Virginia History* 30 (1969): 463–71; Alan Crozier, "The Scotch-Irish Influence on American English," *American Speech* 59 (1984): 310–31.

13. Joseph Wright, *The English Dialect Dictionary*, 6 vols. (Oxford: Oxford University Press, 1898–1905).

14. Crozier, "The Scotch-Irish Influence on American English," 311.

15. Ibid., 328.

16. Michael Ellis, "On the Use of Dialect as Evidence: Albion's Seed in Appalachia," *Appalachian Journal* 19 (1992): 278–97.

17. Ibid., 286.

18. These forty features have been culled from the published research on Appalachian speech as identified in an exhaustive bibliography covering this literature: James B. McMillan and Michael B. Montgomery, *Annotated Bibliography of Southern American English* (Tuscaloosa: University of Alabama Press, 1989).

19. "Southern British" is an inclusive term for patterns whose origin and distribution have been limited to one or more regions of southern England.

20. William Grant and David Murison, eds., *The Scottish National Dictionary*, 10 vols. (Edinburgh: Scottish National Dictionary Association, 1931–84); William Craigie and A. J. Aitken, eds., *A Dictionary of the Older Scottish Tongue: From the Twelfth Century to the End of the Seventeenth* (Chicago: University of Chicago Press, 1933–).

21. For example, William Hugh Patterson, *The Glossary of Words in Use in the Counties of Antrim and Down* (London: Trubner and Company, 1880); John J. Marshall, "The Dialect of Ulster: Glossary of Words in the Ulster Dialect, Chiefly Used in the Midland and North-eastern Counties," *Ulster Journal of Archeology* 10 (1904): 121–30; 11 (1905): 64–70, 122–25, 175–79; 12 (1906): 18–22; Michael Traynor, *The English Dialect of Donegal: A Glossary* (Dublin: Royal Irish Academy, 1953).

22. For example, Sir John Byers, "Dictionary of Ulster English," 1,000–page typescript, Ulster Folk and Transport Museum, County Down, Northern Ireland.

23. Craig Carver, *American Regional Dialects*; Frederic G. Cassidy et al., *Dictionary of American Regional English*, 2 vols. to date (Cambridge, MA: Belknap Press of Harvard University Press, 1985–); William Craigie and A. J. Aitken, eds., *A Dictionary of the Older Scottish Tongue*; Crawford Feagin, *Variation and Change in Alabama English: A Sociolinguistic Study of the White Community* (Washington, DC: Georgetown University Press, 1979); William Grant and David Murison, *The Scottish National Dictionary*; Joan H. Hall, "DARE Items Labeled 'Appalachian,' 'Scottish' or 'Irish' " (n.d.); Edwin R. Hunter, "The American Colloquial Idiom, 1830–1860" (Ph.D. diss., University of Chicago, 1925); Otto Jespersen, *A Modern Grammar on Historical Principles*, 7 vols. (Lon-

don: George Allen and Unwin, 1954); Raven I. McDavid, Jr., "The Dialects of American English"; F. Th. Visser, *An Historical Syntax of the English Language*, 2 vols. (Leiden: E. J. Brill, 1970); Harold Wentworth, ed., *American Dialect Dictionary* (New York: Thomas Y. Crowell Co., 1944); George P. Wilson, "Folk Speech," *The Frank C. Brown Collection of North Carolina Folklore* (Durham: Duke University Press, 1952), 505–618; Walt Wolfram and Donna Christian, *Appalachian Speech* (Arlington, VA: Center for Applied Linguistics, 1976).

24. This influence may in fact be broader than it appears to be because Southern British forms may well have come through Ulster. Many settlers from England, especially from the southwest, participated in the seventeenth-century plantation of Ulster. See Philip S. Robinson, *The Plantation of Ulster: British Settlement in an Irish Landscape, 1600–1670* (New York: St. Martin's, 1984). Twentieth-century novels in Ulster English, e.g., Agnes Romily White, *Mrs. Murphy Buries the Hatchet* (Belfast: White Row, 1989), employ *a-* prefixes and the regularized past form *blowed*. Much of the North American contact between Scotch-Irish and Southern British people and their varieties of English was mirrored three centuries ago in Ulster. This is the subject of a study by Michael Montgomery and Philip S. Robinson, "Ulster English as Janus: Language Contact Across the Irish Sea and Across the North Atlantic," in *Language Contact Across the North Atlantic*, ed. Sture Ureland (Tubingen: Max Niemeyer, forthcoming).

25. Although no formal analysis has yet been pursued by this or any other writer, *ye* appears to be a phonological variant of *you* in unstressed contexts, particularly as the direct object of a verb or the object of a preposition. This form of *ye* is used as both singular and plural and has no connection to the Middle English and Renaissance *ye* that was a nominative plural form.

26. In "The Pragmatics of Multiple Modals in North and South Carolina," *American Speech* 69 (1994): 3–29, Margaret Mishoe and Michael Montgomery identify twenty-three different combinations based on their observations in South and North Carolina, including the following previously unattested ones:

1) It's a long way and he *might will can't*, but I'm going to ask.
2) They're saying we *may shall* get some rain.
3) We *would might* run maybe ten hams a week.

I have developed the transatlantic comparison of modal combinations further in a longer paper: Michael Montgomery, "Exploring the Roots of Appalachian English," *English World-Wide* 10 (1989): 227–78.

27. For many modern-day Southern American speakers, *y'all* and *you all* are apparently unrelated forms. *Y'all* most likely derives from *ye all*, the Scotch-Irish phonological form of *you all*, and not from *you all* directly; see Michael Montgomery, "The Etymology of *Y'all*," *Old English and New: Studies in Language and Linguistics in Honor of Frederic G. Cassidy*,

ed. Joan H. Hall, Richard Ringler, and Nick Doane (New York: Garland, 1992), 356–69. This is supported by the fact that many southerners today who use *y'all* either do not also use *you all* (the "supposed" form from which, according to dictionaries, *y'all* is contracted) or spell the form as *ya'll*, which means they do not associate its derivation with *you + all*; see Michael Montgomery, "The Reanalysis of *y'all*," *American Speech* 64 (1990): 273–75. The contention here is that the contracted form *y'all* was brought by Ulster emigrants, contrary to Crozier's supposition (Crozier, "The Scotch-Irish Influence on American English," 326).

28.   Peter Trudgill, *Dialects in Contact* (London: Blackwell Publications, 1986).

29.   I have made a beginning for vocabulary with my paper "The Diversity of Appalachian English," presented at the 1992 meeting of the Appalachian Studies Association.

12. Scotch-Irish Frontier Society in Southwestern North Carolina, 1780–1840

1.   John C. Inscoe, *Mountain Masters, Slavery, and the Sectional Crisis in Western North Carolina* (Knoxville: University of Tennessee Press, 1989), 7–10.

2.   E. Estyn Evans, "The Scotch-Irish: Their Cultural Adaptation and Heritage in the American Old West," in *Essays in Scotch-Irish History*, ed. E. R. R. Green (London: Routledge and Kegan Paul, 1965), 86.

3.   For Ireland, Sir Robert E. Matheson, *Special Report on Surnames in Ireland* (Dublin: A. Thom and Company, 1909); and Edward MacLysaght, *The Surnames of Ireland* (Dublin: Irish Academic Press, 1978). For southwestern North Carolina, various counties have published "heritage books" that include the work of family genealogists: Alice D. White, ed., *The Heritage of Cherokee County, North Carolina*, 2 vols. (Winston-Salem, NC: Cherokee County Historical Museum, 1987–90); Margaret Walker Freel, *Our Heritage: The People of Cherokee County, North Carolina, 1540–1955* (Asheville, NC: Miller Printing Co., 1956); *Jackson County Heritage, North Carolina* (Cullowhee, NC: Jackson County Genealogical Society, 1992); Jessie Sutton, ed., *The Heritage of Macon County, North Carolina* (Winston-Salem, NC: Macon County Historical Association, 1987); Doris Cline Ward, ed., *The Heritage of Old Buncombe County*, 2 vols. (Winston-Salem, NC: Old Buncombe Genealogical Society, 1981–87). We have especially benefited from John L. Waldroop's genealogical research on Macon and Jackson Counties.

4.   U.S. Census Office, *First Census of the United States: 1790*, Population Schedule, Burke County, NC, 102–3.

5.   U.S. Census Office, *Second Census of the United States: 1800*, Population Schedule, Buncombe County, NC, 158–94.

6.   U.S. Census Office, *Third Census of the United States: 1810*, Population Schedule, Haywood County, NC, 191–203.

7.   Listed in Nathaniel Browder, *The Cherokee Indian and Those Who Came After: Notes for a History of Cherokee County, North Carolina, 1835–1860* (Hayesville, NC: Browder, 1973), 75–76.

8.   U.S. Census Office, *Fifth Census of the United States: 1830,* Population Schedule, Macon County, NC, 1–36; Browder, *The Cherokee Indian and Those Who Came After,* 81–84.

9.   U.S. Census Office, *Sixth Census of the United States: 1840,* Population Schedule, Cherokee County, NC, 231–48.

10.   American Council of Learned Societies, "Report of Committee on Linguistic and National Stocks in the Population of the United States," American Historical Association, *Annual Report of the American Historical Association for the Year 1931,* vol. 1 (Washington, DC: United States Government Printing Office, 1932), table 12, p. 124 (this report was primarily compiled by Howard F. Barker and Marcus L. Hansen); Forrest McDonald and Ellen Shapiro McDonald, "The Ethnic Origins of the American People," *WMQ,* 3d ser., 37 (1980), table 5, p. 198; Thomas L. Purvis, "The European Ancestry of the United States Population, 1790," *WMQ,* 3d ser., 41 (1984): 85–101.

11.   Foster A. Sondley, *A History of Buncombe County, North Carolina* (Asheville, NC: Advocate Printing Co., 1930), 2:457–60, 652–54.

12.   Buncombe County Land Entry and Claim Records, 1788–1810, vol. 1, and Haywood County Land Entry and Claim Records, 1809–1819, vol. 1, North Carolina Division of Archives and History, Raleigh, NC.

13.   Listed in Browder, *The Cherokee Indian and Those Who Came After,* 107.

14.   Robert D. Mitchell, "The Presbyterian Church as an Indicator of Westward Expansion in 18th Century America," *The Professional Geographer* 28 (1966): 293–99.

15.   Ora Blackmun, *Western North Carolina: Its Mountains and its People to 1880* (Boone, NC: Appalachian Consortium Press, 1977), 179–80; Clarence W. Griffin, *History of Old Tryon and Rutherford Counties* (Asheville, NC: Miller Printing Company, 1937), 584–85; Edward W. Phifer, *Burke: The History of a North Carolina Community, 1777–1920* (Morganton, NC: Phifer, 1977), 104–5. The Little Brittain Church (founded 1768) and Quaker Meadows congregation (1977) were particularly instrumental.

16.   Agnes C. Sandifer, "Biographical Sketch of James Hall" (1976; MS at the Presbyterian Historical Society, Philadelphia, PA).

17.   *Minutes of the General Assembly of the Presbyterian Church in the United States of America from Its Organization A.D. 1789 to A.D. 1820 Inclusive* (Philadelphia: Presbyterian Board of Publication, 1847), 131.

18.   "Minutes of the Synod of the Carolinas," 1:111 (MS at the Presbyterian Historical Foundation, Montreat, NC).

19.   "George Newton," manuscript file, Presbyterian Historical Foundation, Montreat, NC.

20.   "Records of the Concord Presbytery," 1:90 (MS at Presbyterian Historical Foundation, Montreat, NC).

21.   Ibid.

22. Sondley, *A History of Buncombe County, North Carolina*, 2:758.
23. Ibid., 702–3.
24. George W. McCoy, *The First Presbyterian Church, Asheville, NC, 1794–1951* (Asheville, NC: First Presbyterian Church, 1951), 12.
25. "Minutes of the Concord Presbytery," 1:291–95.
26. William J. Wade, "The Development of Presbyterianism in Western North Carolina to 1915" (unpublished paper), 8–9.
27. "Davidson River [Church] Book of Records, 1828–1875" (MS at Presbyterian Historical Foundation, Montreat, NC).
28. "Records of the Concord Presbytery," 3:415.
29. Ibid., 85.
30. "Davidson River [Church] Book of Records"; "Hiwassee Church Book" (MS at Presbyterian Historical Foundation, Montreat, NC).
31. Wade, "The Development of Presbyterianism in Western North Carolina to 1915," table 1, nn. 20–23.
32. U.S. Census Office, *Seventh Census of the United States: 1850*, 326–31.
33. James Lemon, *The Best Poor Man's Country: A Geographical Study of Early Southeastern Pennsylvania* (Baltimore: Johns Hopkins University Press, 1972), 106–8.
34. Evans, "The Scotch-Irish," 77n. 3.
35. Ibid., 74, 86.
36. Forrest McDonald and Grady McWhiney, "The Celtic South," *History Today* 30 (1980): 13–14.
37. McDonald and McDonald, "The Ethnic Origins of the American People," 182.
38. Browder, *The Cherokee Indian and Those Who Came After*, 95–97; John Solomon Otto, *The Southern Frontiers, 1607–1860: The Agricultural Evolution of the Colonial and Antebellum South* (New York: Greenwood Press, 1989), 51–57; E. Estyn Evans, "The Scotch-Irish"; E. Estyn Evans, "Culture and Land Use in the Old West of North America," *Heidelberger Geographische Arbeiten* 15 (1966): 72–80.
39. Ester Boserup, *The Conditions of Agricultural Growth: The Economics of Agrarian Change under Population Pressure* (Chicago: Aldine, 1965), 28–34; Otto, *The Southern Frontier, 1607–1860*, 55–57, 65–67.
40. Forrest McDonald and Grady McWhiney, "The Antebellum Southern Herdsman: A Reinterpretation," *JSH* 41 (1975): 156–61; François André Michaux, *Travels West of the Alleghenies*, ed. Reuben Gold Thwaites (Cleveland: A. H. Clark, 1904), 299.
41. Lemon, *Best Poor Man's Country*, 106–8; Harry J. Carman, ed., *American Husbandry* (Port Washington, NY: Kennikat Press, 1964), 241–43.
42. Duane Meyer, *The Highland Scots in North Carolina, 1732–1776* (Chapel Hill: University of North Carolina Press, 1957), 104–6; Carl Hammer, *Rhinelanders on the Yadkin: The Story of the Pennsylvania Germans in Rowan and Cabarrus Counties, North Carolina*, 2d. ed., rev. (Salisbury, NC: n.p., 1965), 78.
43. Boserup, *The Conditions of Agricultural Growth*, 35–42.

44.   A. R. H. Baker and R. A. Butlin, *Studies in the Field System of the British Isles* (Cambridge: Cambridge University Press, 1973), 33; Desmond McCourt, "Infield and Outfield in Ireland," *Economic History Review* 7 (1955): 369–76.

45.   Ruth Sutter, *The Next Place You Come To: A Historical Introduction to Communities in North America* (Englewood Cliffs, NJ: Prentice-Hall, 1973), 33.

46.   James Patton, *Letter of James Patton, One of the First Residents of Asheville, North Carolina, to his Children* (Racine, WI: privately printed, 1845; reprint, privately printed, 1970), 21; for a fuller discussion of Patton, see H. Tyler Blethen and Curtis W. Wood, Jr., "A Trader on the Western Carolina Frontier," in *Appalachian Frontiers: Settlement, Society & Development in the Preindustrial Era*, ed. Robert D. Mitchell (Lexington: University Press of Kentucky, 1991), 150–65.

47.   Record of Wills and Inventories, Haywood County, NC, vol. A, 1808–1828, and vol. 1/2, 1829–1846, North Carolina Division of Archives and History, Raleigh, NC.

48.   Ibid.

49.   Harry Roy Merrens, *Colonial North Carolina in the Eighteenth Century* (Chapel Hill: University of North Carolina Press, 1964), 136–37.

50.   Record of Wills and Inventories, Haywood County.

51.   U.S. Census Office, *Seventh Census of the United States: 1850*, Agricultural Schedule, Cherokee County, NC, 715–38.

Select Bibliography

Adams, William Forbes. *Ireland and Irish Emigration to the New World from 1815 to the Famine.* New Haven: Yale University Press, 1932.

Bartlett, T., and D. W. Hayton, eds. *Penal Era and Golden Age.* Belfast: Ulster Historical Foundation, 1979.

Beckett, J. C. *Confrontations: Studies in Irish History.* London: Faber, 1972.

Berthoff, Rowland. "Celtic Mist Over the South." *JSH* 52 (1986): 523–46.

Blethen, H. Tyler, and Curtis Wood, Jr. *From Ulster to Carolina: The Migration of the Scotch-Irish to Southwestern North Carolina.* Cullowhee, NC: Western Carolina University, 1986.

———. "A Trader on the Western Carolina Frontier." In *Appalachian Frontiers: Settlement, Society, & Development in the Preindustrial Era*, ed. Robert D. Mitchell, 150–65. Lexington: University Press of Kentucky, 1990.

Bolton, C. K. *Scotch Irish Pioneers in Ulster and America.* Boston: Bacon and Brown, 1910.

Brooke, Peter. *Ulster Presbyterianism: The Historical Perspective, 1610–1970.* Dublin: Gill and Macmillan, 1987.

Campbell, John C. *The Southern Highlander and His Homeland.* 1921. Reprint, Lexington: University Press of Kentucky, 1969.

Connell, K. H. *The Population of Ireland, 1750–1845.* Oxford: Oxford University Press, 1950.

Cowan, Edward J. "Back-home and the Back Country: David Hackett Fischer's Borderlands Revisited." *Appalachian Journal* 19 (1991): 166–73.

Crawford, W. H. "Landlord-Tenant Relations in Ulster, 1609–1820." *IESH* 2 (1975): 5–21.

———. "Change in Ulster in the Late Eighteenth Century." In *Penal Era and Golden Age*, ed. T. Bartlett and D. W. Hayton. Belfast: Ulster Historical Foundation, 1979.

Cullen, Louis. *The Emergence of Modern Ireland, 1600–1900.* London: Botsford Press, 1972.

Cunningham, Rodger. *Apples on the Flood: The Southern Mountain Experience.* Knoxville: University of Tennessee Press, 1988.

Devine, T. M., and David Dickson, eds. *Ireland and Scotland, 1600–1850: Parallels and Contrasts on Economic and Social Development.* Edinburgh: John Donald, 1983.

Dickson, D. *New Foundations: Ireland, 1660–1800.* Dublin: Gill and Macmillan, 1987.

Dickson, R. J. *Ulster Emigration to Colonial America, 1718–1775.* 1966. Reprint, Belfast: Ulster Historical Association, 1988.

Doyle, David N. *Ireland, Irishmen and Revolutionary America, 1760–1820*. Cork and Dublin: Mercier Press, 1981.

Elliott, Bruce S. *Irish Migrants in the Canadas: A New Approach*. Kingston and Montreal: McGill-Queen's University Press, 1988.

Evans, E. Estyn. "Cultural Relics of the Ulster Scots in the Old West of North America." *Ulster Folklife* 11 (1965): 33–38.

———. "The Scotch-Irish: Their Cultural Adaptation and Heritage in the American Old West." In *Essays in Scotch-Irish History*, ed. E. R. R. Green. London: Routledge & Kegan Paul, 1969.

Fischer, David Hackett. *Albion's Seed: Four British Folkways in America*. New York: Oxford University Press, 1989.

Fitzpatrick, Rory. *God's Frontiersmen: The Scots-Irish Epic*. London: Weidenfeld and Nicolson, 1989.

Ford, H. J. *The Scotch-Irish in America*. Princeton, NJ: Princeton University Press, 1915.

Gerlach, Russel L. *Immigrants in the Ozarks*. Columbia: University of Missouri Press, 1976.

Gillespie, Raymond. *Colonial Ulster: The Settlement of East Ulster, 1600–1641*. Cork: Cork University Press, 1985.

———. *Settlement and Survival on an Ulster Estate: The Brownlow Leasebook, 1667–1711*. Belfast: PRONI, 1988.

———. "The Presbyterian Revival in Ulster, 1660–1690." In *The Churches, Ireland and the Irish*, ed. W. J. Sheils and Diana Wood. Oxford: Oxford University Press, 1989.

Glassie, Henry. *Patterns in the Material Folk Culture of the Eastern United States*. Philadelphia: University of Pennsylvania Press, 1968.

Green, E. R. R., ed. *Essays in Scotch-Irish History*. London: Routledge & Kegan Paul, 1969.

Greene, Jack P., Virginia de John Anderson, James Horn, Barry Levy, Ned C. Landsman, and David Hackett Fischer, "Forum: Albion's Seed: Four British Folkways in America—A Symposium." *WMQ* 48 (1991): 223–308.

Hanna, C. A. *The Scotch-Irish*. 2 vols. New York: G. P. Putnam and Sons, 1902. Reprint, Baltimore, MD: Genealogical Publishing Co., 1968.

Hook, Andrew. *Scotland and America: A Study of Cultural Relations, 1750–1835*. Glasgow: Blackie, 1975.

Houston, Cecil J., and William M. Smyth. *Irish Emigration and Canadian Settlement*. Toronto: University of Toronto Press, 1990.

Jones, Maldwyn A. "The Scotch-Irish in British America." In *Strangers within the Realm: Cultural Margins of the First British Empire*, ed. Bernard Bailyn and Philip D. Morgan. Chapel Hill: University of North Carolina Press, 1991.

Keller, Kenneth W. "What is Distinctive About the Scotch-Irish?" In *Appalachian Frontiers*, ed. Robert D. Mitchell. Lexington: University Press of Kentucky, 1991.

Kephart, Horace. *Our Southern Highlanders*. New York: Macmillan, 1922.

Kirkham, Graeme. "The Origins of Mass Emigration from Ireland." In *Migrations: The Irish at Home and Abroad*, ed. Richard Kearney. Dublin: Wolfhound Press, 1990.

Klett, G. S. *Presbyterians in Colonial Pennsylvania*. Philadelphia: University of Pennsylvania Press, 1937.

Lemon, James T. *The Best Poor Man's Country: A Geographical Study of Early Southeastern Pennsylvania*. Baltimore: Johns Hopkins University Press, 1972.

Leyburn, James G. *The Scotch-Irish: A Social History*. Chapel Hill: University of North Carolina Press, 1962.

Mannion, John T. *Irish Settlement in Eastern Canada: A Study of Cultural Transfer and Adaptation*. Toronto: University of Toronto Press, 1974.

McDonald, Forrest, and Ellen Shapiro McDonald. "The Ethnic Origins of the American People, 1790." *WMQ* 37 (1980): 179–99.

McDonald, Forrest, and Grady McWhiney. "The Antebellum Southern Herdsman: A Reinterpretation." *JSH* 41 (1975): 147–66.

———. "Celtic Origins of Southern Herding Practices." *JSH* 51 (1985): 165–82.

McWhiney, Grady. *Cracker Culture: Celtic Ways in the Old South*. Tuscaloosa: University of Alabama Press, 1988.

Miller, Kerby. *Emigrants and Exiles: Ireland and the Irish Exodus to North America*. New York: Oxford University Press, 1985.

Mitchell, Robert D. *Commercialism and Frontier: Perspectives on the Early Shenandoah Valley*. Charlottesville: University of Virginia Press, 1972.

Mitchison, R., and P. Roebuck, eds. *Economy and Society in Scotland and Ireland, 1500–1939*. Edinburgh: John Donald Press, 1988.

Montgomery, Michael. "The Roots of Appalachian English: Scotch-Irish or British Southern?" *Journal of the Appalachian Studies Association* 3 (1991): 177–91.

Moody, T. W., F. X. Martin, and F. J. Byrne, eds. *A New History of Ireland: III, Early Modern Ireland, 1534–1691*. Oxford: Clarendon Press, 1976.

Newton, Milton. "Cultural Preadaptation and the Upland South." In *Man and Cultural Heritage, Geoscience and Man*, ed. H. J. Walker and W. G. Haag. Baton Rouge: Louisiana State University Press, 1974.

Otto, John Solomon. *The Southern Frontier, 1607–1860: The Agricultural Evolution of the Colonial and Antebellum South*. New York: Greenwood Press, 1989.

Otto, John Solomon, and Nain Estelle Anderson. "The Diffusion of Upland South Folk Culture, 1790–1840." *Southeastern Geographer* 22 (1982): 89–98.

Perceval-Maxwell, M. *The Scottish Migration to Ulster in the Reign of James I*. Belfast: Ulster Historical Foundation, 1990.

Purvis, Thomas L. "The European Ancestry of the United States Population, 1790." *WMQ* 41 (1984): 85–101.

Robinson, Philip. *The Plantation of Ulster: British Settlement in an Irish Landscape, 1600–1700*. New York: St. Martin's Press, 1984.

Roebuck, Peter, ed. *Plantation to Partition: Essays in Honour of J. L. McCracken.* Belfast: Blackstaff Press, 1981.

Schmidt, Leigh Eric. *Holy Fairs: Scottish Communions and American Revivals in the Early Modern Period.* Princeton, NJ: Princeton University Press, 1989.

Truxes, T. M. *Irish-American Trade, 1600–1783.* Cambridge: Cambridge University Press, 1988.

Westerkamp, Marilyn Jeanne. *Triumph of the Laity: Scots-Irish Piety and the Great Awakening, 1625–1760.* New York: Oxford University Press, 1988.

Williams, Cratis. "Who are the Southern Mountaineers?" *Appalachian Journal* 1 (1972): 48–55.

Contributors

H. TYLER BLETHEN is professor of history at Western Carolina University and director of its Mountain Heritage Center. He is coauthor with Curtis W. Wood, Jr., of *From Ulster to Carolina: The Migration of the Scotch-Irish to Southwestern North Carolina* (1983; 1986) and *A Mountain Heritage: The Illustrated History of Western Carolina University* (1989) and editor of *Diversity in Appalachia: Images and Realities* (1993).

S. J. CONNOLLY, reader in history at the University of Ulster, is author of *Priests and People in Pre-Famine Ireland* (1982), *Religion and Society in Nineteenth-Century Ireland* (1985), and *Religion, Law and Power: The Making of Protestant Ireland 1660–1760* (1992). He was editor of the journal *Irish Economic and Social History* from 1983 to 1989, and he is general editor of the forthcoming *Oxford Companion to Irish History*.

EDWARD J. COWAN, head of the Department of Scottish History at the University of Glasgow, is author of *Montrose: For Covenant and King* (1977) and *The People's Past: Scottish Folk, Scottish History* (1980; 1991). He is currently working with Athol Gow on a history of Scottish prophecy to be published by Edinburgh Press.

RUSSEL L. GERLACH, professor of history at Southwest Missouri State University, is author of *Immigrants in the Ozarks* (1976), *The Heritage of the Ozarks* (1984), and *Settlement Patterns in Missouri* (1986).

WARREN R. HOFSTRA, associate professor of history and director of the Community History Project at Shenandoah University, has published a number of articles about the Virginia backcountry and is currently working on a book examining settlement patterns and community formation in the Shenandoah Valley.

GRAEME KIRKHAM was assistant lecturer in the Department of Political Economy at University College, Dublin, from 1980 to 1981, and research officer for the Garfield Weston Research Project "Emigration from Ulster to North America" at the University of Ulster from 1982 to 1985. He has published work on the economic history of eighteenth-century northwest Ulster and on Ulster emigration and popular literacy. He is currently development officer for Rural Action, an initiative to encourage community-led environmental projects in rural England, and coeditor of the journal *Musical Traditions*.

WILLIAM MACAFEE is lecturer in education at the University of Ulster. His main research interests are local history and historical demography. He has published a number of articles on the population history of Ulster from the seventeenth to the early nineteenth centuries.

MICHAEL B. MONTGOMERY is professor of English and linguistics at the University of South Carolina. He has edited five books on Southern American English and was consulting editor for language for *The Encyclopedia of Southern Culture* (1989). At present he is working on a dictionary of the English of the Great Smoky Mountains and is engaged in a long-term effort to reconstruct the evolution of Scottish and Irish language patterns into varieties of American English, especially those found in Appalachia.

TREVOR PARKHILL worked in the Irish Manuscripts Commission in Dublin and in the Public Record Office of Northern Ireland from 1974 to 1994, prior to his appointment as keeper of history in the Ulster Museum in Belfast. He has published widely on the subject of emigration from Ulster and on emigrants' experiences in Canada, Australia, New Zealand, and North America.

VIVIENNE POLLOCK has worked in the museum service in Northern Ireland since 1986, beginning with Derry City Council. In 1987 she became assistant keeper of agriculture and crafts at the Ulster-American Folk Park. She is currently curator of photographic collections in the Department of History of the Ulster Museum. She has published articles on Irish social and economic history in various journals, including *Folk Life* and *Ulster Folk Life*.

CATHARINE ANNE WILSON is associate professor of Irish and Canadian history at the University of Guelph, Canada. She is author of *A New Lease on Life: Landlords, Tenants and Immigrants in Ireland and Canada* (1994), which has won the Fred Landon Award for the best regional history in Ontario.

CURTIS W. WOOD, JR., professor and head of the Department of History at Western Carolina University, is coauthor with H. Tyler Blethen of *From Ulster to Carolina: The Migration of the Scotch-Irish to Southwestern North Carolina* (1983; 1986) and *A Mountain Heritage: The Illustrated History of Western Carolina University* (1989).

Index